THE WORLD ACCORDING TO JESUS...

his blueprint for the best possible world

Lorraine Parkinson

First published in Australia in 2011
By Spectrum Publications Pty Ltd
PO Box 75, Richmond, Vic Australia 3121
Telephone: (+61) 1300 540 736
Facsimile: (+61) 1300 540 737
email: spectrum@spectrumpublications.com.au
web: www.spectrumpublications.com.au

© 2011 Lorraine Parkinson
All rights reserved.
No part of this publication may be reproduced
in any manner without prior
written permission of the publisher.

Cover Design: xy arts
Typesetting by Spectrum Publications PL
Typeface: AGaramond

ISBN: 978-0-86786-231-7
eISBN: 978-0-86786-222-5

National Library of Australia Cataloguing-in-Publication entry

Author:	Parkinson, Lorraine
Title:	The world according to Jesus ... : his blueprint for the best possible world / Lorraine Parkinson
ISBN:	9780867862317 (pbk.)
Subjects:	Jesus Christ -- Teachings
	Christian Life -- Biblical teaching.
Dewey Number:	248.4

Acknowledgment

I am greatly indebted for the encouragement of my husband Dr John Bodycomb during writing, and for his patience as 'sounding board' for the ideas in this book.

Contents

SECTION I: SETTING THE SCENE
    Introduction   3
1. What of Evil in the World According to Jesus?   12

SECTION II: THE BEATITUDES
2. The Power of Humility   23
3. Creative Comfort   27
4. Courage to Resist   33
5. Justice: the Wide-Angle Lens   43
6. Empathy and Justice: the Necessary Partnership   51
7. The Undivided Heart   58
8. Radical Forgiveness   64
9. Freedom from Fear   70

SECTION III: THE TEACHINGS
10. The Prayer for Builders of the Kingdom   81
11. Salty Followers   87
12. Light Up the Darkness   92
13. On Firm Foundations   97
14. Fulfilling the Commandment   103
15. A Task for Human Beings   109
16. The Picture Broadens   117
17. The Responsive Heart   123
18. Treasure Worth Keeping   128
19. Through the Eyes of Jesus   134
20. Souls for Sale   140
21. What's the Use of Worrying?   146
22. The Clear Sight of the Deliberately Humble   152
23. Ask for What?   158

24. The Rule to End All Rules	164
25. No Turning Back	170
26. Not in My Name!	176
27. Founded on Rock	182
28. Why Parables?	188

SECTION IV: THE VISION OF JESUS AND THE EVENTS OF EASTER

29. Taking a Stand	195
30. Facing the Consequences	201
31. Understanding the Meaning	206

SECTION V: WHERE TO FROM HERE?

| 32. What Jesus Left Behind | 215 |
| Conclusion | 221 |

APPENDIX I: THE JESUS CREED	230
APPENDIX II: 'LOST ON THE WRONG ROAD'	233
ENDNOTES	240
BIBLIOGRAPHY	248

SECTION I

Setting the Scene

Introduction

Many Christian scholars are writing about the need to put aside traditional dogma which divides and separates human beings in the name of a Saviour Christ. Such dogma has now been regarded as irrelevant to life by at least two generations of Western Christians, many of whom have clearly voted with their feet. It is also clear that in an enthusiastic effort to rid the church of ideas destructive to Jesus' followers in the twenty-first century, some writers are in danger of throwing out the baby (both God and Jesus) with the bathwater. Many of their readers have acknowledged the thoroughness of the demolition job being carried out on traditional Christian ideas. Not surprisingly, they have also identified the need for a newly-stated foundation upon which to build a renewed church. It is well to recognize aspects of the church's traditional beliefs which are judged irrelevant and irretrievable in any form for contemporary faith and life. It is something else to see clearly how the church might be reinvigorated and renewed for the future. To that end, this book examines teachings of Jesus as recorded in the Gospel of Matthew and commonly known as the Sermon on the Mount.

Biblical scholarship ancient and contemporary is as sure as it can be that the Sermon on the Mount in Matthew's Gospel represents Jesus' own teaching.[1] Most argue that the contents represent core sayings of the historical Jesus, even though many see the form of the collection itself as a literary creation of Matthew.[2] Matthew is most probably responsible for verses

10-11 of chapter 5, which set out the perspective of Jesus' followers after the disastrous Jewish War against the Romans[3]. With that exception, this work will set out a case for the Sermon on the Mount as a deliberately constructed set of teachings from the historical Jesus,[4] the order of which exhibits a high degree of intentionality and importance. The fact of their inclusion in the Sermon on the Mount (or those included in Luke's Sermon on the Plain) indicates the degree of importance Jesus placed on them, no doubt illustrated by the number of times he would have repeated them to different audiences.

We will keep in mind that the gospel version used in this book is an English translation from Greek.[5] Translations change the meanings of words and there is no evidence that Jesus taught in Greek, even though he may well have known many Greek words. At times I will try to get as close as possible to Jesus' original meaning by looking at his sayings in Aramaic, his own spoken language.

The teachings of Jesus are not simply a loose collection of sayings about being a good neighbour, or a peacemaker, or overcoming prejudice, or being forgiving, or being humble, or refusing to be violent, or taking time out to pray, or treating people as equals. Those teachings and many more are integral parts of a whole – a tightly argued, consistent whole. They are essential elements of what came to be Jesus' holistic vision of what he called the Kingdom of heaven on earth. They are the necessary qualities of an enlightened humanity and therefore of the best possible world. As we will see, all aspects of Jesus' teaching are totally consistent and compatible with each other.

Where did all of this come from? How did Jesus come to possess a vision which has the potential to change the basis upon which human society exists and to bring humanity to its fulfilment? The first thing to say is that the vision was not a consequence of his possessing a 'divine nature' as well as a human nature. Jesus may well be described as a godly man because his life and teachings reflect what Christians believe to be the nature of God. However, I do not subscribe to traditional doctrines of incarnation which understand Jesus to be the divine second person of a triune God. On the other hand, a focus on his enlightened humanity will enable Jesus' teachings to have ultimate appeal and utility for his human followers. This would not be the case if he were believed to possess an other-worldly as well as a human nature. Who could follow a super-human Jesus?

Christians sometimes wonder what Jesus was doing in all the years prior to his public ministry. It is highly likely that he worked as a carpenter to make a living, but there is good reason for arguing that he was also preparing to make known his vision of the best possible world. It is self-evident that this was not thrown together willy-nilly, but that he would have honed it endlessly and meticulously. He would have prayed about it constantly and examined it from end to end, back and forth, up and down, inside out. He would have confirmed its veracity in his own interaction with others. He would most likely have talked about it with other teachers and students of Torah. Eventually he would have known that his vision had the graceful consistency and wholeness of truth. As a person of faith, he would have seen it as reflecting the mind of God. For that very reason his teaching was and is, universal. Although it was originally crafted with his own people in mind, in the twenty-first century world of many faiths it has become apparent that his teaching addresses not Jews only, or Christians only, or men only, or people living then only, or rich people only, or poor people only. Instead it has resonance and compatibility with the lives of all human beings of all time. As Albert Einstein put it:

> *If one purges the Judaism of the Prophets and Christianity as Jesus taught it of all subsequent additions, especially those of the priests, one is left with a teaching which is capable of curing all the social ills of humanity.*[6]

This book contends that if followed, the teaching has the potential to give human beings fulfilment as people attuned to each other and mutually committed to a good purpose for life. The teaching's potential is such that if it were put into practice it could fully establish what Jesus called the Kingdom of heaven (on earth). I acknowledge the difficulties inherent in that process, but I aim to set out reasons why it could be possible.

Because he lived in a time of rule by kings, when God was seen as ultimate king of Israel, Jesus naturally called this best possible state of earthly affairs a divinely-inspired kingdom. We will examine the Sermon on the Mount in the Gospel of Matthew, which uses the term, "the Kingdom of heaven". As Matthew was Jewish, he would not have included in his original gospel manuscript the biblical name for God (YHWH), which was spoken only inside the Jerusalem Temple.[7] In accordance with Jewish practice at the time it is most likely that in personal prayer and conversation Matthew called God *Adonai* ('Lord'), which was the approved spoken version of YHWH. Although it is clear that in Jesus' personal relationship with the divine he stepped outside of these conventions and called God *Abba*, which is the Aramaic word for 'my father', there is every reason to believe he would have expressed the idea of the best possible world as Matthew does: "the Kingdom of heaven". If he had lived in the twenty-first century, he might have called it something like 'the government of heaven'. Most probably he would simply have called it 'the best possible world'.

Whatever it may be called, the meaning is the same. It would be a world in which every human being would shape his or her private and public life by the values which inspired Jesus. Contrary to expectations inspired by Paul's writings and passed on by gospel writers, I oppose the idea that Jesus believed his vision would be fulfilled through an apocalyptic eschatological intervention by God at an End-time in history. David Aune offers a succinct explanation of apocalyptic eschatology:

Apocalyptic eschatology, the belief that God would shortly

SECTION I: SETTING THE SCENE

> intervene in human history to bring a catastrophic end to evil in all its forms, was a widespread ideology in Palestinian Judaism from ca. 200BCE to 100 CE. This belief was a supernaturalistic response to what appeared to many Jews to be a dilemma insoluble by ordinary means: the anxiety, alienation, helplessness, and deprivation experienced in the political, economic, social, and religious spheres of Palestinian life.[8]

My opposition to Jesus' association with apocalyptic eschatology is in contrast with the beliefs of some Christian scholars[9], but is affirmed in recent years by members of the Jesus Seminar. One such scholar, John Dominic Crossan, refers to Jesus' approach to the Kingdom of heaven as "sapiential eschatology":

> *Apocalyptic eschatology is world-negation stressing imminent divine intervention: we wait for God to act; sapiential eschatology is world-negation emphasizing immediate divine imitation: God waits for us to act.*[10]

Expectation that God will intervene to bring about a perfect humanity in a perfect world profoundly compromises the imperative of Jesus' teachings for his followers. Nonetheless, apocalyptic eschatological belief of this kind has persisted throughout the life of the church. It is represented by contemporary Christians who accordingly take little or no responsibility for care of the earth or the development of an ethical society as they wait (mainly in exclusivist groups) for the intervention of God and the second coming of Jesus. The ethics they embrace are essentially group-related rules for deciding whether a person is 'in' or 'out' with God. In September 2010 evangelical Christians joined and supported Jewish settlers celebrating the resumption of building their homes on Palestinian land. John Kietz, a Christian Zionist from Kansas, said:

> We are here because only when the Jews are free to settle God's Land of Israel will Jesus descend from heaven to save humanity.[11]

This kind of eschatological thinking leaves open the potential for injustice on a grand scale. It is a clear example of a preference for triumphalist eschatological Christian doctrine over the universal values taught by Jesus.

The establishment of what Jesus called the Kingdom of heaven can only take place in free-will human agreement with the inclusive values he taught. That requires nothing less than a renewal of the mind and heart for people who choose to follow him. Such a requirement for Jesus' followers has far-reaching implications for a new interpretation of Christianity in the twenty-first century. It indicates self-evidently and unmistakably that Jesus did not see himself as a messiah figure who would soon return after his death when God intervened to save the world. Such an idea is inimical to the aim of his teaching, which placed responsibility for the fulfilment of his ideas about the Kingdom of heaven squarely on the shoulders of humanity: "The Kingdom of heaven is within you" (Luke 17:21).

It needs to be said as clearly as possible that Jesus' teachings are systemic in their scope and politically and socially subversive. They contain ethics which turn on their heads the values upon which human societies have lived, both internally and in relationship with their neighbour societies. There can be little doubt that the church's historical reliance on the second coming of Jesus stemmed from the difficulty of implementing his teachings. They looked like foolishness in a world of corrupt, dominating and exploitative systems of governance, plus the corruption of even well-meaning individuals caught up in those systems. Partly for that reason, the church of the fourth century moved toward a personalized faith focussed on belief in and reliance on, an interventionist God. This belief included God's requirement of Jesus' atoning death for individual shortcomings and left the full implementation of the Kingdom of heaven on earth to God at an eschatological 'end time'.

In complete contrast with the church's traditional understanding of the meaning of Jesus, the view of Jesus and his teachings to be outlined in this book contains huge implications for the way Christianity can be re-shaped and re-established for this century. By taking Jesus' teachings with absolute seriousness it is possible to see in them enormous potential for the unity of humanity, not only within Christianity itself, but beyond particular religions and cultures. The universality of Jesus' teachings can enable interfaith cooperation at a profoundly ethical level. The way is then open even for the inclusion of people of no religion, who, based on those universal values, recognize a genuine vision for an enlightened humanity.

To initiate his vision for the world, Jesus could do no other than stand up and say what he believed he was inspired to say. What he said was bold and far-seeing and absolutely audacious in its dimension, but he knew it was real. It was not just a naïve dream; it could work, if only people would listen to his teachings and follow them. The key to make it work was that anyone and everyone could do it; Jesus did not have to do it for them. Once his teachings were firmly grasped they could be lived without further assistance from him. When he found that people he taught had also caught his vision, he knew it was beginning. He told them they could be creators of the vision now imprinted on their own hearts.

Through his teachings Jesus made it plain that he saw it as his role to make this plan of action known to humanity. This was clearly more important to him than anything else; in the end, it became more important to him than his own life. He could not have failed to know that he faced a deadly threat from a state built on domination and exploitation of its people, but he stood up and taught and lived his vision. The vision has survived for two thousand years, despite attempts inside and outside the church to domesticate its socially subversive message. It was for that message he lived and died and for that reason this book includes reflections on the events of Easter. I will present them as clear indications that Jesus was prepared to die for his belief that his followers could create the best possible world.

Since the late twentieth century the church worldwide has seen the development of what is variously called the postmodern church, or progressive Christianity, or what Marcus Borg calls the emerging church.[12] There are several key aspects to this development, including a move away from christological understandings of Jesus and God. For many people it is characterised primarily by a renewed dedication to the teachings of Jesus as set out in the Sermon on the Mount. For them, those teachings represent the only hope for a world in which the hatreds and injustices which have plagued humanity from time immemorial are eliminated from human experience. That is my own belief, for the reason that Jesus' teachings have the potential to unite humanity in harmony and peace.

At the time of Jesus there were no such religions as Christianity or Islam. He therefore was not formulating teaching about the ordering of human society which took into account the belief systems of Christians and Muslims, as well as his fellow Jews. He did not have to allow for the particular festivals or sacred scriptures or doctrine which characterise those two faiths. It is unlikely that he was familiar with Buddhism, even though it pre-dated him by some five centuries. Nor is it likely that he had the opportunity to be acquainted with the writings and practice of Hinduism.

What he most probably did know about were Greek mythologies and the religions of Aramaic-speaking countries such as Persia and Babylon. Finally, he could not fail to have been acquainted with the polytheism of the Roman Empire, which absorbed the religions of newly-conquered areas into its pantheon of religious expression. The religious tolerance of Roman emperors enabled a polytheistic unity which united and stabilised the Empire. Nonetheless, Roman religion contained little of the high ethical requirements of first century Judaism. Ethics which bolstered the imperial system of power, based on the polytheism of Rome, were challenged profoundly by the values of the teacher of the Law of Moses from the Galilee.

SECTION I: SETTING THE SCENE

Jesus of Nazareth was, first and last, a faithful Jew. He and his fellow Jews worshipped the one God of Hebrew tradition, ruling out acceptance of any Roman polytheistic view of religious unity. Yet the principles upon which Jesus' teachings are based have the capacity to unite all of humanity in peace and harmony. Regardless of particular contemporary religious traditions or proclivities, those principles are universally common to human experience in the twenty-first century as the loftiest ideals to which human beings can aspire. Jesus' teachings give these ideals clarity and expression which can bring them into the realm of the possible for all humanity, for all time.

For that reason an intentional adherence to these teachings has in the first instance the capacity to revitalize and reunite the fractured, disillusioned and diminishing church of twenty-first century Western society. A church reunited and reinspired by its founder's teachings will not continue to embrace doctrine that divides Christians from Christians and Christians from all others, religious or non-religious. A revitalized church carrying out the teachings of Jesus will find unity on the basis of those teachings with people of other faiths, or of no faith. The church which reclaims Jesus' teachings will be the church which reclaims his vision for the best possible world – the vision he knew was worth dying for.

This book aims to underline the urgent need in today's world for Jesus' understanding of an enlightened humanity. Further, it aims to show how a comprehensive implementation of his foundational teachings might yet become reality. It will proceed by examining individual teachings and noting their inter-relationship with all others in the Sermon on the Mount.

Lorraine Parkinson,
Melbourne, 2011

1

What of Evil in the World According to Jesus?

> *But I say to you, Love your enemies and pray for those who persecute you, so that you may be children of your Father in heaven; for he makes his sun rise on the evil and on the good, and sends rain on the righteous and on the unrighteous.*
> *(Matt. 5:45)*

Some readers may already be wondering whether this book will outline a case for a utopian paradise in which all human beings have reached a state of perfection and life on earth is totally devoid of pain and suffering. For that reason I begin with an attempt to make clear my thinking about what Jesus' vision of the world is not. In short, I do not see it as a vision of a world completely devoid of evil and its effects. My approach to this all-important issue is based on my belief that Jesus' own thinking did not require a world completely free from evil.

One of the subjects that commonly causes puzzlement and downright consternation in people of faith is the presence of evil in a world they believe to have been created by a good God. Jesus certainly acknowledged the presence of evil; his whole teaching is aimed at the defeat of evil in human affairs. That surely begs the question: will there be evil in the kind of world Jesus envisioned? More particularly, why should evil exist at all if everyone were to live in accordance with the blueprint Jesus offered for an enlightened compassionate humanity? Why should there be any negative emotions or physical pain and suffering in such an environment? How could the world Jesus taught about be the best possible world if it still included evil?

The subject of theodicy (the problem of evil) is far too complex to address fully in the framework of this book, but it cannot be avoided entirely in a discussion concerning Jesus' vision of the world. Even in such a desirable state of affairs, evil would of necessity continue to exist. More specifically, the potential for evil would remain, which means that the development of the society Jesus called the Kingdom of heaven and the continuing existence of evil, must somehow be reconciled. This chapter will address the apparent contradiction.

We cannot know precisely how Jesus may have thought about the existence of evil in a world he believed to have been created by a good God. We can, however, glean some knowledge of his thoughts about evil from the images of God he presented in his sayings and stories. Jesus' teachings indicate clearly that he was a competent scholar of the Hebrew scriptures. Given that, there is no reason to doubt that he had a good knowledge of the quintessential biblical textbook on the problem of evil, the Book of Job. Job is recognized as the one biblical resource which wrestles seriously with the question of why good people have bad things happen to them. It presents the various ways Job's friends try to explain why Job and his family have suffered ill fortune, including financial catastrophe, substantial health problems and the untimely deaths of close family members. The explanations offered always involve the direct action of God. They also place the blame for Job's trials and tribulations at the feet of Job himself. He must have done something wrong; he has not confessed his sin; his children who died must also have sinned.

In essence, his friends argue that Job's suffering is caused by his unrepented offences against God. The various kinds of evil he experiences are understood to have been inflicted by a God who intervenes and punishes to bring about what the three friends regard as justice. Their theological explanation of the presence of evil in Job's life and his family's life is that it was created and inflicted by a judgmental God to punish these unrepentant human beings. This view of evil has lingered in the thought world of some Christians for almost two thousand years.

Yet even where people do not believe in a judgmental, even vindictive God, but do believe in a God who is both omnipotent and ultimately good, there remains a real problem. If God is all powerful and all good, then surely God could easily eliminate evil. Many of the world's great thinkers have wrestled with that thought and been unable to find a satisfactory answer. Among them is Epicurus, a Greek philosopher of the third century BCE[13]:

> *God either wishes to take away evils, and is unable; or He is able, and is unwilling; or He is neither willing nor able, or He is both willing and able. If He is willing and is unable, He is feeble, which is not in accordance with the character of God; if He is able and unwilling, He is envious, which is equally at variance with God; if He is neither willing nor able, He is both envious and feeble, and therefore not God; if He is both willing and able, which alone is suitable to God, from what source then are evils? Why does He not remove them?*[14]

The closing view of the Book of Job is that there is no answer to the question of why bad things happen to good people. It has Job admitting that God and God's ways are a mystery that no human being can penetrate and understand. Many Christians have given up asking why evil things happen after reading the Book of Job. "There is no answer to it", is all they can say.

A much more helpful book in the Hebrew Bible is Ecclesiastes. Its writer is sometimes called The Philosopher, for good reason. The best known passage in Ecclesiastes is in chapter 3, verses 1-8. A popular song is based on its opening verse: "For everything there is a season, and a time for every matter under heaven". The ensuing seven verses express the moral points and counter-points of ordinary living, such as "a time to weep, and a time to laugh;" "a time to kill, and a time to heal;" "a time to love, and a time to hate". These opposing concepts are part and parcel of life as humanity experiences it. In a philosophical and a practical sense they enable humanity to understand opposing moral concepts such as better or worse. It is self-evident that were there no such idea as 'worse', there would be no corresponding understanding of what it means to get better – to become a better piano player or a better human being. This leads not only to the basic differentiation between the concepts of good and evil, but also to recognition of their necessary partnership.

Evil must exist, if only in potential, if humanity is to understand the concept of 'good'. Evil choices must be real possibilities if humanity is to struggle to avoid them, or defeat them. All of Jesus' teachings are designed to help human beings oppose evil and increase the amount of good in the world. Through the application of those teachings, his followers can develop the moral strength to resist and surmount evil influences in themselves and others. For that reason the potential for evil is, and will remain, a necessary part of the best possible world.

There are two primary types of evil; the suffering which results from natural causes and that which results from human immorality, ignorance or foolishness. Luke's gospel contains a small glimpse of Jesus' thoughts about both kinds of evil. Chapter 13:1-5 indicates his belief that God is not the cause of two tragic events which happened to people who (he says) were no better or worse than anyone else. The first event was the collapse of the Tower of Siloam near Jerusalem, which killed eighteen people. Jesus knew it was not punishment caused by God because the people concerned were evil. They were simply victims of a tragic accident caused perhaps by poor building techniques or perhaps by natural forces such as an earthquake. The falling tower illustrates natural evil as pain, suffering and premature death experienced through the operation of the natural laws of gravity and motion. Quite simply, the structure of the universe relies on those laws for its continued existence. Even in a world where human beings lived entirely according to the wisdom of Jesus, the sharp edges of the natural world controlled by the laws of physics would still have the potential to cause pain and suffering to soft-fleshed creatures. Weakened or earthquake damaged buildings will always collapse on the unfortunate.

Some Christian leaders still regard that kind of occurrence as punishment from an interventionist God. One American televangelist suggested that the 2010 Haiti earthquake was God punishing Haitians for "aligning themselves, at times, with the devil." In 2008 one Nebraska state senator went even further than that; Senator Ernie Chambers attempted to sue God. He wanted the court to order God to stop causing "widespread death, destruction and terrorisation of millions upon millions of the Earth's inhabitants". He cited as evidence of God's wrath, fearsome floods, hurricanes, earthquakes, plagues, famine, genocidal wars and birth defects. The suit claimed that the "defendant" had "manifested neither compassion nor remorse". The judge, however, ruled that the plaintiff must be able to serve papers on the defendant for a law-suit to go ahead. They could not do that, as the Almighty has an unlisted address!

The second instance of evil (this time morally based) cited in the passage from Luke is the Roman massacre of Galileans going about their religious duties. Jesus says they did not deserve to die in that way any more than anyone else did. The implication is that the blame lies in an immoral approach to governance, where tragic events occur because dominating governing bodies exert their authority through violence. Again, Jesus does not blame God.

In contrast with these examples of Jesus' apparent view of God as non-interventionist, the passage ends on a decidedly messianic note.[15] Luke places in Jesus' mouth an exhortation to his listeners to "repent" before the messianic age begins, when evil and evil-doers will be destroyed by God: "unless you repent, you will all perish just as they did." This book does not make a case for Jesus' vision as the attaining of a perfect world of perfect human beings. For that reason it will not argue for Jesus as an eschatological teacher who believed that the present world would end with the intervention of God to destroy evil and restart the world in the pristine perfect mould of a second Garden of Eden. There is no evidence from history or science that the world ever was perfect. Neither is there evidence in the Sermon on the Mount that Jesus believed the world would become perfect, including humanity itself, either by intervention of God or by human effort in following his guidelines for life.

Even in the best possible world as Jesus saw it, human and animal suffering will continue to be caused by the action of violent weather-based phenomena such as cyclones, lightning and floods. The fact is that the planet sometimes behaves in ways that cause pain and death to creatures who inhabit it. Volcanoes, earthquakes and tsunamis obeying natural laws will continue to have the potential to cause untimely mass deaths and great suffering. Destructive bushfires caused by heat and lightning will always be a feature of dry areas of the earth such as the continent of Australia. Deadly diseases potentially will continue to exist as part of the interaction between biological processes and living creatures.

The question is whether the creation of Jesus' vision can be expected to have any deterrent effect on pain and suffering caused by features of the natural world. If the natural order will and must remain the same, destructive natural events can continue to occur. If the potential for moral evil must remain in order that human beings learn to become morally strong and discerning, immoral acts may continue to occur. The question then becomes, if the cards are so stacked against Jesus' vision of the best possible world, why should anyone bother to follow him?

Acknowledgment of this question is inherent in all of Jesus' teachings discussed in this book. At present humanity spends overwhelming resources on weapons of death and destruction and the waging of war between national, religious and ideological groups. Yet Chapter 24 (on the Golden Rule) describes the transformed world which could occur if that rule were applied. If human beings avoided doing to others what they would not want done to themselves, there could be a world without war and crime. Instead of wasting the world's resources on destructive warfare, humanity could apply them to developing warning and rescue systems to relieve the effects of cyclones, floods, tsunamis, blizzards and bushfires. Where natural disasters occurred, universal goodwill could ensure that adequate help is swiftly given to restore the necessities of life. Acknowledgment of the equal rights of all people could also ensure that none were disadvantaged because they lived in flood or drought-prone areas. An enlightened compassionate humanity could ensure that huge resources were made available to eradicate disease and genetically-based abnormalities.

This holistic view of the world as Jesus saw it would include intentional protection of the welfare and well-being of animal species, as well as the preservation of earth's life-giving eco-systems. Jesus' vision identifies the moral qualities needed to enable human cooperation for the good of all. On a world-wide scale this could create the impetus and energy to cope with or prevent the potential for suffering caused by natural evil.

In the moral sphere the aim would be different. In a world where humanity as a whole had learned to live in the best way possible, the potential for evil could finally have taken its rightful place as intellectual counter-point to a profound understanding of what is good. In such a world, human freedom in partnership with a belief in the triumph of goodness would have reached the pinnacle of its possibilities. For believers in God, the English theologian and specialist in theodicy, John Hick, has the last word:

> *It is logically possible that a universe might have been created in which the created beings respond to God in a freely given love and trust and worship which he has himself caused to occur by his initial formation of their nature. But such a universe would be a poor second best to the one in which created beings, whose responses to himself God has not 'fixed' in advance, come freely to love, trust and worship him.*[16]

Clearly Jesus' vision is not of a perfect Utopia where there is no pain and suffering and no potential for either natural or moral-based evil. Yet even taking into account the physical nature of the created order and humanity's essential need for freedom of choice, the world Jesus envisaged does contain the potential to become the best possible world. Such a world would not be perfect because it was divinely re-created at an eschatological End time, or because it became perfect through a perfect observance of Jesus' teachings.

Crucially, there must be a qualification of what the best possible world might be. Plainly, it could only be the best possible world for its own time. After all, Jesus' vision of the best possible world in his time would not have included cures for diseases such as diphtheria and bubonic plague, or corrective surgery for heart disease. What might be the best possible world in 2011 would not include cures for various forms of cancer, or for multiple sclerosis. The best possible world in 2070 may well be free of those two scourges. In other words, the best possible world is not a point of arrival – it is the best way the world can be at any given period. The world will never be perfect; there will always be room for improvement.

Followers of Jesus do not have the potential to develop a perfect world, but through their change of mind and heart each can help to bring about the best possible world in their own time and place. This is the all-inclusive possibility behind the teachings of Jesus of Nazareth.

A note of clarification in all of this concerns the end of the teachings in Matthew chapter 5 (v.48). Here there is a command of Jesus that has become a stumbling block for many people: "Be perfect, therefore, as your heavenly Father is perfect." Contrary to what I have said about Jesus not pointing the way to a perfect world, this would appear to be clear expectation that his followers themselves should become perfect. In fact this command has been continually cited throughout Christian history as primary reason why the Sermon on the Mount ought to be regarded purely as an 'ideal' for discipleship, not as actual guidelines for following Jesus.

Here I turn the reader's attention to the word *tamam* in Jesus' language Aramaic. It has been filtered through the Greek word *teleioi* in Matthew's gospel and finally into English as 'perfect'. Both *tamam* and *teleioi* have the meaning of something which is whole or complete. This does concern moral fulfilment, but is most closely related to the idea of human integrity in a personality which contains no corrupting or divisive elements.[17] The English word 'perfect' here is misleading. This saying does not mean that Jesus' followers must be without fault or the potential for fault as they begin to follow Jesus. His saying is actually a command which is really a promise – if you follow my guidelines for life on earth, you will reach your own completeness or fulfilment as a human being. In that sense Jesus' saying is incentive to follow him, not the disincentive it has often been taken to be.

QUESTIONS FOR DISCUSSION CONCERNING ISSUES RAISED IN SECTION I

1. How do you see the Kingdom of heaven as proclaimed by Jesus?

2. Do you think Jesus meant it to be brought into being by God at the End Time? If not, why not?

3. Do you think Jesus meant the Kingdom of heaven to be a perfect world? Would that be possible?

SECTION II

The Beatitudes

2

The Power of Humility

When Jesus saw the crowds, he went up the mountain; and after he sat down, his disciples came to him. Then he began to speak, and taught them, saying: "Fortunate are the poor in spirit, for theirs is the kingdom of heaven." (Matt. 5:3)

In accordance with Matthew's version of the Sermon on the Mount we will first consider nine sayings which could be understood as a creed for followers of Jesus (see Appendix I). The nine sayings set out the qualities and characteristics of people who are equipped to create the world of Jesus' vision. In Aramaic, the language of Jesus, the root word translated into English as 'blessed' is *ashar*, meaning to be strong and happy, or fortunate. Accordingly, in the quotations from scripture at the chapter headings I have substituted the word 'blessed' with 'fortunate'.

The nine sayings have become known as the beatitudes. The first is expressed in Luke's gospel (6:20) differently, as "Blessed are you who are poor, for yours is the kingdom of God." Matthew's version understands poor to mean poor in spirit. Either way, Jesus made reference to the poor in the first of these primary statements about what he called the Kingdom of heaven on earth. The key to understanding this teaching is that there are three ways to interpret the word 'poor' in scripture. In Aramaic the one word (*anavim*) translated into English as poor has three different meanings. First there is 'poverty-stricken' as opposed to rich. Second there is 'oppressed' as opposed to dominant. Third there is 'humble-minded' as opposed to egotistical. Jesus referred to the poor in all three of those meanings. In the first meaning, poor is understood in a passive sense; the poor are simply those who are not rich. In fact they suffer because they are poor. They are victims, helpless before the circumstances of their birth, or the forces of nature, or the events of their lives. In Jesus' eyes the poverty-stricken poor are always to be helped. They are to be fed, their diseases are to be cured, they are to be clothed and housed. From Israel's prophets the constant plea is on behalf of the poor and the oppressed. This is echoed in Jesus' teaching.

Luke's gospel includes Jesus' statement of purpose at the beginning of his public appearances. In the synagogue at Nazareth he quotes from the prophet Isaiah: "The spirit of the Lord is upon me, to bring good news to the poor."[18] Because of this and other prophetic quotations associated with Jesus in the gospels[19], some scholars regard Jesus as having the self-understanding of a prophet. This is certainly the view of Muslims. There is no doubt that he found an enormous amount of inspiration in the prophets, particularly in the writings of the prophet Isaiah. He may well have seen himself as having a prophetic voice in his proclamation of the Kingdom of heaven. Both prophets and teachers commonly had an inner circle of students or 'disciples'.

Yet given Jesus' powerful and constant teaching role and the forty-seven references to him as 'Teacher' in the gospels, it is not unreasonable to come to the conclusion that he saw himself primarily as a teacher. It is true that essentially there is no contradiction between the role of prophet and that of a teacher calling his followers to alter the future, but many of Jesus' teachings are not so much prophetic utterances as aphorisms, or wisdom sayings. For that reason I see him as teacher proclaiming the way to the best possible world, who sometimes performed prophetic actions such as the 'cleansing of the Temple' and sounded prophet-like in his condemnation of the unjust.

The word in Isaiah and the first beatitude which is translated into English as poor was originally in Hebrew, which is the biblical form of Aramaic. It therefore carries that three-fold meaning: poverty-stricken, oppressed and humble. Jesus knew that. He saw the best possible world as a state of affairs where no one was poor and no one was rich, no one was oppressed and no one was dominant. In the face of earth's sometimes harsh climatic conditions, all would have sufficient food, clothing and shelter. The primary question remains: why are the poor fortunate? The answer is in the second half of the saying: "for yours is the Kingdom of heaven."

Yet the best possible life for all had definitely not become reality in Jesus' time. Nor has it become reality in the twenty-first century. As well as victims of cyclones, bushfires and earthquakes, there are millions of poverty-stricken and hungry people on Planet Earth in the third millennium CE. Millions of people are not just hungry, they are starving to death. Millions are still living under the dominance of dictators. What then does Jesus mean by, "Fortunate are you who are poor, for yours is the kingdom of heaven"?

As already mentioned, we have no reason to believe that Jesus taught in Greek. What if in the first beatitude he had used the Aramaic word *anavim* (translated into Greek and then into English as 'poor') actually to mean humble, which is one of the basic meanings of *anavim*? "Fortunate are the humble in spirit, for theirs is the kingdom of heaven". It is clear that humble-mindedness (or humility) need not be a passive state. To be poverty-stricken and oppressed is to be a victim. To be deliberately humble is to take a highly pro-active stance. The deliberately humble are people of great courage and strength. It is much easier to push in and take what is on offer than to stand back and make sure others first have their fair share. What if the first beatitude addressed the deliberately humble, those who do not push themselves ahead of others? What if it meant people who are willing to share what they have for the good of everyone? What if it meant people who do not insist on their own way? What if it meant people who use peaceful means to resolve conflict? Could that be the reason Jesus placed this beatitude first? Could it be the key to understanding how his vision can become reality?

The stunning thought here is that it is the deliberately humble people, not the proudly powerful and self-important, who have the real power. It is the deliberately humble who are equipped to change the world. It is they who will reform systems that distribute resources unequally. It is they who will break down systems that use force and violence to keep the peace. It is they who will release humanity from pervasively powerful political and religious institutions which corrupt even the best-intentioned individuals. It is they who will bring about reconciliation between all people.

Matthew grasps this truth in his stating of the first beatitude: "Fortunate are the poor in spirit, for theirs is the Kingdom of heaven". Matthew was obviously a well educated Jew. In addition to Hebrew he would have been able to read and write Greek, a common element of upper class Jewish education in his time. It is also most likely that he spoke the common language of the first century Middle East – Aramaic. He was therefore linguistically equipped to know that Jesus was not talking about the poor purely as those who live in poverty. He would have understood Jesus to mean that the poor in spirit are the deliberately humble in spirit – in their hearts and minds. That is why the best possible world belongs to them! Jesus continued to develop aspects of this same theme throughout his teaching. It is no wonder that it comes first.

3
Creative Comfort

Fortunate are those who mourn, for they will be comforted.
(Matt. 5:4)

It is understandable that the distressing emotional state of mourning should be addressed by someone who claimed to be announcing the way to the best possible world. Mourning is universally one of the most painful of human experiences and almost no one goes through a whole lifetime without experiencing the painful loss of someone (or something) very dear. This fact begs a question: if Jesus' aim was to comfort those who are mourning, does this mean that mourning, or grieving, would not exist in the world he imagined?

The answer to that must emphatically be: No! Of course not! Death will always be a necessary part of life and nothing can remove from human experience the pain of losing someone near and dear. Even if the best possible means of dying were to become the experience of every creature, each person (or animal) would still leave behind those who mourned them. To imagine a world without mourning is to imagine a world of robots without feeling. Of course people will continue to die; of course they will be missed by those who love them. There will always be the potential for pain like that of the anonymous mother who wrote this verse:

I never feel the sun… I never feel the rain…
all I feel is pain… since you've gone.

> *My son I miss you so… I never thought you'd go… before me.*
> *You are so loved… You are so missed.*

To love deeply is to risk the pain of loss, yet to be without love is to be deprived of the best that life can offer. Jesus knew that when he urged his followers to love one another.

In this beatitude Jesus was speaking to people who were mourning in his time, yet his words apply to people who mourn in any age. His emphasis is on the comfort that will be offered, although what he says is paradoxical: "Fortunate are those who mourn." The justification for this seeming contradiction is in the second half of the saying: "for they will be comforted". In the context of the beatitudes the comfort Jesus is announcing is related to the coming of a better world. It is also legitimate to see this saying simply as a call to comfort someone whose loved one has died and it has often been put to that use. Yet even in those circumstances a helpful way to offer comfort is eventually to point out that the mourner's own life has not ended. It is possible for him or her to begin something new and find solace and contentment in that. Even so, one would hardly say that mourners are fortunate, or blessed. There is mystery here.

Given that, it is useful to determine whom Jesus might have meant when he referred to "those who mourn". If we keep in mind that all of the beatitudes are focussed on Jesus' vision, the answer to the question is easier to find. The Hebrew scriptures reveal long-established traditions concerning comfort offered to those who mourn. The books of the Prophets describe the conquests of Israel and Judea and the exile of the people in foreign lands. Over and over again the invader comes; over and over again the people mourn. They mourn for their past wiped away, for their homes destroyed, for their loved ones killed in military invasion or taken into exile. They mourn for their homeland, for their way of life, for their religion, for their place of worship, for their city, even for their God. All of that seems dead, or destroyed.

The prophet Jeremiah poignantly captures the grief of

people left behind when their loved ones are taken into exile in Babylon. The wives and mothers and children try to keep the home fires burning while they await the return of the exiles. Eventually they grieve the loss of their final asset – hope. Jeremiah has a message for them: "Thus says the Lord: a voice is heard in Ramah, lamentation and bitter weeping. Rachel is weeping for her children; she refuses to be comforted for her children, because they are no more" (31:15). Then comes the answer from God: "Keep your voice from weeping, and your eyes from tears; for there is reward for your work, says the Lord: they shall come back from the land of the enemy; there is hope for your future, says the Lord: your children shall come back to their own country" (31:16). In Isaiah 40:1 the message is addressed to the exiles themselves: "Comfort!" or "take comfort!" You are released; get up and go back to Judea. New life is beginning!

In both cases the comfort offered is not just consolation; it has an active intention. There is encouragement to let go of the past and to embrace a new future. The word Jesus would have used in Aramaic for comfort (*nakham*) contains that active meaning. In Jewish tradition the mourner is offered bread by a 'comforter' as a means of strength for the days to come. Even the English word comfort has the root meaning of 'with strength'. As I noted in the previous chapter, the root Aramaic word translated into English as 'blessed' is *ashar*, which includes the meaning of strength.

Jesus called people to be involved actively in creating the best possible world and he knew they could not do it while they clung to the old certainties of the past. In this beatitude he addressed the pain of grieving, or mourning. With the coming of his envisaged world in mind he said, "You will be comforted." There are two helpful ways to understand Jesus' saying. The first is that when Jesus said, "you will be comforted" he meant that the mourners would be strong enough to let go of their reliance on the past. Jesus knew very well that the pain of grieving means at least a temporary withdrawing from active involvement in life. For a time the focus of the bereaved is inevitably on the past, when the beloved was still around. There is little involvement in the present, let alone an active embracing of the future.

A famous example of this was the widowhood of Queen Victoria. Her beloved Prince Albert had died of typhoid fever, probably due to primitive sanitary arrangements at Windsor Castle. Victoria, however, blamed her son Edward for his father's death. Edward had been playing up at Cambridge, necessitating Albert going there to give him a fatherly pep-talk. Immediately on his return to Windsor Albert succumbed to typhoid fever, at which point Victoria put on black and went into mourning for the rest of her life. She conducted the affairs of the monarchy from the seclusion of Balmoral or Windsor and never again went out in public. She was unable to be reconciled with Edward. She mourned from 1861 (when Albert died) until her own death in 1901. There is the rumour that comfort came to Victoria in the person of a certain John Brown. Be that as it may, in Jesus' terms being comforted is being helped to gain the strength to let go of the past. The past, after all, cannot be altered; to cling to the past is to maintain the pain and helplessness of being unable to change it.

In Jesus' own context, when he thought about people in mourning he would have had particular mourners in mind. He would have seen them as people who had lost their loved ones and were longing for their past. He would also have understood "you who mourn" as people longing for Israel's past. It is probable that he personally knew people who yearned for a time when Israel lived in security and peace, free from exploitation and persecution. In fact that golden time was not far behind Jesus' own life-time. After Jewish patriots called Maccabeans rose against Greek occupation in the second century BCE, Israel was then ruled by its own leaders from 164–63 BCE. Because that period ended less than two generations before Jesus was born, there would have been older people around during his childhood who remembered what it was like to live in freedom. To their dismay, in the year 63 BCE a new occupying empire had arrived in their homeland – the Romans. Like Jeremiah and Isaiah, Jesus and his contemporaries were looking for an end to the violence of occupation, when the people would be free to follow their religion as they pleased and live without fear of the Romans.

Yet the second beatitude is a call to something far better than a return to the rule of the Maccabeans. The people are now to take an active role in shaping the future. The way to do that is not through violent revolution but by the carrying out of Jesus' teachings. Through an active expression of them, people who mourn will be able to let go of the past, take hold of the future and find their comfort.

This kind of active comfort is illustrated in a poem written by Wilhelmina Stitch.[20] Wilhelmina wrote the poem from her own experience of an active recovery from grief:

THEN JOY STEPPED IN

Said she, 'I will not live with Grief from morrow unto morrow.
My heart cries out for some relief. Good-bye, my little sorrow.'
She closed the windows of her home and pulled down every blind.
'I'm going forth,' she cried, 'to roam. You, Grief can stay behind.'
Grief wanly watched her go away into the warmth and light;
with quickened step and brightened eyes she mingled with the throng.
Instead of pale Grief's moans and sighs she heard Endeavour's song.
She saw a sister, crossed the road and asked her how she fared:
then helped to lift her heavy load and in the burden shared.
Throughout the day Self was suppressed whilst Service took its place.
When she returned at night to rest – of Grief there was no trace!
But Joy stepped forth and sweetly said, 'May I be your friend instead?'

The poem is simple, the wisdom is profound.

In the second beatitude comfort for those who mourn is encouraging, but not just that, it is also a call to action. It is the kind of comfort that breaks down barriers to involvement in the new. Jesus knew it would not be easy for people in his time to let go of their mourning for Israel's past. He also knew the wisdom he taught would enable them to create a positive future. An apparently simple concern with caring for the bereaved contains a crucial aspect of his plan of action to bring to reality the best possible world.

4
Courage to Resist

Fortunate are the meek, for they will inherit the earth.
(Matt. 5:5)

What sort of word is meek? The problem here is that it is hard to imagine anyone with Jesus' kind of courage telling his followers to be meek! There are few words in English that create a clearer picture of a spineless wimp than the word meek. Given that, why did Jesus think the meek will inherit the earth? How could they? They would not have the courage. Or so I thought before I actually looked up meek in English. I consulted a good selection of dictionaries and some said meek meant submissive, yielding, non-resistant, gentle. None came close to the meaning in Jesus' language until I consulted the Macquarie. It said meek meant 'humbly patient under provocation from others'.[21] There is nothing spineless about that. Being meek as Jesus understood it is not about being a door-mat. Here Jesus would again have used the Aramaic word *anavim*, albeit with a different connotation from its meaning in the first beatitude. In this case the meaning of *anavim* is again humble, but specifically we will see that it is humble as in non-violent.

Patience in the face of provocation takes real courage. It implies the strength of character to refrain from retaliating when provoked. It implies moral courage of the highest order. Most importantly, it captures the essence of Jesus' central ethic of non-violent resistance to evil, an essential qualification for creators of the world according to his vision. After all, human society has almost always been run by the rules of violence. Violence has usually been the solution of choice for problems between individuals and between nations. Wars of the early twenty-first century such as in Iraq and Afghanistan are continuing testaments to the dominance of the rule of violence. On the sporting field and in film and on TV, violence is accepted as the norm. To oppose violence is to oppose a whole culture largely influenced and driven by violence. Aspiring followers of Jesus should not fool themselves; non-violence is not an easy option. Yet it has the capacity to turn upside down the violent norms of the contemporary world.

It is essential to understand what non-violent resistance is, and is not. Some people have opposed the whole concept of non-violence by citing the case of the Jewish people under the Nazis. They have argued that the Jews adopted non-violence as their response to murderous power, and that it was completely ineffective. In fact that was not the case. The reality was that the Jews were scattered in small groups throughout Europe. As small minorities in each society they became isolated victims of state-sponsored violence. Because of their limited numbers in any one location, they were unable to mount a concerted, united campaign of non-violent resistance to Hitler without the support of Christian majorities in those countries. Needlessly (and shamefully) it must be said that they were not offered that help. On one of few occasions when the Jewish people had sufficient numbers in one place to mount a resistance against their murderers, they took up arms to fight the Nazis in the Warsaw Ghetto.

June 6 is the anniversary of the assassination of former US Attorney-General, Robert Kennedy (1925-1968). Also on June 6 but two years earlier, Kennedy had addressed a rally of black South Africans looking for freedom from the shameful system of Apartheid. In supporting their non-violent resistance to Apartheid, he said:

> *Moral courage is a rarer commodity than bravery in battle or great intelligence. Yet it is the one essential, vital quality of those who seek to change a world which yields most painfully to change.*

Nelson Mandela, who was able to turn the tables of white domination, adopted non-violence as his modus operandi, as did Mohandas Gandhi and Martin Luther King. Gandhi saw clearly the strong connection between humility of mind and the ability to practice non-violence: Non-violence is impossible without humility.[22] M. Fethullah Gülen, the Muslim scholar and writer, advocated a non-violent attitude toward the 'ill-natured':

> *Return good for evil, and disregard discourteous treatment. An individual's character is reflected in his or her behaviour. Choose tolerance, and be magnanimous toward the ill-natured.*[23]

The Tibetan Buddhist spiritual leader, the Dalai Lama, also has expressed his commitment to non-violence.[24] With that in mind, the third beatitude can appropriately be expressed as: "Fortunate are the deliberately humble non-violent, for they will inherit the earth." Non-violent resistance to the practice of evil is a highly pro-active stance.

Jesus knew that violence is the great destroyer, not just of bodies but of souls. Six points can be deduced from Jesus' teachings on non-violent resistance to violence:

1. Non-violent resistance creates shame in the violent one. It can lead to an awareness of harm being done and a desire for reconciliation.
2. Non-violent resistance is resistance to the power of evil itself. It does not mean running away from confrontation.
3. Non-violent resistance is an expression of love. The focus is on turning the violent opponent to repentance and from an enemy into a friend.
4. Non-violent resistance accepts the possibility of suffering to defeat the power of violence.
5. Non-violent resistance leads to justice for the powerless.

6. Non-violent resistance can establish on earth the peaceful, just world Jesus called the Kingdom of heaven.

A clear modern example of Jesus' policy of non-violent resistance is contained in the words of Martin Luther King in a sermon preached at Dexter Avenue Baptist Church, Montgomery, Alabama, in 1957:

> *To our most bitter opponents we say: We shall match your capacity to inflict suffering by our capacity to endure suffering. We shall meet your physical force with soul force. Do to us what you will, and we shall continue to love you. We cannot in all good conscience obey your unjust laws, because non-cooperation with evil is as much a moral obligation as is cooperation with good. Throw us in jail, and we shall still love you. Bomb our homes and threaten our children, and we shall still love you. Send your hooded perpetrators of violence into our communities at the midnight hour and beat us and leave us half dead, and we shall still love you. But be ye assured that we will wear you down by our capacity to suffer. One day we shall win freedom, but not only for ourselves. We shall so appeal to your heart and conscience that we shall win you in the process, and our victory will be a double victory.*

Given that non-violence is a foundational aspect of Jesus' plan of action for the best possible world, it deserves our closest attention. As I noted before, there is plenty of opposition to non-violent resistance and not just from people who actually use violence. Most of humanity still believes that violence is the answer to society's ills and unfortunately, the church has a history of acquiescence to violence that most Christians prefer to forget. For many years church-goers sang hymns that used the imagery of soldiers victorious in war. Who can forget 'Onward, Christian soldiers, marching as to war'? Or, 'Stand up, stand up for Jesus, ye soldiers of the Cross'? Many more hymns of that sort have been sung in both war-time and peace-time. The military imagery testifies to the church's long-term tacit support for involvement in war.

Even though millions of good people have gone to war willingly in defence of home and nation they are nonetheless victims of war, the continuing vicious cycle of violence and counter-violence. Paradoxically, when Christian nations went to war it was usually done with the blessing of the church in the name of Jesus, whose clear and passionate call was to non-violence. Christian empires in all ages have used their religion to reinforce their desire to conquer and dominate, or to defend themselves violently from the violence of other empires.

In defence of violence as the solution to violence, many have argued that non-violent resistance would not have worked in the world wars of the twentieth century. Veterans of wars have described how turning the other cheek to a soldier of an opposing army would only have resulted in their being shot. They have not understood that non-violent resistance has nothing to do with wars and armies. Once the decision to go to war has been made, the option of non-violent resistance has implicitly been rejected. A soldier cannot engage in non-violent resistance; he is doomed to participate in the giving and receiving of violence.

Non-violent resistance refuses to arm itself and be involved in warfare or military-based coups, but many Christians do not rule out using violent defence in order to protect the innocent from a violent robber or intruder, etc. On the large scale, this is the essence of Just War theory, which may be traced back to the fifth century writings of Augustine. He declared that Christians had a loving obligation to use violence if necessary to defend the innocent against evil. This theory was adopted by a church which had become a part of the war-oriented Roman hegemony. That position has ever since influenced the church, which has led Christians to be identified as among the most warlike people on the planet.

The New Testament scholar Walter Wink has written extensively to explain the concept of non-violence in Jesus' teachings. He has identified the full consequences of the church's acquiescence to the norms of empire and the Just War theory:

The price the church paid was embracing violence as the means of preserving empire. But the removal of non-violence from the

> *gospel blasted the keystone from the arch, and Christianity collapsed into a religion of personal salvation in an afterlife jealously guarded by a wrathful and terrifying God – the whole system carefully managed by an elite corps of priests with direct backing from the secular rulers now regarded as the elect agents of God's working in history.*[25]

Obviously Jesus did not want his followers to stand idly by while the innocent suffered; he expected them to resist violence and injustice, but to do it non-violently (Matt. 5: 38-42). It is crucial to note that non-violent resistance cannot be equated with the standpoint of pacifism.[26] Jesus did not teach passivity without resistance in the face of evil. That kind of accepted powerlessness or resignation is the very thing he was trying to overcome, the very thing he confronted in his teachings. The past history of violence on a large scale cannot be changed. A genuine embrace of non-violent resistance to evil in civilian and international life can ensure the inheritance of a very different kind of earth.

Another advocate of non-violence was Sheikh Abdul Aziz Bukhari, Co-Director of Jerusalem Peacemakers and founding member of the Abrahamic Reunion group of religious leaders. Sheikh Bukhari dedicated his life to promoting peace, harmony and unity in Jerusalem, in the Middle East and the world until his death in 2010. He made this commitment clear in a 2008 interview with the Globaloneness Project:

> *The stronger one is the one who can absorb the violence and anger from the other and change it to love and understanding. It is not easy; it is a lot of work. But this is the real jihad. Two wrongs do not make a right. We need to transform violence through love for the other and change him through showing him goodness.*

In his book *God & Empire*,[27] John Dominic Crossan sets out clearly the difference between the beliefs of empire and the beliefs of Jesus.[28] He defines the religious beliefs of the Roman Empire as "piety which leads to war, which leads to victory, which leads to peace", in that order. He defines the beliefs of Jesus as "covenant with the God of justice, which leads to non-violence, which leads to justice, which leads to lasting peace". The emphasis of pious Romans on war and victory before peace was repeated in later empires, including those called Christian.

None of this reliance on war was taught by Jesus; for him, lasting peace depended on the existence of universal justice. His original followers lived in a time when violence was a common part of daily life and twenty-first century people cannot begin to imagine the extent of violence used by the ruling class of those times against ordinary people. To oppose actively that kind of violence took courage of an extraordinary kind. Specifically, Jesus called people not to run away from violence but to resist it non-violently. Those who could do that, he said, would "inherit the earth". They would have victory over evil.

The following are two recent examples of justice achieved through the non-violent method of Jesus. The first is set in Nigeria, the world's sixth largest producer of oil. To say the least of it, most Nigerians do not benefit from the enormous wealth which results. People living in the oil producing areas of the Niger Delta have to drink, cook with and wash in polluted water. They eat fish contaminated with oil and their farming land is being destroyed. Oil spills, waste dumping and gas flaring are endemic. The air reeks of petrol and communities complain of breathing problems, skin lesions and other health problems. The estimated six hundred billion dollars US in oil revenue already extracted has done little to alleviate the problems of the region. Instead, the contrast between the wealth of a few and the deepening poverty of many has fuelled discontent and anger.

In the summer of 2002 hundreds of Nigerian women took a non-violent initiative aimed at raising the living standards of ordinary people in the area. Ranging in age from 25 to 90, they succeeded in shutting down an operation that produced half a million barrels of oil per day. Not a shot was fired, not a soul was injured. After a sit-in by its female employees which lasted ten days, the company agreed to provide jobs which brought much needed infrastructure and economic independence to villages where extreme poverty had been the norm.

In 2008, hundreds of taxi drivers sat peacefully in the middle of a Melbourne intersection, protesting against violence in their workplace. The state reacted positively to their non-violent protest by putting into place measures for their increased safety.

Nonetheless, even non-violent demonstrations for justice are sometimes regarded by law-abiding citizens as unacceptable behaviour. In the 1960s many well-meaning Christians were uneasy about Martin Luther King's civil rights demonstrations, even though the protestors were completely non-violent. For those uneasy Christians, law and order in the streets seemed closer to the sacred than justice for the oppressed. In 1963 Martin Luther King responded to this in his famous 'I have a dream' speech:

> *There are those who are asking the devotees of civil rights, "When will you be satisfied?" We can never be satisfied as long as the Negro is the victim of the unspeakable horrors of police brutality. We can never be satisfied as long as our children are stripped of their self-hood and robbed of their dignity by a sign stating: "For Whites Only." We cannot be satisfied as long as a Negro in Mississippi cannot vote and a Negro in New York believes he has nothing for which to vote. No, no, we are not satisfied, and we will not be satisfied until "justice rolls down like waters, and righteousness like a mighty stream."*[29]

Followers of Jesus in Australia can never be satisfied until there is no place where Aboriginal children are treated as less than the equals of white children. Followers of Jesus in Australia can never be satisfied until there is no community where peaceful Muslim Australians are denied the freedom to build a school for their children. Toward the end of the "I have a dream" speech, Martin Luther King said:

> *I have a dream that my four little children will one day live in a nation where they will not be judged by the colour of their skin but by the content of their character.*

It can only be imagined how he might have viewed the news that a former US Senator whose father is a black man had become President of the United States. Martin Luther King gave his all non-violently so that such a thing could come to pass. The past cannot be changed; the future certainly can be different.

The church has often endorsed war as the rightful reaction of the righteous to the unrighteous; hence the war-like language of some of its hymns, the consecration of regimental colours in cathedrals and the blessing of soldiers marching off to expand or defend empire. Fortunately there are increasing differences between the church's historic celebrations of the military and the way mainstream churches view war in the twenty-first century. All Australians welcomed home individual soldiers who had served in Iraq. At the same time, as followers of Jesus the mainstream churches could not endorse Australian involvement in the Iraq war. In 2003, before the war began, there were protest marches in six hundred cities around the world, including Melbourne. In Berlin three hundred thousand people protested, in Madrid there were six hundred thousand on the streets, in London between one and two million, and in Rome three million people protested peacefully against a war in Iraq.

In spite of this widespread opposition to the war, by 2007 millions of Iraqi mothers and fathers, grandmothers and grandfathers, brothers and sisters, children and grandchildren were dead, dreadfully maimed and injured, or driven from their homes. In 2010 this scenario is being perpetuated among innocent civilians in Afghanistan. No amount of reparation or justification from world leaders will alter those facts. This conclusion is supported by the Muslim teacher M. Fethullah Gülen:

> *Humanity is a tree and nations are its branches. Events that appear as heavy winds hurl them against each other and cause them to clash. Of course, the resulting harm is felt by the tree. This is the meaning of "Whatever we do, we do it to ourselves."*[30]

Jesus' followers and those who agree with his teachings cannot be satisfied until war and violence disappear completely from the earth. Where injustice occurs in their own countries the response is clear: peacefully resist the unjust powers and so deprive them of a subservient population. Where injustice occurs in other countries, the task of Jesus' followers is to support those who resist it non-violently. It is high time the church stopped its dithering between a confused pacifism and support for war on the basis of Just War ideas. It is high time that it made a commitment to follow the non-violent way of Jesus. As Walter Wink expressed it:

> *Jesus, in short, abhors both passivity and violence. He articulates, out of the history of his own people's struggles, a way by which evil can be opposed without being mirrored, the oppressor resisted without being emulated, and the enemy neutralized without being destroyed.*[31]

Universal justice remains the only foundation for a permanent universal peace. Fortunate are the meek (the deliberately humble non-violent); through their love and courage they can inherit the earth.

5

Justice: the Wide Angle Lens

*Fortunate are those who hunger and thirst for righteousness,
for they will be filled. (Matt. 5:6)*

One of the grandest, most colourful and ostentatious entrance scenes in history is recorded in the first book of Kings. George Frideric Handel attempted to represent its magnificence in music with his *Arrival of the Queen of Sheba*. If readers of the story take a moment to turn on their imagination, they can picture it all. They can see the gorgeously attired Queen of Sheba, dripping with jewellery, reclining on a magnificently-draped horse-drawn conveyance under a sun-roof, fanned by servants. They can smell her perfumed clothes as she goes by. They can see heavily-laden camels led by richly clothed attendants. They can catch a whiff of exotic spices. They can see the dusty clouds blowing up from the camels' feet and feel the hot sun. They can hear the excitement of the crowds as this fabulous procession approaches the court of King Solomon. It looks like the height of wealth and power in ancient times.

In fact, the Queen of Sheba is on a mission. She has heard that Solomon is the wisest of monarchs and she has come to "test him with hard questions" (1 Kings 10:1). Perhaps there is a hint of rivalry here; after all her realm is large and influential, probably including all of modern-day Ethiopia and Yemen. She has come to see what made Solomon so wise that he is known for it throughout the ancient world. Accordingly she asks her 'hard' questions. He answers them all. Meanwhile the Queen is observing Solomon's household. She notes how well it is run, with everything done in accordance with royal protocol. Yet there is something else; the king's servants are happy! Given that the happiness of servants was not a known preoccupation of kings in antiquity, why are these servants happy? The clue comes in the following verse where the Queen of Sheba says to Solomon, "Because the Lord loved Israel forever, he has made you king to execute justice and righteousness." The author of the first book of Kings points here to a vital connection between human happiness and justice.

The fourth beatitude in the Gospel of Matthew is: "Fortunate are they who hunger and thirst for righteousness, for they will be filled." Again the reader is confronted with a difficult word. Righteousness sometimes carries the idea of a person who is terribly pious, 'holier than thou'. In fact, in both the Greek language of the gospel writers (*dikaiosune*), and the Aramaic language of Jesus (*ts'dakah*), righteousness is related to the concept of justice. The righteous person is one who brings justice for others. In turn, justice brings happiness.[32]

When Jesus taught the beatitudes he had in mind the way life could be. He saw what would happen if humanity lived according to principles for life that build up good human relationships. This beatitude says that people who "hunger and thirst for righteousness" will be satisfied. There are two possible ways to understand this. The first is that people hungry and thirsty for righteousness are those who are deprived of it. They are oppressed by injustice; they are starving for what Australians would call a 'fair go'. Jesus had a clear vision of how the world could be if justice were applied equally to everyone.[33] Plainly he was passionately inspired by the call to justice of the prophets of the Hebrew Bible and accordingly he was not talking only about individual instances of justice or injustice. In this teaching he reveals his big picture thinking about changing the whole world. Obviously he did not know the whole world as we know it, but doubtless he would have believed that the principles he taught are applicable to human society of any time and place. The obvious questions to ask about Jesus' vision are: how realistic is it, and how likely is it that everyone will ever be given a fair go? The most crucial question is, who will put it into practice?

One of the contemporary thinkers trying to come to grips with these questions is Wesley J. Wildman, Associate Professor of Theology and Ethics at Boston University School of Theology. In an article called "What's Radical about Christian Ethics?"[34], he makes the reasonable claim that:

Christianity is dominated by the ideal of love: God's love for the world, Jesus' love for his disciples, his disciples' love for one another, and Christian love for the suffering and the poor.

Wesley Wildman is not talking about love only as between friends. He means invincible goodwill that puts other people and their well-being first. He asks how that would work in relations between nations. How would a US government guided by the ethics of Jesus of Nazareth have responded to the 9/11 terrorist attack? Would it have saturated the area from which the terrorists came, not with bombs, but with gifts to target poverty and childhood illness? By that response would it have begun to correct the comprehensive imbalance of the world's resources that creates resentment and hatred? Would a US government guided by the ethics of Jesus of Nazareth have tried to institute a universal form of restorative justice? Wildman then lists reasons why that strategy might not work. Not least is because the US would be a laughing stock for people who have no use for kindness in international relations.

The reality is that when it is applied to relations between nations, Jesus' ethic of the fair go can look like foolishness, but in 2010 as the US and its allies leave a still-violent Iraq and look to extricate themselves from a faction-ridden, blood-soaked Afghanistan, the same question is still being asked. Could the bloodshed have been avoided if the 'the coalition of the willing' had 'bombed' those countries (plus Pakistan) with material goods and practical aid?

A natural reluctance to appear foolish has often been behind the church's hesitation to push governments too far. It is fair to say that churches have never yet seriously pushed for a radical, universal implementation of Jesus' teaching. It is one thing to say there should be justice for all. It is another thing altogether to put it into practice. This being the case, why did Jesus teach it?

To consider that, there is a need to look at the other side of the equation – that the "righteous" themselves, the people who bring justice for others, are fortunate or happy. Scripture says humanity is created "in the image of God" (Genesis 1:27). That does not mean there is a God who is like a great big androgynous human being. It does mean that humanity can adopt and act on principles it regards as reflections of the divine nature. Specifically, Jesus' followers are called to look at the big picture of the world through what we might call a 'God's eye' perspective – the universally applicable ethics that Jesus articulated. This does not come naturally; most of humanity has a very small picture of the world. The smaller the world picture, the greater the isolation of groups and ideas and the stronger the belief that the other (group) is not like 'us'. The smaller the world picture, the smaller the urge to become acquainted with and understand the 'other'.

When I studied anthropology the first article distributed for reading was called "Body Ritual among the Nacirema", by Horace Miner[35]. It described weird rites among the Nacirema tribe, including all kinds of rituals associated with household shrines. One such ritual involved the mouth:

> The Nacirema have an almost pathological horror of and fascination with the mouth, the condition of which is believed to have a supernatural influence on all social relationships. The daily body ritual performed by everyone includes a mouth-rite. Despite the fact that these people are so punctilious about care of the mouth, this rite involves a practice which strikes the

uninitiated stranger as revolting. It was reported to me that the ritual consists of inserting a small bundle of hog hairs into the mouth, along with certain magical powders, and then moving the bundle in a highly formalized series of gestures."

It took us students quite some time to realise that this was an American cleaning his teeth! (Nacirema is 'American' spelt backwards). Much of human behaviour can look weird to an outsider until an effort is made to understand it.

Further, the smaller the world picture the stronger the tribalism; the stronger the tribalism, the stronger the drive to win goods for 'my tribe' and defend them. This applies whether it is my family, my ethnic group, my religion, my social class, my nation. A recent television commercial features a rich woman, haughtily complaining that the cheaper fur coats being advertised are now within the reach of what she calls the lower classes. "Disgraceful!" she huffs. It is of course meant to be funny, but it is not altogether divorced from truth. The smaller the world view, the stronger the likelihood of injustice toward people 'not like us'. That kind of thinking also applies on the scale of one nation's view of another. To Australians, the Japanese are those weird people who eat the meat of intelligent and magnificent whales. To Japanese, the Australians are those weird people who eat their cute national symbol.

Through this beatitude Jesus' followers have a wide-angle lens on the world. People pictured through the Jesus lens can be seen more clearly as 'like us'. The injustice they suffer can be recognized immediately. They may be starving children in Ethiopia or Pakistan, Americans deprived of adequate medical care, industrial workers without safety measures, bullied children in the playground, African girls with no education. Through the wide-angle Jesus lens all of those examples of injustice, and countless others, can be seen clearly. Why then do so many of Jesus' followers not follow his lead? As Wesley Wildman notes, Christianity too often simply abandons its own core ethical ideals and lines up behind the values of the wider culture.[36]

Yet the teachings of Jesus are crucial to the future of the world. As long as the universal principles they contain are ignored, there will be people who hunger and thirst for righteousness, or justice. As long as they are ignored there will also be people who hunger in vain to be givers of justice. When justice is freely given and freely received, both giver and receiver are blessed with a just and peaceful world. As the beatitude says, "they will be filled".

JUSTICE FOR THE WHOLE CREATED ORDER

It follows then, that if justice is a truly inclusive value, justice for one is justice for all, including justice for inanimate aspects of creation. It must be said that universal justice includes justice for trees and plants and rivers and seas. Would Jesus have seen it that way? No one could seriously doubt that if he lived now he would be concerned for the well-being of the natural order. In his time nature was not threatened by human population expansion, pollution and exploitation, as it is now. Yet the gospels are replete with sayings of Jesus where he displays a clear awareness and appreciation of the natural world. Aspects of nature he uses as illustrations in his teachings are: crops, figs, fruit, grapes, grass, hills, lilies, logs, mountains, rocks, sand, seeds, sky, stones, thorn bushes, trees, vineyards, weeds, wheat, yeast, manure and salt.

The ultimate aim of justice is that all will have sufficient resources for their needs, without taking more than the amount needed. Protection of the natural order is inextricably linked with the aim of justice for human beings. There is plenty of evidence that people whose own lives are diminished by poverty and crime and the effects of war have what Australian scientist and writer Tim Flannery refers to as a tendency to discount the future. Because their own lives do not produce hopes for a different and good future, they are also inclined to discount the future of the natural world:

> *The tendency to discount the future helps explain why people sometimes act to destroy their environment, whether by cutting down rainforests, continuing to pollute the atmosphere or*

destroying biodiversity. And people without prospects are created in a number of ways – through grinding poverty, through greatly unequal societies and through war, famine or other misfortunes. If you're concerned about our future, it's not just desirable that we eradicate poverty in the developing world, create more equal societies and never let ourselves fight another war; it's imperative, for the discount factor tells us that failure to do so may cost us the Earth.[37]

When nature is protected so that it flourishes and produces good and sufficient food for humans and other creatures, there is a mutual experience of justice. Universal justice therefore includes protection of the ecological systems of the earth, including the seas and skies.

People who put the welfare of the natural order ahead of profit-making are sometimes given derogatory names and their views are disregarded. Those who have a passion for the preservation of pristine wilderness are often regarded as plain foolish. Yet if they were asked why they were so concerned with the conservation of trees, they would probably connect old growth forests with clean air, the absorption of carbon from the atmosphere and the efficiency of water catchments, not to mention the preservation of animals and birds and plants whose habitats would otherwise disappear.

Such 'foolishness' is essential for the health and even the survival of life on Planet Earth. People engaged in this task are often found to have a profound understanding of other issues of justice for all living things. Whether or not they are followers of Jesus, they have nonetheless caught his vision for a universal kind of justice. Their focus on justice for the natural order is completely in accordance with the all-inclusive harmony envisioned for the world by Jesus.

In the context of this discussion about responsibility for the natural order it is appropriate to include here a definition of human imperfection (or 'sin') which fits with Jesus' view of human efforts to follow him. I have not specifically used the word sin before this, purely to avoid the kind of baggage which comes trailing after it. For many Christians sin means particular kinds of human failings, principally those concerned with the personal life such as envy, vengeance, sexual offences, issues relating to abortion and homosexuality, abuse and unfaithfulness in relationships. There is also good reason to define sin as a failure to act according to the rule of love – "love the Lord your God with all of your heart, soul, mind and strength …… and your neighbour as yourself".

That rule of love calls Jesus' followers to take responsibility for the rights both of their fellow human beings and of members of the animal kingdom (see Chapter 6). Sometimes it calls them to look foolish in the eyes of many as they stand up for the rights of other 'neighbours', including inanimate aspects of creation such as the sea, the air and the plants of the earth. Until Jesus' followers are able to be foolish in the eyes of the world, the best possible world cannot become reality. It is as clear and as urgent as that.

6
Empathy and Justice: the Necessary Partnership

Fortunate are the merciful, for they will receive mercy.
(Matt. 5:7)

Through the northern winter of 1995-96 I was in Cambridge, England. As November turned into December the air grew colder until the streets were covered in snow and ice and the night-time temperature was commonly below zero. As I went from my warm room to warm libraries, I could not help noticing people sitting on freezing footpaths holding signs saying 'unemployed', or even worse, 'homeless'. Passers-by were contributing coins here and there, but it all looked grim. Cambridge, with its wealthy colleges, was the last place I expected to see that sort of need. Then one Sunday morning in the Methodist Church where I worshipped, the youth group announced that the following Saturday night they would sleep outdoors with the homeless. The morning after they did that, they were back in church still looking blue around the ears. They had endured a miserable night but they had gained a thoroughly empathetic outlook on what it felt like to be homeless. Armed with that insight they passionately challenged the congregation to fund accommodation for people without homes. The difference was that now they were aware of the suffering – they could actually feel for the unfortunates on the streets.

What has that to do with the beatitude "Fortunate are the merciful"? Many would say that being merciful is surely about being forgiving. Certainly that is a widespread understanding, but it is also incorrect. In English and in the languages of the Bible, the merciful are those who show kindness and compassion, or empathy. They empathize with people in need, as did that youth group in Cambridge. The Aramaic word Jesus is most likely to have used is *rakham*, which means loving kindness or compassion.

While I intend to make a case for mercy as another essential quality for an enlightened humanity, it is instructive first to identify the opposite of mercy. It is not hate or violence; it is indifference. People who do not know how to be merciful (or kind and compassionate) do not understand another's needs, do not understand how someone else might feel. In other words, they lack empathy with the other – the ability to appreciate how he or she feels.[38]

Psychologists know that a lack of empathy is characteristic of a sociopath. The American Psychological Association claims that three per cent of American males are sociopaths and that prisons are full of sociopaths, criminals unable to empathize with the feelings or suffering of their victims. They simply cannot feel and appreciate the pain they inflict on other people. Many psychologists believe that this disorder of the normal brain results from a profound disturbance in early childhood. A little boy somehow fails to bond with his parents, perhaps because of abuse or neglect. As a result he does not develop the capacity for the warmth and caring which is imparted by loving parents. When he has his own children the danger is that the pattern will be repeated in them and the odds are that they too will not possess the capacity for empathy. On the other hand, people whose positive life experience has enabled them to develop a capacity for empathy are equipped to enter into the other's distress, or longing, or sadness. Such persons are qualified to know the deepest needs of the other because they can feel what he or she is feeling and respond compassionately. Empathy opens up the power of love in human relationships.

The previous chapter identified Jesus' teaching about universal justice as worth dying for. The beatitude about mercy follows naturally from that. Mercy understood as compassion, or kindness, or sympathy, or empathy, oils the wheels of justice. Mercy treats human beings as individuals with individual needs, not simply as a deserving collective. Without mercy, justice cannot recognize individual need; without mercy, justice is cold comfort indeed. Justice without mercy will provide a measure of food or clothing or shelter for people in need, but without kindness and compassion, justice will not understand how to deliver its benefits.

There have been countless examples of this in human experience. The horrors of the nineteenth century orphanage and work-house illustrate the coldness and inadequacy of justice without compassion or empathy. Charles Dickens' *Oliver Twist* was given shelter, food, clothing and a job. Much of that was donated by worthy citizens in church and community, but none of it was accompanied by a kind word or any understanding of a little boy's need for love. The result was an under-nourished, poorly clad, abused and terrified child, starving most of all for a kind word. Oliver's birth to a single impoverished mother in a work-house set the scene for the remainder of his childhood. As Dickens describes it:

> *He was badged and ticketed, and fell into his place at once – a parish child – the orphan of a work-house – the humble, half-starved drudge – to be cuffed and buffeted through the world – despised by all, and pitied by none. Oliver cried lustily. If he could have known that he was an orphan, left to the tender mercies of churchwardens and overseers, perhaps he would have cried the louder.*

Charles Dickens' frequent writings about orphaned, abused children were inspired by his own experience of being separated from his loving parents at the age of twelve. As often happened then to the unfortunate, they had been imprisoned for unpaid debt. Charles was spared that but he was sent to work in a shoe blacking factory. His experience there as a child labourer haunted him for the rest of his life, but eventually his own suffering qualified him to write about the plight of abused children. Quite simply, Charles Dickens was able to empathize with them and his writings reveal in stark clarity the extent of cold-heartedness that passed for justice in Victorian England. It need hardly be said that this is not the kind of justice Jesus envisaged in the fourth beatitude.

Tragically, the shadow of cold-hearted attitudes to justice still falls over the descendants of Charles Dickens' England. In February 2010 the British Prime Minister Gordon Brown delivered a national apology to the approximately ten thousand British people taken as children from single mothers or impoverished families and sent overseas, ostensibly for a 'better life'. In reality they were regarded as potential labourers for countries such as Canada and Australia and the means of boosting their populations with 'good white stock'. One former child migrant who arrived in Australia as a six-year-old voiced the pain of so many:

> *I was only six years old when I arrived. It was a terrible place for young children and there was never a day I felt safe. I still feel that way today; lost, forgotten and uncared for ... There was nobody on my side.*

The traumatized children were placed into institutions and robbed of their childhood. They never celebrated a birthday, never received a Christmas present, rarely were allowed to play and were never hugged. There is good reason why the beatitude concerning mercy follows the beatitude addressing justice. In Jesus' vision of the world, justice and mercy are intertwined and that truth is still not fully recognized. Justice may see society's wrongs and try to correct them, but mercy sees the individual and individual needs.

The 1960s movie Ben Hur is famous for the thrilling chariot race between the 'prince of light' Judah Ben-Hur and the 'prince of darkness', the Roman tribune Messala. There is also a scene in the film that illustrates the power of mercy, or compassion. Through a terrible injustice Ben-Hur is condemned by Messala to slavery. On the way through the hills of Galilee to the coast the line of beaten, suffering slaves is in agony from thirst. When they stop at a small village the people rush to give them water and among the villagers is a carpenter. The Roman soldier in charge forbids anyone to give water to Ben-Hur and he collapses on the ground in the hot sun. Then a shadow falls over him and the carpenter kneels beside him, gently pouring water on his face and stroking his head. At this he revives and drinks deeply.

The soldier notices and advances furiously on the carpenter. His tirade of threats is halted when the kneeling figure – obviously Jesus – rises to his feet. He does not speak, but silences the Roman with a look. Although his back is to the camera, the audience knows that the look is not one of rebuke, but of pure compassion. Jesus' compassionate empathy is not only for Ben-Hur but for the soldier as well, a man caught up in a system of violence and heartlessness. The soldier is disarmed by Jesus' compassionate gaze and turns away in total confusion. No word is spoken, no force is needed. The moral force of justice, strengthened by the power of compassion, is enough. Justice gives mercy its focus. Mercy gives justice its love.

At the turn of the 20th century the American Methodist church released what it called the Social Creed. The creed expressed the church's outrage about injustice in the lives of millions of workers in factories, mines, mills, tenements and company towns. It cited "Maureen", an Irish-American girl who from the age of 13 worked in a woollen mill in Massachusetts. For $3.50 a week she worked from 6 am until 7 pm, 6 days per week. Ten cents per day was deducted from her pay for polluted drinking water and she witnessed multiple deaths and disfigurements of workers caught in unguarded machinery. One of the authors of the Methodist Social Creed was Dr Frank Mason North.[39] He concluded the list of justice demands for workers with this:

> *To the toilers of America and to those who by organized effort are seeking to lift the crushing burdens of the poor, and to reduce the hardships and uphold the dignity of labour, this Council sends the*

greeting of human brotherhood and the pledge of sympathy and of help in a cause which belongs to all who follow Christ.

EMPATHY WITH THE CREATURES.
This exploration of universal compassion or empathy in Jesus' teaching would not be complete without consideration of what that might mean for the animals, birds, fish and insects which share planet Earth with humanity. None of it has any legitimacy unless it includes compassionate empathy for all living creatures. The best possible world would not be confined to the human species; it would extend to include the life experience of all species that have their home on earth. In the absence of a specific teaching from Jesus concerning compassion for the animal kingdom, we are required to look for evidence that non-human creatures came within his ethical concerns. His awareness of them becomes clear on considering the list of creatures named in his sayings. They are: birds (in general), calves, camels, chickens, dogs, doves, fish, foxes, goats, hens, oxen, pigs, ravens, serpents, sheep, snakes, sparrows, vipers, wolves, gnats, moths and scorpions. In particular, Luke's gospel has Jesus convinced of God's concern for a form of life as small and apparently insignificant as sparrows (Luke 13:15).

Luke also includes Jesus' chosen illustration of possible exemptions from the law of the Sabbath. In chapter 10 verse 29 Jesus notes that his listeners already disregard Sabbath law every time they untie their ox or ass on the Sabbath and lead the animal to a drink of water. Implicit in this is Jesus' belief that the welfare of living creatures outweighs even laws thought to have been sent from God. Any commandment believed to be of God which puts at risk the well-being of one of the other creatures of earth should be interpreted according to the overarching law of love. Clearly Jesus taught that following such a commandment to the letter ought to come second in importance to the rights of needy animals.

English law reformer William Wilberforce (1759-1833) found his empathy with human beings sold into slavery reinforced by his compassion for members of the animal kingdom. Those two causes occupied a huge amount of his passion and energy, but even they were part of a holistic theology of compassion out of which he also championed social reform and regular education for the children of the poor. He came to see that all creatures deserved to be treated with dignity and love. His love for earth's non-human species led him to establish the Society for the Prevention of Cruelty to Animals.[40] Jesus' teachings about compassion must apply to all forms of life or they are irredeemably compromised.

The German doctor, musician, missionary and theologian Albert Schweitzer (1875-1965) also championed the cause of the animal kingdom in his system of ethics called Reverence for Life. He had been searching for a foundation for his ethical thinking when one evening in Equatorial Africa the answer came to him:

> ... at the very moment when, at sunset, we were making our way through a herd of hippopotamuses, there flashed upon my mind, unforeseen and unsought, the phrase: "Ehrfurcht vor dem Leben" ("reverence for life").

In 1952 he was awarded the Nobel Peace Prize for his philosophy of Reverence for Life. In 1936 his article concerning this philosophy was published in the periodical *Christendom*. He concluded it with these words:

> *This, then is the nature and origin of ethics. We have dared to say that it is born of physical life, out of the linking of life with life. It is therefore the result of our recognizing the solidarity of life which nature gives us. And as it grows more profound, it teaches us sympathy with all life. Yet, the extremes touch, for this material-borne ethic becomes engraved upon our hearts, and culminates in spiritual union and harmony with the Creative Will which is in and through all.*[41]

Mercy, compassion, sympathy, kindness or empathy; no matter how it is expressed, mercy for all things living is the essential companion of justice. This exploration of universal compassion in Jesus' teaching would be incomplete without consideration of what that might also mean for the animals, birds, fish and insects which also live on Earth.

7

The Undivided Heart

Fortunate are the pure in heart, for they will see God.
(Matt. 5:8)

The sixth beatitude acknowledges that the first five are hard! Jesus doubtless knew they would be very difficult to accept and carry out. Nevertheless in this beatitude he is naming another essential quality needed to bring his vision to reality, in addition to humility, courage to begin again, non-violence, justice and compassion. This time he identifies what he calls a "pure heart". Those who have this pure heart will "see God" (or the divine) in their life. A pure heart is sometimes explained as belonging to a good person, someone who does not indulge in loose living, or criminal activity, or anything morally corrupt. Yet that is only a part of what Jesus is saying in this beatitude.

The word translated from the Greek of Matthew's Gospel into English as 'pure' occurs in both Hebrew and Aramaic as *bar*. It has the meaning of something pristine and unadulterated, like wild uncultivated forest or land. It also means moral purity - of the mind and heart. Something which is *bar* has not been corrupted or compromised and has an integrity of its own. *Bar* is also translated from Aramaic into English as 'clear, bright and clean'. To apply *bar* to the heart means the person concerned is not corrupted, but is a person of integrity.

A further, corresponding sense of what Jesus might have meant by the word we translate as 'pure' can be found in his own scriptures. Psalm 86, verse 11 says: "Teach me your way, O Lord, that I may walk in your truth; give me an undivided heart to revere your name." This is doubtless the kind of thing Jesus wishes for his followers; it is what he knows is essential if people are to 'walk in the truth' of his teaching. The pure heart is uncorrupted, undivided in its loyalty.

Yet people have many different loyalties – to family, friends, football club, tennis or bridge partner or city. They can be loyal to their religion, political party and nation. What does it mean to have a heart undivided in its loyalty? One of the reasons given for the requirement that Roman Catholic clergy be celibate is the idea of the undivided heart. It is thought that a married priest will necessarily have divided loyalties and will not be able to give full attention to his flock, as well as to his family. Be that as it may, a closer look at the word in Psalm 86 that we translate as 'undivided' adds further clarity. The Hebrew (and Aramaic) word (*yakhaid*) means something joined together; all parts of it are 'with each other'. In relating this to a personal characteristic most people would use the word integrated, which comes from the root word (in English) integrity. In the heart of a person of integrity nothing is at odds with anything else. The word *yakhaid* also associates this with the idea of harmonious community, where all are in agreement. Clearly the idea of a pure heart relates to a person whose way of thinking is free of corruption and whose loyalty is not compromised or divided.

Here Jesus is acknowledging the difficulty his followers will experience in holding together and living his teaching so far. To accomplish that, they will need clean (pure) or undivided hearts. It is also helpful to see the flip side – what can happen when the heart of Jesus' follower does become divided. I look for illustration to the American theologian Reinhold Niebuhr (1892-1971). He wrote the famous Serenity Prayer, which looks for grace to accept the unchangeable, courage to change what can be changed, and wisdom to distinguish one from the other. In 1932 Niebuhr wrote a book called *Moral Man and Immoral Society*. In it he issued a dire warning about how difficult it is for human beings to apply their personal morality to the public sphere – in other words, how hard it is to keep the heart from becoming divided in its loyalty. He wrote this:

> *Individual men may be moral in the sense that they are able to consider interests other than their own in determining problems of conduct, and are capable, on occasion, of preferring the advantages of others to their own. All these achievements are more difficult, if not impossible, for human societies and social groups. In every human group there is … less ability to comprehend the needs of others and therefore more unrestrained egoism than the individuals, who compose the group, reveal in their personal relationships.*[42]

One of countless possible illustrations of that insight proves the difficulty of maintaining the undivided heart. It comes from the greatly respected nineteenth century ethical philosopher John Stuart Mill, who was famous for his treatise *On Liberty*. Mill has been rightly praised as a passionate defender of human rights and fierce opponent of slavery. Yet even he was capable of writing this:

> *The British government in India was not only one of the purest in intention but one of the most beneficent in act ever known among mankind. I do not doubt that this is still true now.*[43]

To that, Reinhold Niebuhr commented: "This judgment combines the blind pride of a ruling nation with the arrogance of a ruling class." It is without doubt a warning to affluent followers of Jesus.

In the 1980's I was a regular preacher in a little church on the outskirts of a country town. The church was to all intents and purposes run by one of its laypeople – a dairy farmer I will call Jack Richardson. Jack was the very soul of good humour and eagerness to do what he could for the church. He extended his commitment to the whole community to support the local branch of the Country Fire Authority, the community hospital and the Cubs and Scouts. He was a great conversationalist, always eager to hear other people's opinions and offer help where he could. In spite of my inexperience in ministry, Jack gave me the utmost respect as an interpreter of scripture. He was obviously well educated, but vague about his past.

It was not until I had known this man for several years that a stock and station agent told me about Jack's background. The agent had worked in Western Australia 20 years beforehand and had known Jack in a very different context. It turned out that he had been a businessman – not just a businessman, but CEO of a large corporation. His career came to an abrupt end just as he was being touted to head the company in London. At that point he realised he could no longer accept that the company's resources were being bought from poor landowners for less than half their real value. Jack's integrity was being violated by the profit-driven values of the corporation. He resigned amid great consternation, yet when I knew Jack he was a happy man. His heart was no longer corrupted and divided; he had discovered how to follow Jesus.

There are many stories like that about members of the church. As Reinhold Niebuhr argued, the individual can be a dedicated follower of Jesus in his or her private life. There are countless examples of such people making a huge difference to the lives of the disadvantaged. The problem of divided loyalties for followers of Jesus often stems from their experience of corporate life in business and politics. It is easy enough to save the planet by using less power and creating less pollution at home. It is easy enough to offer a struggler a helping hand in the local community. It is not so easy to do those things when they threaten profits in business and the ire of shareholders.

In a similar way the church itself has sometimes been found to have a divided heart where its relationship with the state is concerned. That relationship has caused the church to have a less than whole-hearted commitment to the teaching of Jesus. As G. K. Chesterton wrote:

> *The Christian ideal has not been tried and found wanting; it has been found difficult and left untried.*[44]

Jesus meant his followers to speak as prophets, critiquing the institutions of power. Historical records show that the church's prophetic voice and loyalty to Jesus has often been compromised by its close connection with the state. By the fourth century CE the church was well established around the Mediterranean Sea. In spite of dreadful persecution by Rome, most of Jesus' followers were trying to put his teachings into practice. The persecutions finally ended in the mid-fourth century when Constantine (soon to be Emperor Constantine) declared that the Christian cross had helped him to victory over his rival to the throne, Maxentius. It looked as if the church's troubles were finally over but the truth is they were actually just beginning. When successive bishops' conferences defined the Nicene Creed and the Doctrine of the Trinity to the satisfaction of Roman emperors, Christianity was well on the way to becoming the state religion of the Roman Empire. In 380 CE the emperor Theodosius declared Christianity to be the only legitimate imperial religion, which meant that Christianity had become the theological arm of empire – a pyrrhic victory if ever there was one. Experience shows that the worst thing which can happen to religious dogma is that it becomes linked with the power of the state.

In that process the heart of the early church became profoundly divided between its adherence to the message of Jesus and its desire to emulate power structures in society. An early sign that the religion first founded on the teachings of Jesus was in danger of corruption happened almost immediately following Christianity's appointment as state religion. Before 380, ordination into the Christian clergy had often meant a one-way ticket to meet wild animals in the arena. Now it was suddenly the door to a safe, secure, lifetime position, paid for by the state, exempt from taxes, military service and all other public duties. Predictably, men offering then for the priesthood were not always those with 'pure (or undivided) hearts'. Since then the institution of the church has often been compromised by association with the power and

SECTION II: THE BEATITUDES

prestige of the state or with particular political parties. Throughout church history the church's heart has been divided – between loyalty to the vision of Jesus and loyalty to human wealth and power.

For the follower in the pews, the result has often been confusion between conflicting loyalties. On the one hand, the teachings of Jesus have been passed on through the church. On the other hand, the doctrine of Christian superiority has been presented as integral to the faith. Where Christian empires have spread, much good has been accomplished at both individual and societal levels. At the same time, Christianity has been associated with the exploitation and excesses of colonialism. Alongside the growth of empire the imperative to convert the world to the Christian religion has also compromised relationship with people of other faiths. In all of this the heart of the sincere individual follower of Jesus has often been both divided and confused.

Jesus knew how hard it would be for his followers to implement his plan for the best possible world, and "see God" in relations between individuals and society. If he had known his followers would become rulers of the world through the Roman Empire and other subsequent 'Christian' empires, he may well have despaired. He may well have agreed with G. K. Chesterton.

8

Radical Forgiveness

*Fortunate are the peacemakers, for they will be called
children of God. (Matt. 5:9)*

As we begin to examine the seventh beatitude – about peace-makers – the reader may assume that the subject is opposition to war. After all, peacemakers try to stop people from fighting. Yes, they do and there are different ways of doing that. Perhaps one way is to demonstrate in the streets and another is to write letters to members of parliament. All of that is true, but in this chapter I will explore the idea of peacemakers differently. I will argue that when Jesus spoke of people who make peace, he had in mind those who are able to forgive. The seventh beatitude brings Jesus' followers face to face with the toughest requirement of all. Even when creating a world where universal sacred values such as humility, justice, compassion and peace are the norm, the creators will find they cannot move an inch without radical forgiveness. To ensure the best possible future, human beings must first forgive each other for the past.

One of humanity's most common characteristics is the tendency to hold on to past hurts or grievances. Every tribe and nation has ancient feuds that are still active, or at least they maintain active memories of past feuds. Examples that spring to mind are Campbells and McDonalds, Albanians and Serbs, Catholics and Protestants, Israelis and Palestinians. They represent a tiny proportion of innumerable possibilities. We could argue that all of the above-mentioned antagonists eventually called truces with each other, or made peace treaties. Unfortunately, with the passage of time each attempt at peace has become the precursor to another conflict. Even when there is no active fighting, even when there is so-called peace, hostility remains beneath the surface ready to break out again. The dilemma is that in human society each group's identity is more often than not based primarily on its perceived difference from its rival or enemy group. Here there are echoes of primordial times when human tribes expanded their territories to include better resources of food. Aeons later each side is still accusing the other of stealing what both regard as 'our territory'.

Where there is a religious element in territorial disputes, the belief that "God says this is our land" enormously exacerbates the intractability of conflicts. The other side is sometimes regarded as morally inferior to 'our people', a belief which leads to more conflict and a stronger likelihood of the abuse of the other's rights. The outcome is that the original reason for the fighting may never be finally resolved. From all of this it is possible to see the extent of the problem Jesus raised in this beatitude. For the peace-makers Jesus refers to, there is one way only that such dead-end stand-offs can be resolved. I mentioned it before – it is forgiveness.

In Matthew's version of the prayer attributed to Jesus the Greek words literally translated are: "Forgive us our debts; for indeed we ourselves are forgiving everyone indebted to us." The assumption addressed to God in this section of the prayer is that those who pray are actually claiming to have cancelled unpaid debt! It is crucial to allow what is often said unthinkingly every Sunday to sink in. The Lord's Prayer has the people praying, "God, we are making peace in the world by forgiving, or foregoing what is owed to us (or forgiving those who have sinned against us[45]). We have decided to let go of our grievance, or our hurt, or our claim to something taken away from us. On that basis we are looking for your forgiveness of our own debts (or sins)." Most church-goers would be amazed to find that this is what they actually pray each Sunday. How could Jesus expect human beings to forgive to that extent?

In recent years there have been clear illustrations of how challenging forgiveness can sometimes be. I doubt there could be a more difficult example than the case of parents trying to deal with the destruction of their children's lives by clergy in a church setting. The perpetrators concerned have betrayed their vocations as representatives of the Catholic Church, as well as the trust of children and parents in their parishes. It is not for anyone to tell someone else they must forgive. Forgiveness must come without pressure or coercion from the hearts of those offended against. But in cases of clergy abuse of children, real peace for both victims and church may come only when forgiveness is offered by each party to the other.

Forgiveness that finally brings healing will clearly have to come initially from the Catholic Church's ruling elite. They have acted first to protect the church institution and apparently cannot (as yet) forgive those who have exposed its shortcomings. It may be that only when those who wield power in the Catholic Church find the compassion to forgive victims of clergy abuse for demanding justice and exposing cover-ups, that forgiveness of church leadership by the victims may become possible. Forgiveness of this kind is clearly of a different order from the apologies church leaders are offering to victims. It involves acknowledgment of the sins of the institution as well as of its servants.

All of this involves pain and the letting go of pain, and given how costly forgiveness of the kind Jesus promoted really is, it is important to see clearly the benefits it can bring. It is helpful to look at a primary idea behind Jesus' vision of the best possible world. The idea is called Jubilee, the biblical concept of forgiveness of debt. Jubilee requires that everyone give up things legitimately owed to them in the name of equality, or justice. It usually means foregoing money or property or territory.[46] In human terms it can also mean giving up the right to feel hurt – "he did wrong to me (or exposed my own shortcomings); I have a right to be angry, resentful, grieving, even vengeful". Giving up the right to anger or vengeance is a crucial step in developing the capacity to be forgiving. It is the first step in the establishment of lasting peace and reconciliation.

On a world-wide scale the idea behind the Jubilee has the potential to bring peace that lasts, yet it is not just peace as the absence of conflict. The Aramaic words Jesus would have used for "peacemakers" are *osai'r shalom* (makers of Shalom). *Shalom* certainly does mean the absence of war, but it also means good health, sufficient food and shelter, good relations with neighbours and security for children. The best description of *shalom* in scripture comes from chapter 65 of the Book of Isaiah, where the writer sets out three major elements of a world characterized by *shalom*. First, people live out the full span of their natural lives. Second, they are free to eat the food they have produced. Third, they are free to live in the houses they have built. Those three things are interrelated; they all rely on a world in which there is universal peace and freedom, where no one need fear premature death from violence. It is a world where no one need fear starvation because their crops are destroyed by warfare, or by famine caused by war. It is a world where no one need fear losing family and home to violent invaders. In short, it is a world of freedom from war and they are the benefits of a world at peace. Implicit in the seventh beatitude is the knowledge that it takes forgiveness of old hurts to bring about that kind of peace. The forgiving makers of *shalom* also make possible the best kind of world. Yet the question remains – how can human beings forgive like that? Jesus believes they can. The full text of the seventh beatitude is "Blessed are the peace-makers, for they will be called children of God". Here is the strongest possible affirmation of a human being. To call a person a child of God is to say he or she has characteristics that humanity equates with goodness. There is good reason to say that together these characteristics add up to love for other people. In essence, the person called child of God is capable of putting aside personal needs to care first for the needs of other people. An essential characteristic of the loving person is that he or she is radically forgiving.

There is another clue in scripture about how this kind of forgiveness may be possible. In Chapter 13 of Paul's First Letter to the Corinthians, he sets out a superb description of love. Where the English (NRSV) version says, "love … is not … resentful", the original Greek words mean 'love does not keep a record of wrongs'. The surest way to prolong pain caused by offences against an individual and pass it on to a whole tribe, is for the victim to hold on to hurts and seek revenge. Others in his or her community then feel obliged to act in solidarity with the injured member.

History has demonstrated continuously how difficult it is to break out of this kind of thinking and acting. Revenge creates revenge, which creates revenge. The underlying problem is that a person who feels wronged also feels diminished – that his or her humanity has been disregarded as of no account. It is very difficult to let go of that reaction, and the pain and resentment of the abused are understandable. Yet their pain can ultimately be passed on to a whole nation. The world saw a prime example of this in the invasions of Afghanistan and Iraq following the attack on the World Trade Centre on September 11, 2001. In 2010 the cycle of pain and resentment and vengeance and pain, from both internal and external sources, continues.[47]

The reaction of Jesus' forgiving followers is to heal the pain of offences committed against them through making peace with the offender, rather than through seeking vengeance. This is radical forgiveness and it takes something very powerful in the forgiving person for this to happen. It is called the power of love. Love says to victims of violence and hate who intend to avenge this with more violence, "You are important; your pain is acknowledged." Love's affirmation of the victims/potential offenders can be sufficient to rule out their need for revenge and ultimately it can lead them to a healthy view of the self. Psychologists know that a healthy self-esteem depends on whether or not an individual is loved. Love is the buffer against life's slings and arrows and it is mostly those who see themselves as unloved or rejected who seek revenge for a wounded sense of self. Persons who are loved and have given love develop the emotional resources to overcome offences against them. Such persons have the inner strength to let go of the pain, which can result in a cessation of the vicious cycle of offence and revenge and the establishment of lasting peace. I say again that the key is love. It is not for nothing that the Japanese Christian writer Toyohiko Kagawa wrote these words:

> *Love is the only eye that visions God. With this wonderful eye of Love, God and man behold one another. In Love, the eye of man becomes the eye of God. In Love is first achieved the interfusion of Divinity and humanity.*[48]

At this point, a word of caution is needed. The reader is not being invited here to imagine a world in which there will no longer be a need to learn to be forgiving, as though human nature had undergone a divine transplant. As I pointed out at the beginning of this book, human beings learn what is better through knowledge of its flip side – that which is worse. Children will always need to be taught by loving and forgiving parents how to forgive hurts and disappointments. The best fulfilment of Jesus' vision will come when all parents are equipped to pass on to their children the love they themselves have experienced.

9

Freedom from Fear

> *Fortunate are those who are persecuted for righteousness'
> sake, for theirs is the kingdom of heaven. Fortunate are you
> when people revile you and persecute you and utter all
> kinds of evil against you falsely on my account. (Matt.
> 5:11)*

We have noted that the principles contained in the beatitudes can be seen as personal characteristics for creators of the best possible world. Now there is a definite change in focus. The previous seven beatitudes concern what will come – what can be brought about day after day, year after year, by followers of Jesus. The eighth and ninth concern what can happen right now – if the previous seven are taken seriously.

In 1989 a fantasy film called *Field of Dreams* was released. It concerns a man longing to tell his late father that he loves him – a common and often bitter human predicament. The man receives a message that they will reconnect through the sport of baseball, which his father loved. If the son builds a baseball pitch, they will meet there. The actual message he receives is, "If you build it, he will come." The message from Jesus to humanity is, "If you in your own lives build the Kingdom of heaven among you, it will come!" Jesus is saying that if his followers are deliberately humble, able to recover from setbacks or failures, non-violent, bringers of justice, undivided in their willingness to follow Jesus, and radically forgiving, they will create the world according to his vision. They will not even have to decide to do it; it will happen as they live their lives.

This chapter concerns the final two beatitudes, which are focussed on stark reality as experienced by Matthew and his community in the eighth decade of the first century. These two sayings contain warnings about what is actually happening to people living in accordance with the beatitudes more than forty years after Jesus' death. The warnings are blunt; such people may be persecuted. These two beatitudes are most likely to have been added by Matthew (they are not in Luke) as a caution to his readers that creating the world Jesus envisioned will inevitably lead to confrontation with both religious and secular authority. During the whole time frame covered by the New Testament writings, the risk of offending Rome was real; we know what happened to Jesus.

For those who ask why Jesus taught his gospel of non-violence and love for the other, the question must also be, why then, and why there? Why did this man who taught the guidelines for a better world appear among the Jewish people in the era of Roman occupation, with all of its attendant violence and degradation of the ordinary people? After all, Jesus knew the Roman penalty for people who stood up 'against the government', and particularly for leaders who looked as if they were challenging the sovereignty of Caesar. How can we doubt that it was largely the nature of the world in which he lived that galvanized him into action and gave his teaching such urgency?

Jesus was born in the period immediately before or following the death of Herod I (or Herod the Great) in 4 BCE. After that, Herod's son Herod Antipas became Tetrarch of the Galilee and ushered in a period of 'Romanizing' the area where Jesus grew up. Antipas eventually transferred his capital to Tiberias and imposed hardship on the fishermen of the Sea of Galilee by means of heavy taxes on fish. Unsurprisingly that period was turbulent, with several messianic figures inciting the Jewish people to rebel against the power of both Rome and Herod. In all cases the messianic aspirants were brutally killed along with many followers. As Jesus grew up he could not have failed to know about these leaders, several of whom came from his home territory in the Galilee. They included Judas the Galilean as well as Athronges and his four brothers from Judea and Simon from Perea. Judas had been joined by a Pharisee called Zadok and together they had founded the party known as Zealots. Zealots were those who had 'zeal for Torah', and defended it with the sword. In this period, when Jesus was a small boy, Varus the Roman legate of Syria was sent by Rome to punish Judas and the Zealots. The punishment was multiple crucifixions, as described by Josephus the Jewish historian:

> *Varus sent a part of his army into the country, to seek out those that had been the authors of the revolt; and when they were discovered, he punished some of them that were most guilty, and some he dismissed: now the number of those that were crucified on this account were two thousand.*[49]

All of these things could not have failed to have a profound effect on the young Jesus. They were the circumstances in which he developed his vision for a very different kind of world. Jesus' teaching about loving the enemy was totally opposite to the norms of the empire under which he lived. As such it was just as socially subversive as any militaristic rebellion and he would have known it was bound to attract the attention of those who considered him a rival to Roman authority. It is clear that he was willing to risk his life for the sake of his teaching. It is also clear why Jesus was so passionate about his non-violent vision of a far better world. Given the brutal methods of government all around him and the hopelessness of violent rebellion against it, the time had come for his teaching and he knew it.

More than forty years later, when Matthew wrote his gospel, the risk to followers of the teacher from Nazareth had clearly not disappeared; in fact it was still growing. The passion of Jesus' followers for his vision of a better world was still seen by Rome as treason, an insult to Caesar. Those who understood Jesus' teachings as ultimate truth for human community were calling him 'Lord', one with ultimate authority. The problem was that

Rome required its subjects to say "Caesar is Lord". To proclaim Jesus as Lord was to challenge the absolute power of the emperor.

It is easy to see why the earliest Christians were persecuted by Rome, but at the same time they faced persecution from the leadership of mainstream Judaism, which saw them as promoting a failed or false Messiah. The first century CE idea of a Jewish Messiah certainly did not allow for him to be killed. His traditional role was as an anointed warrior king who would liberate the people by military means, or as anointed 'messenger' who would call the people to repentance before God intervened to liberate Israel from Rome in a decisive victory of good over evil. Following that, the Messiah would come in glory to reign from God's right hand for a thousand years. At the time of writing the gospels it was therefore understandable that most Jews could not accept the crucified Jesus (who, fifty years after his death, had not returned) as the Messiah of their traditions.

Also understandably, after the disastrous defeat of the Jews in the war against Rome (66-70 CE) when they were led by messianic figures such as Menachem of Galilee, any continuing Jewish association with a Messiah figure was regarded as a threat to the security of the Jewish people and religion. In short, because the gospel writers' proclamation of Jesus as Messiah was at odds with both secular and religious authority, the followers of Jesus were persecuted. Significantly, that kind of persecution from fellow Jews did not happen to Jesus in his lifetime, from which (apart from the New Testament's messianic proclamation) there is no evidence that he saw or promoted himself as a Messiah. Given its traditional militaristic associations, it is highly unlikely that Jesus would have sought or accepted the title Messiah.[50] Later Christian attempts to see him as a different kind of Messiah (the 'risen Christ') are based on expectation of a so-far unrealised 'second coming'.

According to the book of the Acts of the Apostles, the earliest followers were not just religious/political activists; they actually lived the teachings of Jesus found in the beatitudes. In their everyday lives they tried to act compassionately and justly. They considered the needs of others ahead of their own and even when they suffered the loss of loved family and friends they refused to respond to violence with more violence. They were willing to forgive people opposed to them (that is, to love their enemies); they were committed to living in accordance with Jesus' teaching. In other words, they were free. By committing themselves to Jesus' plan of action to establish the best possible world and by seeing it begin to grow, the people being persecuted had freed themselves from fear of three things. They were free from fear of authority; they were free from fear of exclusion; they were free from fear of failure.

No one can risk retribution from secular or religious authorities without some degree of trepidation. There is a natural fear of what the authorities might do to me if I defy the law. Severe punishment can also be a strong deterrent and courts often refer to the hope that a harsh sentence handed down to an offender might deter others from committing the same offence. In the first century CE, punishment was not just deprivation of liberty. A law-breaker could risk various levels of torture including flogging and burning, being sold into slavery, or, in the ultimate government obscenity, crucifixion. For Jesus' original followers, fear of authority was much more warranted than it is for people in this age, yet they went on doing and saying what they knew to be truth. Perhaps that was the key to their courage, as in the case of the third century Roman Christians, Valerian and Cecilia. They had been the ultimate upper class power couple in Roman society and he was expecting a career as a Roman senator. When Valerian and Cecilia became convinced by the teachings of Jesus everything changed. In spite of their natural fear of persecution they practised their Christianity openly, including giving away their possessions to the poor. Their palace became a meeting place for Christians until Roman authority caught up with them. The test of loyalty to Caesar was to burn incense in his honour, but they refused and were condemned as disloyal to the state. For them Jesus was Lord, not Caesar, and for that commitment to Jesus' way they were tortured and killed. Their punishment was carried out in secret, for fear that the people of Rome would rise up against the state. How did Valerian and Cecilia overcome their fear of authority? Perhaps the key is that as they practised the teaching of Jesus they found it was the ultimate guide to realising their full human potential. They knew they were on the side of Jesus and that knowledge freed them from fear.

Fear of exclusion from institutions of power is one thing; exclusion from one's own religious community and even from family and friends, is something else. That is precisely what happened to some of Jesus' first followers. Matthew 23 shows us what was going on in his time between Jews who believed Jesus was the awaited Messiah and other Jews who argued that according to their criteria he was a failed or inauthentic Messiah. It was not a pretty picture, and one quote from chapter 23 will suffice. Matthew places it in the mouth of Jesus, but it describes bitterly polemical conditions between mainstream Jewish leaders and messianic Christ followers toward the end of the first century. According to Matthew, Jesus says: "I send you prophets, sages and scribes, some of whom you will kill and crucify, and some you will flog in your synagogues and pursue from town to town." These were not the conditions for Jesus' followers during his own lifetime. Clearly the Jews of Matthew's time who saw Jesus as Messiah/Christ were regarded as heretics, particularly since Messiah figures were now associated with the disastrous defeat of Jews in the Jewish War.

Yet even today some followers of Jesus are excluded by their own families and friends. I refer here not only to exclusivist Christian sects but to members of mainstream churches. One of the risks faced by people trying to put Jesus' teachings into practice is ridicule from their own peers. People committed to sharing their possessions with the disadvantaged can be an unwanted challenge. They can find themselves at odds with families and societies which place high value on acquiring and retaining material possessions and it takes a brave person to withstand being called foolish. Perhaps the key is that in the practising of Jesus' inclusive teachings they find themselves profoundly connected with all of humanity. It follows that because of this they are freed from fear of exclusion.

The third freedom for Jesus' followers is freedom from fear of failure. At some point in life most people have ruled out trying something new because they fear failure. Paradoxically, some of the highest achievers are those who can also become resistant to trying something new. By definition, high achievers are successful people who like to win and achieve high standards in work and play. They build their lives on success at school, university, sport, hobbies, work and even parenting. Eventually there comes a point when the idea of failure is unthinkable to such people, to be avoided at all costs. The simplest way to avoid failing is never to take a risk, to stick rigidly to what is already known and to what has already been done. That is often the hallmark of conservatives in both secular and religious life. It is not a characteristic of people equipped to create the best possible world.

On the other hand, people of faith can see failure merely as a set-back, even as an invitation to try again. As Martin Luther King once wrote: "Faith is taking the first step even when you don't see the whole staircase." Jesus clearly believed that real faith in God is faith in a God who forgives. Forgiveness offers the freedom to recover from failure and begin again. People of faith, practising the teachings of Jesus, need not despair if their efforts fail. The radical forgiveness he taught overcomes fear of failure.

The only way Jesus' vision will become reality is if his followers actually put it into practice. The warnings from Matthew in beatitudes 8 and 9 say that they may face persecution, ridicule and even exclusion from their own community. In spite of all that, Jesus' followers find that when they carry out his teachings they are freed from fear and are actually living as he hoped they would. If they fail, they can try again. Jesus' message to his followers then and now is the same: if you build it, it will come. That is why they are fortunate.

THE BEATITUDES RE-STATED

For the reader's clarification, the following are the beatitudes re-stated in accordance with the way they have been interpreted in the preceding chapters:

Fortunate are the humble-minded, for they will live in the best possible world.

Fortunate are the mournful, for they will face the future with strength.

Fortunate are the non-violent, for they will govern the earth.

Fortunate are those whose passion is for justice, for they will receive justice.

Fortunate are the compassionate, for they will receive compassion.

Fortunate are the undivided in heart, for they will commit to the way of Jesus.

Fortunate are the peacemakers, for they will forgive and reconcile humanity.

Fortunate are those in danger for living Jesus' way; for they will be freed from fear to follow him.

QUESTIONS FOR DISCUSSION CONCERNING ISSUES RAISED IN SECTION II

1. Do you think the Beatitudes could form the basis of a new creed for Jesus' followers? How would you state it?

2. Why do you think many people have regarded Jesus' teachings as too hard to follow? In what ways have you seen them carried out?

3. If the Beatitudes are a kind of blueprint for the best possible world, what would be the first step toward making it reality?

SECTION III

The Teachings

10

The Prayer for Builders of the Kingdom

> *Pray then in this way: Our Father in heaven, hallowed be your name. Your kingdom come. Your will be done, on earth as it is in heaven. Give us this day our daily bread. And forgive us our debts as we also have forgiven our debtors. And do not bring us to the time of trial, but rescue us from the evil one.*
> *(Matt.6:9-13)*

There is an old saying: be careful what you ask for; you may get it! That may also apply to what is prayed for. This chapter will explore one of the most often-prayed prayers in history. In Christianity, the Our Father and the Hail Mary are the most popular prayers of all. The Lord's Prayer, as Protestants call it, has been foundational to Christian experience since long before Matthew and Luke included it in their gospels. There is scholarly agreement that it comes originally from Jesus. Significantly, it fits beside what I have called the plan of action for Jesus' followers – the beatitudes. His prayer is the outcome of a habitually spiritual way of life which can be glimpsed in the gospel references to his long nights spent in prayer, where he was open to the promptings of the Spirit.[51] Given Jesus' own spirituality, the Lord's Prayer represents encouragement of his followers to be in close contact with the source of his inspiration. The prayer naturally relates closely to his core teaching about what he called the Kingdom of heaven.

Firstly – "Our Father in heaven, hallowed be your name." "Our Father" gathers all of humanity into one family. It uses the familiar term father to address a God who regards human beings with love, as parents love their children. There is a whole world of Jesus' experience of God, plus his hopes and dreams for a united humanity, in those two words, "Our Father". They point to the inclusive gospel of Jesus in which all are equal in the eyes of God the parent. "In heaven" refers to the ideal pattern for the earthly Kingdom that Jesus felt called by God to inaugurate.

"Hallowed be your name." To hallow something is to regard it as beyond reproach. To hallow God's name rules out the swearing of false oaths in God's name. It rules out using God's name (or sacred or ultimate values) lightly, or loosely, or as a swear-word. For most committed Christians the same would apply to the name of Jesus, including those (such as myself) who do not regard Jesus as co-equal with God. In the 1960s I worked for an insurance company where the branch staff included inspectors who travelled around from Monday to Thursday. On Fridays they were back in the office with new policies and new insurance claims. One Friday a young office-boy was having trouble with an adding machine and each time he made a mistake he uttered the name of Jesus – as an expletive. One inspector, who had seen it all among all kinds of people, was observing the office boy's performance. Eventually, he lost patience: "Mister Jesus to you, boy! You obviously don't know him very well."

Misusing God's name or even Jesus' name is one way to disregard that line of the Lord's Prayer. Using the name of God to justify privilege is another, as did the family whose front-yard tree had blown onto their house in a storm. When they were interviewed on television the reporter said: "You were so lucky that the tree didn't fall on bedrooms where you were sleeping." The mother of the family said: "No, not lucky. God saved us! We just know that God made the tree fall on the empty lounge-room." In the same news service there was a report that a car had hit another fallen tree, this time killing a young mother and her baby. What might the first mother have said to the bereaved husband and father? In effect, she had said on TV that God saves special 'chosen' people. By implication she was saying that the mother and baby who were killed had been regarded by God as dispensable. Hallowing the sacred means avoiding giving God a bad name.

Secondly: "Your kingdom come. Your will be done on earth, as it is in heaven." Here it is; this is what is prayed for every time Christians mumble their way through the Lord's Prayer. How many realise what it is they pray for? Notice that the prayer does not say, "Our Father, make your kingdom come!" The person praying is not asking God to do it; he or she is simply expressing the desire that life on earth will become the best that life can be. Prayer of that kind does not actually ask God for anything. It does not assume that God is an interventionist deity who moves things around in response to prayer. Instead, it expresses the wishes or longing of the people praying. Through that expression of desire for something better there is openness to inspiration. The outcome may well be that those praying realise it is up to them to become the answer to their own prayer. They may be inspired and encouraged by the idea of the best possible world, but also aware that its realisation is up to them.

"Give us today our daily bread". Again we could see this as a simple request: God, we don't know where our food is coming from. Please arrange it so that we have enough to eat! Many devout Christians have seen it that way. Stories abound of people going off to do 'God's work' without the certainty of income or supplies, yet food and other necessities have appeared just when needed. Apparently the real probability that someone, Christian or not, took pity on them and provided it, does not stack up against the belief that God specifically arranged for its delivery. Most Christians these days see this section of the prayer as a longing for justice, which fits beside one of the major themes of the beatitudes. Justice ensures there is sufficient food for everyone and people who see the need for daily bread in others are inspired to express personally their compassion, or mercy. Praying the Lord's Prayer is not meant to be an end in itself; it is meant to be the beginning of a response to the needs of humanity.

Thirdly – "forgive us our debts, as we also have forgiven our debtors". We have noted in the beatitudes that people who make peace are those who are capable of foregoing or forgiving debt. The Lord's Prayer assumes that the persons praying have already done that. They are not asking forgiveness from God in the absence of practicing forgiveness toward others themselves. In that regard people who pray this prayer might occasionally ask themselves whether what they are saying in the prayer is actually true. In essence, the prayer focuses the mind on personal pre-requisites for creating the world as Jesus saw it, a strong indicator that he intended it to be prayed on a regular basis. The words are extremely challenging, yet they are often prayed unthinkingly. In countless cases Christians have domesticated the prayer and turned it into mindless repetition. It is important to be careful about what is prayed for.

Fourthly, "do not bring us to the time of trial". Here we have another reference to persecution. This part of the prayer expresses a natural desire to escape the kind of opposition to Jesus' teaching that was faced by his first followers. The Lord's Prayer comes from a world where it was highly dangerous to express a different view from that of the authorities and the prayer looks for God's help in coping with or even avoiding such trouble and challenge. That is one of the reasons why modern Christians tend to gloss over this part of the prayer, thinking, "That's not about me". Others simply see it as a reference to temptation. In the modern version of the prayer this section says, "save us from the time of trial".

Many have protested that this line of the prayer is not realistic, as everyone has testing times and a life with no trials would be like one cocooned in cotton wool. The type of trial the prayer might refer to is limited only by human experience and one example may be temptation to do something illegal, or selfish. Or perhaps the trial is one of endurance, such as experienced by many parents whose lives are one long test of their fortitude. To love a healthy child is challenge enough, but to love and care for a child with disabilities is to face a lifetime need for the virtues of endurance and patience. A recent Deakin University (Melbourne) survey found that well over half of full-time carers for frail, disabled or mentally ill relatives have moderate depression, compared with less than a sixth of the general population. Because of that kind of trial and countless other examples, many people feel that "save us from the time of trial" might be better expressed as "save us in the time of trial".

There is a good case for understanding this section as a prayer for strength to endure life's testing times. The world Jesus envisaged is not a perfect world in which there is no longer the possibility of physical or mental illness or injury caused by accidents. It is, though, a world in which all creatures in pain receive love and compassion and in which humanity dedicates its resources to the cure or eradication of illnesses.

Finally, the prayer asks: "rescue us from the evil one." In the ancient world evil was personified as Satan, although contemporary Christians should not be misled by that word. Satan here is not the stereotypical devil with horns and red pitchfork, presiding over hell. At the time of Jesus, Satan was believed to be sent by God to test people in situations of challenge or decision-making. In other words, Satan was sometimes seen as the prosecutor in God's 'court'. He appears in this role in the Book of Job. He also visits people to test them in 1 Chronicles (21), Zechariah (3), and in Psalm 109, verse 6.

The same understanding of Satan appears in the account of Jesus' temptations in the Gospel of Matthew (4:1-11). This last line of the prayer reflects Jesus' own experience of temptation and he knew his followers would face something similar to that. The role of Satan in the story is typically from Jesus' time and place, where Satan is not the devil as we know the concept, but God's prosecutor, who brings people to face "the time of trial". The temptations story depicts Jesus going through trials of indecision concerning how to bring his message to the world. Through the inclusion of that story the gospel writers indicate clearly that Jesus also was tempted to do things the world's way. He appealed to his own scriptures and to his knowledge of God to overcome the lure of the easy way. Later christologically-driven interpretations of this story have invested Jesus with divine strength so that he was not really tempted, but was actually teaching Satan a lesson as well as proving he was the 'Son of God'. That kind of approach to this story is helpful to no-one.

When Jesus called people to bring into being the best possible world, he gave them the wisdom to carry it out. He knew they would face a time of trial when they would be tempted to take short cuts, or even to declare it all too hard and leave it to someone else. He knew about this because he had experienced it himself. It was for that reason that he gave them this prayer.

11

Salty Followers

You are the salt of the earth; but if salt has lost its taste, how can its saltiness be restored? It is no longer good for anything but is thrown out and trampled under foot.
(Matt. 5:13)

Sometimes people are described as "the salt of the earth", which usually means they are good, kind and generous. Yet even that does not cover what Jesus meant when he said to his followers, "You are the salt of the earth." It is important to explore ways of understanding what he meant by that. For example, most people in my family like mashed potato, lots of it. Some of them also like porridge, every day! In themselves neither of those foods have much taste. To become their true selves they need help and the help they need is salt. Salt is one of earth's enigmas. By itself it is impossible to eat, yet without it the potential full flavour of food remains hidden and unfulfilled.

Salt also needs to be added to food in the correct proportion. My sister and I would often ask our parents to repeat a particular family story. We thought it was very funny, although it was not so funny for one person in the story. When our parents became engaged to be married our grandmother made a big fruit cake for the engagement party. When the time came to cut the cake it looked rich, smelt good, and had just the right amount of moisture. Unfortunately, when the 200 or so relatives and friends were served the cake they started gagging and pulling awful faces. Grandmother was dreadfully embarrassed when it was realised that instead of a cup of sugar she had mistakenly put a cup of salt into the cake! The postscript to the story is that an uncle of ours took the cake to his farm and gave it to his cattle as a salt lick. They refused it.

In the right proportion with the right partner, salt and food are the perfect combination. Salt does not actually add flavour to food, but when it is added the latent flavour already present in the potato or oatmeal comes to life. Food scientists believe it does that by suppressing bitterness in the food and enhancing its natural sweetness. That is surely the perfect explanation of people who are described as 'salt of the earth'.

This metaphor, which Jesus used to describe his followers, comes in two parts. First, "You are the salt of the earth"! To whom is Jesus speaking? Matthew places this saying immediately after the beatitudes. The implication is that people reading it have already embraced the qualities Jesus describes in the beatitudes. It is important to keep in mind that these are also the qualities of Jesus. The implication is that if his followers do as he did, they will become like him. Why does his metaphor call them "the salt of the earth"? One explanation for Jesus' choice of metaphor is that in the ancient world salt was regarded as a very valuable commodity. It was not readily available to everyone as it is in the modern world and was often transported long distances by camel trains or in ships across the Mediterranean and even traded for gold. Cakes of salt were used for currency and Roman soldiers were sometimes paid in salt. The word 'salary' comes from *sal*, the Latin word for salt.

The point is that salt was valuable. In many ways the metaphor reflects the time of Jesus, indicating that he regarded people he called "the salt of the earth" as very valuable individuals. Significantly, there are also links in the metaphor with religious practice among the Jews of his time. In the Book of Leviticus, which contains instruction about sacrifices and how to carry them out, there is a rule concerning adding salt to sacrifices made on the altar. This applies to every kind of sacrifice, including offerings of grain. In Leviticus the idea is that salt preserves, so the salt offering signifies something everlasting, like the covenant with God. In fact the salt is called "the salt of the covenant with your God" (Lev. 2:13). We also know that salt is sometimes used as a preservative as in salted meat or fish and it is easy to see why Jesus' metaphor might also contain the idea of salt as something which preserves. Those who are the "salt of the earth" can enhance and preserve the goodness in human lives and save that goodness from corruption.

After listening to Jesus, these 'salty' followers are also wise. In the writings of Jewish teachers in Jesus' time, salt is a metaphor for wisdom. If Jesus thought of it in that way he no doubt linked it with the wisdom to be learned from what came to be called the beatitudes. That wisdom includes knowing salt does not add a strong flavour of its own to food. As salt of the earth, Jesus' followers are called to enhance the good already present in people they meet.

Bill Woodfull's father did just that. Most older Australians know that Bill Woodfull was the Australian Test Cricket captain in the 1930's, through the notorious Bodyline series. When the team was in England in 1930 they were approached by a well-dressed gentleman who invited them to tea at his nearby mansion. Over tea the man asked their names. When he heard 'Woodfull', he said, "Do you know if your family is related to a Methodist minister in Melbourne?" "Yes", said Bill Woodfull, "he's my father." The man became very excited. "If it were not for that man, we would not be sitting at this table today," he said. Then the story came out. This gentleman had gone to Australia to try his luck but had lost everything, including his self-respect. On a fateful day he was standing on a footpath in Melbourne, thinking he would end it all. Then a horse and buggy stopped and the driver offered him a lift. The man on the footpath was dirty and dishevelled and the worse for alcohol, but the driver insisted.

They soon arrived at the Flemington Methodist parsonage and the Rev T.S.B. Woodfull invited the man into his home for a meal. He could see that the stranger was uncomfortable about being dirty so he offered him a hot bath. It was when he handed this unkempt stranger a clean towel that the message got through. The man realised that he was being treated as if he were not a derelict but someone worthwhile, and all the good strength that lay dormant in him came to the surface. After accepting the compassion of a stranger he was able to pick himself up and return to England, where his life took on new meaning and purpose. No doubt those who knew the Rev T.S.B. Woodfull could easily have called him 'the salt of the earth'.

The second half of Jesus' saying is curious: "but if salt has lost its taste, how can its saltiness be restored? It is no longer good for anything, but is thrown out and trampled under foot." How is it possible for salt to stop being salty? How can it lose its saltiness? After all, sodium chloride is an extremely stable element. The answer is that with this saying Jesus takes us into his own world. In those days salt mining was much less sophisticated than it is now and salt was often adulterated with sand and soil, or by unscrupulous merchants who were known to add other substances to it. This saying of Jesus could also be a reference to rock salt that had been too long exposed to the elements and gradually become less salty. Salt degraded in such ways was often spread by the Romans on muddy roads, where it increased traction for marching soldiers and wagon wheels. This is the reason for Jesus' reference to salt being "trampled under foot". Impure salt is still spread on icy roads to stop cars from sliding.

Through this metaphor Jesus warned that the saltiness of enthusiastic, 'salty' followers could become corrupted and weakened by other claims on their lives. By this means they could lose the Jesus-like character they had embraced when they first heard his teaching. They also could lose their saltiness by allowing it to lie dormant, like rock salt. It would then be incapable of bringing out the dormant flavour in their own lives, let alone in the lives of others.

Here Jesus was being realistic; he knew how enthusiastic people can be in the first flush of inspiration. He also knew that life's complexities have a way of taking over good intentions and putting them on the back-burner. For that reason the people actually listening and taking notice were very precious to him, like salt. He was relying on them to put his teachings into practice and he knew it was only by doing this that they could also draw out the good potential in people they encountered. Only in this way could his vision become reality. In Jesus' saying about salt losing its flavour, he was urging his followers not to lose their own saltiness.

12

Light up the Darkness

> *You are the light of the world. A city built on a hill cannot be hid. No one after lighting a lamp puts it under the bushel basket, but on the lamp stand, and it gives light to all in the house.*
> (Matt. 5:14-15)

The creation myth in the first chapter of the Book of Genesis offers a magnificent perspective on why the universe exists. Genesis is hardly scientific; it is a work of faith, but the writer of chapter 1 believes implicitly that God's essential nature is creative and life-giving. The acts of creation occur because God speaks to the chaos of lifelessness and disorder. Significantly, the first words God speaks as Creator are: "Let there be light." Light comes first; light comes even before the creation of the sun, moon and stars. This gives the clue – it is not sunlight or starlight; it is the 'light' of God's creativity. Contemporary readers might associate it with light first created by the 'big bang'. In any case, in this metaphor of Jesus, light is the beginning of what gives life and order to the formless void of nothingness. Light is the divine signal for illimitable creative energy to explode in the void and power every step and process in creation. In Genesis, when God's creativity is let loose all else becomes possible and God sees that it is good. It brings life into being and it brings that life to its full potential. Out of the blackness of oblivion comes the magnificent light of creation.

We have no way of knowing exactly what Jesus believed about the creation of the universe aside from his belief in a Creator. For his present-day followers, belief in the creation of the universe as the intention of a Creator does not rule out the theory of Evolution. Science has shown beyond reasonable doubt that Evolution is the means by which the changing conditions on earth are compensated for in every species of life. It is not unreasonable to propose that by evolutionary means an ongoing creative genius who intentionally initiated the big bang and all its consequences, continues to create new life. In his splendid book explaining the theory of Evolution, the evolutionary biologist and atheist Richard Dawkins describes this ongoing creativity:

> As we look back on the history of life, we see a picture of never-ending, ever-rejuvenating novelty. Individuals die; species, families, orders and even classes go extinct. But the evolutionary process itself seems to pick itself up and resume its recurrent flowering, with undiminished freshness, with unabated youthfulness, as epoch gives way to epoch.[52]

Jesus' metaphor draws connections between creativity and the coming of light out of darkness. All through a long cold grey winter most people yearn for the return of the light. Longer days signal to the trees that it is time to blossom, to the birds and animals that it is time to produce new life of their own. In fundamental terms the coming of light brings with it the potential to create new life. In John's gospel Jesus is called "the light", meaning the creative genius in his life and teachings that produces enlightenment and new life in his followers. As bearer of this light, Jesus awakens the creativity of those who follow his way and encourages them to pass on that creative light to others. Jesus gathered up a whole world of meaning when he told his followers: "You are the light of the world".

In purely physical terms, light is fundamental to making sense of life. Many have experienced the tour of underground caves when the guide says, "I'm going to turn off the lights for a moment so you can experience real darkness." The lights go off and there is a total absence of light. You literally cannot see your hand in front of your face. Along with that is a sense of disconnectedness from the people with you. You know they are still nearby but there is a feeling of complete isolation from everyone and everything and great relief when the lights are switched on again. On reflection, it is possible to see that along with light other things had also disappeared, such as communication and confidence.

At first glance this teaching looks like another of the conundrums Jesus sometimes offered. It looks to be in contradiction with other teachings about doing good things in secret. "Let your light shine before others" seems to have a similar meaning to the derogatory saying, 'he blows his own trumpet'. In fact there is a real difference between those two things. The latter is concerned with showing the world "what a good person I am; look at how much I have given to charity." The light Jesus speaks of does not originate from personal effort done for the purpose of building up the ego. He means something that originates in the divine creativity but which can shine through the lives of human beings. As salt enhances the flavour of food, this kind of light also enhances good characteristics already present in humanity. It is the illumination that lights up the potential for goodness, beauty and truth already present in human life.

Following the saying about light, Matthew adds these comments from Jesus: "A city built on a hill cannot be hid"; "no one after lighting a lamp puts it under the bushel basket, but on the lamp stand." In the Galilean hills five miles from Nazareth there was a city built on a hill and called Sepphoris. Ancient Nazareth lay in a hollow basin surrounded by hills, totally hidden until the traveller came up close to it. By contrast, Sepphoris was built deliberately on a hilltop to command a view of the surrounding countryside. That also meant it attracted the traveller, who could see it from miles away. Sepphoris was clearly not a city trying to stay unseen; its light shone for everyone to see.

In his words about the city on the hill Jesus is encouraging his listeners to communicate with the world as his followers. He is telling them to let their creative light reach as many people as possible – to "give light to all in the house". In darkness, the reaction is self-preservation or a drawing inwards, like the child in bed in a dark room, buried under blankets for security. In the creative 'light' shining through Jesus' teachings there is no fear, only openness and communication with others. In this light his followers can see more clearly the potential for good in the future. The message from Jesus is that there is no point in following him if his followers keep hidden what that means to them. The essence of being his follower is to reach out to enlighten others as he did. The beatitudes say this means being humble, merciful, hopeful, compassionate, non-violent and courageous.

All of those ideas are about good communication with other people. There is substantial evidence from the early years of the Jesus movement that his followers actually did that. Their commitment to Jesus gave them confidence to communicate to others what they had heard him say. People saw clearly from their words and example what it meant to follow Jesus and create the best possible world. Referring to Jesus' metaphor, we could say there was light shining in the lives of Jesus' followers. Its effect is summed up by the second century Christian writer Tertullian. In the middle of his description of how Christians lived in those days, he includes a famous observation made about them by outsiders: "See how they love one another."

In accordance with that, the sociologist Rodney Stark sums up the influence of the early followers of Jesus:

> *Christianity served as a revitalization movement that arose in response to the misery, chaos, fear and brutality of life in the urban Greco-Roman world. It revitalized life by providing new norms and new kinds of social relationships able to cope with many urgent problems. To cities filled with the homeless and impoverished, Christianity offered charity as well as hope. To cities filled with orphans and widows, Christianity provided a new and expanded sense of family. To cities torn by violent ethnic strife, Christianity offered a new basis for social solidarity.*[53]

This is the kind of light Jesus wanted his followers to shine into a dark world. In complete darkness the absence of light creates fear, loss of self-confidence and a focus on self-protection against the dangers of the dark. When confidence in the self disappears it is very difficult to help anyone else. I noted before that light is like salt – it does not actually add anything; it illuminates what was already there, and brings out confidence and energy and commitment to action.

Consider what happens each morning. People who get up early know what it is to watch light return as the earth turns toward the sun. At first the colours are grey, until a cosmic paint-brush seems to splash everything with pink, orange and yellow. Then all of the rainbow's colours appear and overcome the darkness. As John's gospel proclaims, light cannot be overcome by darkness. Darkness is not a thing in itself, but merely the absence of light. In the same sense, darkness in the life of an individual is not something objectively real; it is merely the absence of positive, life-giving creativity. Light brings out the colour of life. When the sun lights up the magnificent colours of the world, humanity says, "What a beautiful morning!" The light of which Jesus spoke brings out beauty in human life. As it does that, it also reveals the beauty of its creator. A poetic expression of how light awakens life already present in the world was penned in the 19th century by the American preacher and hymn-writer, Phillips Brooks:

> *When the sun rose this morning it found the world in darkness, torpid and heavy and asleep, with powers all wrapped up in sluggishness; with life that was hardly better or more alive than death. The sun found this great sleeping world and woke it. It bade it to be itself. It quickened every slow and sluggish faculty. It called to the dull streams and said, 'Be quick;' to the dull birds and bade them sing; to the dull fields and made them grow; to the dull men and bade them think and talk and work. It did not make the world. It poured strength into the essential processes which belonged to the very nature of the earth. It glorified, intensified, fulfilled the earth.*[54]

The metaphor about light is a further example of the dimensions of Jesus' thought and teachings. His teachings are focussed not only on specific issues in the lives of individuals; they are as far-reaching and profound as it is possible to be. They throw light on humanity's potential to live positively in one world-wide family.

13

On Firm Foundations

Do not think that I have come to abolish the law or the prophets; I have come not to abolish but to fulfil. For I truly tell you, until heaven and earth pass away, not one letter, not one stroke of a letter, will pass from the law until all is accomplished.
(Matt. 5:17-18)

When my husband and I travelled around the UK and Ireland I was fascinated by a characteristic of the houses. In the rows and rows of terraced houses, in street after street of semi-detached or detached one and two-storey houses, in grand manor houses, in new houses on new estates, or in small village cottages, they all held one thing in common; they were all traditional in style. There were variations of style of course, but unmistakably they all came from the same background. They were not African, or American, or Australian. No matter how big or how small, how grand or how humble, they were all products of the house-building traditions of the Scottish, English, Welsh and Irish people.

Even so, all is not what it seems there. Even the village cottages with thatched roofs are not entirely the traditional housing they seem to be. Under the ageless thatch, behind the white-washed walls with shuttered windows, are modern kitchens and bathrooms, widescreen television sets, up to date computers and computer-driven washing machines. Yet those developments are simply the latest in a steady stream of household appliances that have been developed and used over millennia. The traditional exteriors of the houses are inextricably linked with an evolution in housing and family life over the centuries. In essence, no one has assumed that these new developments in the contents of houses should mean the abandonment of traditional basic housing styles. After all, the houses are perfectly adapted to the climate. On the firm foundation of traditional house design, new thinking and new technology are incorporated and integrated with the old.

This fact throws light on a timeless truth about human wisdom. Everyone lives in the twenty-first century in a certain way, using certain technologies, only because that has been built on the knowledge and skills of the past. Development upon development in all manner of areas has brought humanity to where it is today. In that sense, each generation has stood on the shoulders of those who have gone before. Not so clear, but nonetheless equally as true, is the fact that the same developmental issues apply to religious advancement. There have always been new developments in religious thought and practice. Beliefs about God have undergone a continuing evolution of thought since the earliest days of primitive religion. No Uniting Church member in 2010 believes that God is the exclusive God of the Uniting Church, or that God lives in a cloud on top of Mount Dandenong (near Melbourne). Yet that is the kind of parochialism that determined the way the first people of the Hebrew scriptures thought about God. Since then there has been endless speculation about the divine, and different conclusions have been reached in every culture and generation.

There is no reason to think that reinterpretations of the old religion for a new era will not continue. That does not mean the fundamentals will be thrown away. It does mean that the terms in which they are expressed will cater for new eras of human experience. The new ways of interpreting religious truth will ensure that the fundamental wisdom of religion will continue to be accessible to each new generation.

Matthew's gospel records the thinking of Jesus about this same issue. In his comments about fulfilling his own religion, Jesus appears to be responding to fellow Jews who ask if he is proclaiming a new religion. His answer is crystal clear; he tells them in no uncertain terms that he does not advocate abolishing the precepts of the Law and the prophets. In fact, he is more emphatic than that: "until heaven and earth pass away, not one letter, not one stroke of a letter will pass from the Law until all is accomplished." Jesus expects that the people will go on observing and respecting the ethical precepts they received through Moses and the prophets. The clue about his intention regarding the traditions of the past is this: (he says) "I have come not to abolish but to fulfil." There is every reason to believe that Jesus would associate fulfilment of the Torah with the contemporary Jewish concept *Tikkun Olam*, which means 'repair of the world'. Contemporary Progressive Judaism describes its approach to Torah in these terms:

> *Judaism is built on the history and laws set out in the Torah. It emphasises ethical behaviour and prescribes a way of life. We put particular emphasis on Tikkun Olam (repairing the world), the belief that through social and environmental action we are partners with God in creating the world as it should be.*[55]

The French writer Voltaire once observed that it might be a very good thing if Europe decided to try Christianity. He was implying that in the Christian world there had never been a serious attempt to put into practice the code of ethics set out in the Sermon on the Mount. In effect, Jesus was saying the same thing about his own religion, first century CE Judaism. In his teachings and in the way he lived, he explained and lived the ideals of Torah[56]. His aim was to retrieve its original meaning and intention for humanity, and accordingly, his teachings illustrated foundational truths contained in scripture. Everything he said could be summed up by the so-called Golden Rule: treat others as you would have them treat you. His contemporary the Pharisee Hillel, who was a liberal teacher of the Jewish Law, reached the same conclusion.

If Jesus' teachings, which sound so radical when opened up and examined carefully, are not about a new religion in his day, neither are they about a new religion in this age. In this saying Jesus makes it clear that the basic laws believed to be from God are still to be followed; the scriptural foundations of faith are to remain for all time. He will not repudiate them; he will build on them. He will not bring their antiquity into disrepute; he will illustrate ways to carry them out in his time. Therein lies the key to this teaching. It is obvious that time has moved on since the ancient teachers first taught the Law of Moses, including the Ten Commandments. Even by the time of Jesus the society in which the Law of Moses emerged had all but disappeared and the world was profoundly different. Empires had risen and fallen, the Hebrew nomads had settled in towns and cities and the rule of clan chieftains had given way to the rule of kings. Prophets had appeared in response to corruption of the monarchy and bureaucracies had developed to impose taxes, establish standing armies and build the successive Temples that stood in Jerusalem. The life of the average Jew in Jesus' time would have been unrecognisable to people who first observed the Law of Moses.

For that reason, teachers such as Jesus of Nazareth were sorely needed. The people needed to hear how the ancient Law (or Torah) could be reinterpreted for their time. In fact Jesus was an interpreter of scripture; he showed the people how scripture could actually be fulfilled. He explained that fulfilment as the coming of the best possible world (the Kingdom of heaven) among human beings, and his way of explaining it was to put his finger on the spirit of the Law. His scholarly colleagues at the time were the Pharisees, who were extremely well versed in the letter of the Law, both written and oral. That is, they knew exactly the words in which the Law is expressed and most could recite them from memory. For some Pharisees, although doubtless not for all, attaining holiness meant following the 'letter of the Law' in exact detail. This did not mean that when they failed they were inevitably hypocrites, as they have so often been described by Christians; they were merely human.

For Jesus it was possible to interpret the Law's requirements in accordance with human need. One example is his attitude to observing the Sabbath Day. In word and action he illustrated how exceptions could be made to the letter of the Law without damage to the original spirit of wisdom in which it was written. The gospels say the people who heard him interpret the Law in this way "received him gladly". The gospels also say that those who upheld religious forms for tradition's sake accused him of rejecting it. Jesus obviously knew that even though religious traditions addressed to a particular age eventually fall into disuse and pass away, the spirit of the Law is timeless. For that reason his message also is timeless. Details in his stories about kings and servants are not from our age, but the values his stories illustrate are every bit as relevant to this age and concern his followers still. That is the point Jesus was making. It is also the point the American Jewish Rabbi Lawrence Kushner was making when he wrote this:

> *We reread scripture not to learn about what happened to our ancestors but to learn about ourselves. The stories of the Torah are true not because they happened but because they happen. We reread the sacred text, and our hands tremble.*[57]

Christians have always read and reinterpreted Jesus' stories for their own time. In the early centuries of the church, Greek-speaking Christians wrote down ideas about who they thought Jesus might have been. They drew their ideas partly from Jewish tradition and partly from Greco-Roman religion with its pantheon of gods and sons of gods, particularly Zeus and his son Apollo. Because of that influence, Jesus was re-imagined as a god-like figure beside the throne of the father God, the ultimate ruler of heaven. Because in Greek thought the father God was perfect and unchangeable and likely to be polluted by direct contact with sinful humanity, Jesus became the cosmic mediator between heaven and earth.

In scientifically enlightened times, Christians have allowed God to step down from the seclusion of a heavenly throne on the clouds and be re-imagined among them and around them, even in their own hearts. Along with that reinterpretation of understandings of God there has been an ongoing reinterpretation of Jesus. Scholars studying the original Jesus have thrown off him the doctrinal chains of two millennia and also allowed him to step down from beside a mythical heavenly throne. They have revealed Jesus as a godly man whose vision of the best possible world inspired his followers to risk their own lives to make it reality.

As the process of reinterpreting Christian belief about Jesus has gathered pace, something wonderfully ironic has occurred. In their attempt to find a new Jesus for a new era, Christians have in fact rediscovered the original Jesus of old. Many these days are encountering the Jesus who lived and worked and prayed and taught among the hills and valleys of ancient Galilee. They are rediscovering why he was willing to die for what he believed in and taught. They are reconnecting with the rock-solid foundations upon which he built his own life. It is not often acknowledged that without those foundations the church would not have survived to this day. Even when it turned its back on Jesus of Nazareth and embraced the trappings of an imperialistic, hierarchical religious institution, the faith of its adherents in a God of love could be restored when they remembered Jesus the teacher of abundant life.

God and Jesus have been imagined and re-imagined over and over throughout the past two millennia. Yet along with changes in understanding, basic Judaeo-Christian traditions about God and life have been preserved and applied in each new era. In following them, Christians continue to stand on the shoulders of those who came before them. Along with changing interpretations of Christianity, the church preserved and passed on the sacred values first discovered by the Hebrews. Followers of Jesus receive them anew in his timeless teachings.

14

Fulfilling the Commandment

You have heard that it was said to those of ancient times, 'You shall not murder'; and 'Whoever murders shall be liable to judgment.' But I say to you that if you are angry with a brother or sister, you will be liable to judgment; and if you insult a brother or sister, you will be liable to the council; and if you say, 'You fool,' you will be liable to the hell of fire. So when you are offering your gift at the altar, if you remember that your brother or sister has something against you, leave your gift there before the altar and go; first be reconciled to your brother or sister, and then come and offer your gift. (Matt. 5:21-24)

In this teaching there is a clear, concrete example of what Jesus meant by fulfilling the requirements of the Torah (see Chapter 13). For understanding here, it is essential to remember that in this regard Jesus was talking to his fellow Jews, not to people who much later became known as Christians. Matthew the gospel writer was not addressing Christians, only Jews (and some Gentiles) who saw Jesus as the Messiah. On examination, the illustration Jesus gives about fulfilling Torah can be seen to concern personal fulfilment of the commandment, "You shall not murder." The instructions he gives are uncompromising; if you have offended someone and have not been reconciled to him or her, go and sort that out before you come to worship God.

In fact the offences Jesus refers to are not murder itself; they look much more ordinary than that. The first is about being angry with someone, the second is about insulting someone, the third is about a particular form of insult – calling someone a fool. Jesus says people who do any of those things should be held to account. They should not set out to worship God until they have admitted their guilt and asked forgiveness. The clear message is that until they have been reconciled with people to whom they have done wrong in this manner, they cannot properly be reconciled with God. Church-goers might wonder what would happen to church attendance if people actually took notice of these words of Jesus. How many might find themselves disqualified from worship if they were first required to reconcile with people they had offended?

I will leave the reader to ponder that as I point out a misunderstanding about the sixth commandment. In the 1611 Authorized King James Version of the Bible, it is translated as "Thou shalt not kill." Therefore the commandment is understood as prohibition on killing of any sort, including killing by soldiers on a battlefield. Based on that translation, many Christians sent to war as soldiers have seen themselves at odds with one of the Ten Commandments. The New Revised Standard Version of scripture gets it right; it says, "You shall not murder." I am not saying that the sixth commandment excuses killing in war; it simply does not refer to that. Just as there is in English, in Hebrew there is a word that means the deliberate taking of another's life for personal reasons, that is, *ratsakh* ('murder'). There is another word in Hebrew that means the taking of life in war, or accidentally, or in the killing of animals, that is, *harag* ('kill'). The Bible uses the word for murder when it describes the killing of Abel by his brother Cain. Jesus' teaching in this section of the Sermon on the Mount is designed to prevent the crime of murder. Ultimately, its aim is to help humanity fulfil the commandment against murder.

That brings a more urgent perspective to Jesus' instructions about making amends or reconciling with someone offended against. We can begin to see that this teaching is preventive medicine for murder. For that reason it is important to look very carefully at the three offences Jesus mentions. They have frequently been proven to be antecedents for the crime of murder. The first concerns anger. Anger is one of the necessary emotions, designed as part of basic human equipment for survival. It usually manifests as part of the flight or fight response to an external threat. Most angry people point to something they believe has 'happened to them' as the cause for their anger.

Controlled anger is something else. It can actually help a person put right a wrong or injustice. Sometimes it is even referred to as righteous anger, but that is not what Jesus refers to in this teaching. He means uncontrolled anger, where the angry person is less able to think clearly and less able to monitor his or her behaviour. Examples are the angry husband who bashes a helpless wife, or the angry parent who uses a weapon to break the bones of a little son or daughter.

Jesus would doubtless have observed the effects of uncontrolled anger. In the violent world in which he lived he may even have witnessed an angry person commit murder. He may also have known of an angry person whose ill-treatment of someone had sparked a murderous revenge. We can be sure that Jesus knew very well what can happen when anger is allowed to control a person's behaviour.

Secondly, Jesus' teaching prohibits insults. Insults come in many shapes and sizes, including the one George Bernard Shaw wired to Winston Churchill to invite him to the opening of his new play Pygmalion:

> Am reserving two tickets for you for my premiere. Come and bring a friend – if you have one.

Churchill wired back:

> Impossible to be present for the first performance. Will attend the second – if there is one.

Although decidedly spiteful, those insults at least have the calming influence of humour. But even little children know the power of real insults. No one believes the little rhyme: 'Sticks and stones can break my bones, but names can never hurt me.' That simply is not true; insulting names do hurt.

Insults can take away a person's dignity in the eyes of others and rob the victim of self-respect. Children insulted or called names for slowness in school or ineptness on the sports field can grow up lacking the confidence to reach their real potential. In a twenty-first century development, internet bullies use written insults that can be lethal to their victims. In extreme situations, insulting language inflicted on school children can lead to revenge in the form of the mass murder of their fellow pupils and teachers.

That kind of response to perceived insult or rejection has become all too real in relations between religious groups and between nations. Clearly, terrorism does not arise out of a vacuum. International security consultant David Wright-Neville and Monash University's Anna Halafoff have edited a new book which spells out the links between terrorism and social exclusion. The contributors to the book see an inclusive social policy as the answer. The summary statement encapsulates their point of view:

> *As a causal factor of terrorism, social exclusion can be remedied by inclusive, participatory and deliberative measures. It would be beneficial to recalibrate counter-terrorism policies to unite rather than divide multi-ethnic, religiously diverse and multicultural societies, stressing the importance of understanding and addressing underlying causes of social tensions.*[58]

In this teaching of Jesus, the Greek language of Matthew's gospel contains an intriguing type of insult in the form of a loan word from Aramaic. In Greek, Matthew states that Jesus said (literally): "whoever might say to his brother, *Raca!* will have to account for it to the Sanhedrin" (or council of Mosaic Law). *Raca* is not a nice word; it is about as insulting a word as one can utter, and it was in use at that time. It originates from an Aramaic word (*racab*) meaning something that is rotten, decaying and full of maggots, like a corpse. Given that a corpse is regarded by the Law to have the power to corrupt and render impure any man having contact with it, the effect of calling a man *Raca* was to say that he was not worthy of the company of other human beings. Jesus the Jew knew very well the power of this kind of insult. He knew it could well provoke the subject of the insult to murder his tormentor.

Thirdly, Jesus' teaching prohibits calling someone a fool. On the face of it this sounds a lot less problematic than the first two offences. After all, most readers will have had fun with April Fools' Day jokes. Yet even they can go wrong, like the time employees at the London City Hall decided to play a joke on a fellow office worker who was then on vacation. They sent him a memo stating that the really big report he had been working on was now due early, in just two weeks. The tip-off was that the memo was dated April 1st. Very 'funny'. The problem was that the victim did not realise it was a joke. He immediately cut his holiday short and flew home to return to work. As he thought about the closer deadline he worked himself into a panic and collapsed from the stress. As he was recovering he decided it wasn't worth risking his health to finish the report on time, so he notified the City Hall of his early retirement. At that point someone finally told him about the so-called joke. Fortunately, in preference to murdering them he responded to being taken for a fool by successfully suing the perpetrators for damages. The outcome of this April Fool's Day joke makes it clear just who were the fools.

The usual definition of a fool is someone who lacks judgment or common sense, or discretion. The definition may not always genuinely apply, but if someone is labelled a fool the label is inclined to stick. It can injure that person's heart and mind and result in low self-esteem and even isolation from community. In New Testament Greek the word used by Matthew is *moré* which means 'stupid', and is the root word of the English word 'moron'. In Aramaic, the word Jesus would have used is *nabal*, which means someone who is either intellectually or morally foolish. In Greek, Aramaic or English, to be called a fool is to have one's dignity and humanity degraded or dismissed. I referred before to the fact that when school children are made to feel foolish it sometimes has devastating consequences such as school massacres.

Similar outcomes occur in universities or other work places, where sacked employees sometimes take violent revenge for what they have experienced as unfair or degrading treatment by employers or other workers. In 1999 a Canadian bus driver entered the bus company's headquarters carrying a high-powered rifle. "It's judgment day!" he shouted, and then gunned down four men and wounded another. After that he shot himself to death. It was later revealed that his job was the last of many he had left because he had been made to feel foolish. The problem was that he stuttered and people taunted him about it, robbing him of his self-esteem. In the end his revenge on them left children without fathers, wives without husbands, and a community with unnecessary tragedy.

Jesus knew the possible connection between uncontrolled anger or insulting language and the crime of murder. He knew that anger can lead to bad judgment in treatment of others. He knew that insults can rob a person of self-respect and create a desire for revenge. He also knew that the best way to prevent murder is to avoid those pre-conditions for it. Jesus' instructions to his hearers are quite simple, but very clear. If there is someone you have hurt through your anger, or because you've insulted someone or called him or her a fool, your responsibility is to apologise and restore the relationship. Unless you are in good relationship with other human beings, your attempts to worship God are in vain. You cannot be reconciled with the source of the ultimate ethics for harmonious life unless you are first reconciled with people you have hurt.

Reconciliation restores right thinking in the perpetrator. It restores self-respect to the person offended against. It can bring peace between individuals, and in the wider sense it can bring peace on earth. When examined carefully, we find that this teaching of Jesus has the potential to prevent murder. It can bring about fulfilment of the sixth commandment: "you shall not murder".

15
A Task for Human Beings

> *It was also said, 'whoever divorces his wife, let him give her a certificate of divorce.' But I say to you that anyone who divorces his wife, except on the ground of unchastity, causes her to commit adultery; and whoever marries a divorced woman commits adultery.* (Matt. 5:31-32)

In any given week in Australia about two thousand people marry and hope to live happily ever after. Also in any given week, about a thousand people are divorced, ending the marriage they had fondly expected to last for ever. Marriage can be bliss or misery, or anything between those extremes, but it is never easy. It is rarely as good as the classic love stories with their perfect endings would have it, for the reason that there have never been perfect people. In this section we look at one of the most common examples of human imperfection – marriage breakdown and divorce – and how Jesus deals with this vitally important subject.

The invitation to follow Jesus is not for perfect people and he did not assume that any of his followers were perfect, or that they would become perfect. His aim was that they become the best people they could be. Why else would his major teachings concern human failings and how to overcome them? Why else would he teach about a God who forgives when humanity stumbles and falls – again and again? Even if his vision of the best possible world became reality, it would not be a state of affairs in which nothing could go wrong. Getting it right all the time is an impossible challenge for human beings and Jesus believed in a God who loves imperfect human beings even when they try and still fail. His hope for the difference between the present world and the best possible world was that when human beings fall short of perfection, they forgive each other, pick themselves up and start again. They can try and fail, but still be accepted and loved.

At this point it is important to remember Jesus' own humanity, and therefore his own imperfections. Most Christians have been taught from childhood that Jesus could not possibly have done anything wrong. The reason given is that according to traditional Christian doctrine, he was the perfect 'Son of God'. Many readers will recall the old Sunday School hymn favourite, 'A Man There Lived in Galilee'. The first verse is:

> *A man there lived in Galilee,*
> *unlike all men before,*
> *for he alone from first to last*
> *our flesh unsullied wore;*
> *a perfect life of perfect deeds*
> *once to the world was shown,*
> *that all mankind might mark his steps*
> *and in them place their own.*[59]

The obvious response to those words is, how could they do that? How could anyone follow a perfect person? New Testament scholar Paul Trudinger addresses the subject of the immense difficulty that would be experienced by his followers if Jesus had indeed been a perfect God-man. If that had been the case, he would have had a unique relationship with God that especially empowered him to live his own teachings:

> *It may be comforting to know that God loved us enough to want to take on our form, but it doesn't show us how that it is possible for us to live in the kind of intimacy with God that Jesus had, because that intimacy would have been in-built: God feeling at one with God's self; God, the first person of the Trinity, feeling at one with the Son, the second person.*[60]

Fortunately the gospels contain many instances of Jesus' humanity, his anger (the 'cleansing of the Temple') being an often-cited example. The gospel writers had no problem in noting that he also felt anxiety and fear, as well as pain and physical exhaustion, in facing up to the brutal wielders of power. Given his humanity, who could doubt that there were times when he failed to achieve his best? The power of Jesus' teachings is that they come from a spiritually enlightened but vulnerable human being who nonetheless was able to put them into practice.

At some time in life every person experiences trying his or her hardest to get something right and still failing. An unfortunate example of this occurred during a recital given in Bangkok by a promising young American pianist. The recital had only just begun when the pianist discovered that due to excessive humidity the D key of the treble clef was stuck. As luck would have it, his program was Bach's Toccata and Fugue in D minor, and Prelude and Fugue in D major. A reviewer in the *Bangkok Post* also noted that the swivel-type piano stool had been greased rather more than necessary. During a particularly vigorous section the pianist found himself facing the audience instead of the piano. Abandoning the Toccata in D minor, he moved on to Liszt's Fantasia in G minor, whereupon the G key of the bass clef also stuck. To try and free these notes the pianist started kicking the lower section of the piano, but its right leg gave way and the whole instrument tilted over at thirty-five degrees. At this point the pianist rose, bowed to the audience and left the stage. The audience responded with tumultuous applause. He may not have succeeded in what he set out to do, but the audience gave him full marks for trying.

In all confirmation groups I have led I gave the participants one essential thing to remember. If they remembered nothing else, I urged them to hold on to the good news of the gospel according to Jesus. Summed up in just two words, it is: God forgives. That is worth keeping in mind as we consider one of

Jesus' most difficult teachings – the one concerning divorce. In Matthew's gospel he says: "Anyone who divorces his wife, except on the ground of unchastity, causes her to commit adultery; and whoever marries a divorced woman commits adultery."

This teaching has always bothered Christians. It has divided families and churches and it has also been the basis of the church's position on divorce and on the remarriage of divorced people. Because of that, this teaching has profoundly affected the lives of countless Christians and continues to do so. There is so much disparity between those words of Jesus and much of contemporary Australian society's view of divorce, that there seems little chance of reconciling the two. Yet there are very few families untouched by divorce, and for that reason it is important to think through these sayings of Jesus.

In this exchange Jesus responded first to a question from Pharisees. At the time there was a vigorous debate among the Pharisees about divorce and remarriage, with one major school of thought (the Pharisaic House of Hillel) saying that a man could divorce his wife for trivial reasons such as burning the dinner. He could also divorce her if he found another woman more attractive. If we think that preposterous, we might remember that there are similar reasons behind many divorces in our time. The Pharisaic House of Shammai also followed Deuteronomy 24:1, which says a man could end his marriage ("because he finds something objectionable about her") by giving his wife a document of divorce. While the House of Hillel allowed more grounds for divorce, the point is that the two Pharisaic schools allowed for divorce. Instead of identifying with one or the other school, Jesus interpreted Deuteronomy in a new way. He advocated the view that apart from "unchastity", a man who divorced his wife made both of them adulterers should they marry again. Matthew's version gives us the disciples' reaction to that: they were staggered. "In that case," they said, "it is better not to get married!"

To come closer to Jesus' meaning here, we need to look at what he might have said in Aramaic. The word "unchastity" in

Jesus' reply to the Pharisees is the rather modest effort of NRSV translators to convey the original meaning. In Greek manuscripts the word is *porneias*, which means every kind of unlawful sexual intercourse. Jesus would have used the Aramaic word *zanah*, which means illicit intercourse or 'fornication'. *Zanah* could mean homosexual acts and it also means prostitution, including cultic prostitution such as occurred at shrines and sanctuaries when the Law of Moses was first formulated. In the Book of the Prophet Hosea (6:10), where the relationship between God and Israel is expressed as a marriage bond, *zanah* refers to infidelity as the people of Israel's apostasy with the gods of other nations. In that case God forgave the unfaithful wife (Israel). The meaning in Jesus' time is most likely to have been adultery.

The primary problem for Jesus in his conversation with the Pharisees about divorce was that in both schools of thought there was more interest in what was legal than in what was loving. Before Christians run away with the idea that this proves Judaism to be a 'legalistic' religion, it should not be forgotten that many Christians today ask first what the church says about divorce. Only secondly do they ask what is best for the people involved. Yet the question remains: what can be done with this teaching of Jesus?

In other parts of the gospels we see clearly that Jesus was not limited by a literal observance of the precepts of his religion; instead he emphasized how following the spirit of the Law can lead to human wholeness. He consistently took into account human imperfection, and we can see clearly that forgiveness is the heart of his approach to the Law. In Mark's version of this teaching we see Jesus' thinking more fully than we do in Matthew. This is not to say that Mark contradicts Matthew, but it does contain helpful detail not present in Matthew. According to Mark, rather than align himself with one Pharisaic party or another on the question of divorce, Jesus opened up the background behind the Law's precepts on marriage. From Genesis he quoted the Bible's ideal for marriage: "… from the beginning of creation God made them male and female. For this reason a man shall leave his father and mother and be joined to his wife, and the two shall become one flesh. So they are no longer two, but one flesh. Therefore what God has joined together, let no one separate." (Mark 10:6-9).

The point is that instead of concentrating on the question of when divorce is right, Jesus reminded his listeners of when marriage is right. He focussed their thoughts on how marriage partnerships could be in the best possible world. Crucially though, his quoting of what the Bible sees as God's ideal for marriage did not mean that Jesus had no understanding of human frailty and imperfection. His teachings are given with love, to encourage imperfect humans to love and forgive one another. They are all based on his foundational conviction that God first loves us.

Therefore (in Mark 10), when Jesus was asked what he thought about the stipulation in the Law which allowed a man to divorce his wife, he replied: "Because of your hardness of heart he [Moses] wrote this commandment for you." In Greek, *sklerokardia* literally means a hardened heart. In Aramaic, *kashah lav* means a hard heart in the sense of being severe or angry. Hardness of heart is Jesus' way of expressing the absence or even opposite of love. Many would acknowledge that although the opposite of love can be anger and hate, but it can also be indifference. A heart indifferent to the other has developed a hard shield that blocks the giving and receiving of love. This can happen whether or not one partner or the other has been unfaithful.

When unfaithfulness in marriage does happen, some couples are able to work their way through the crisis and forgive and stay together. In that case the wronged partner's heart has not become 'hardened' to the other. In other cases, divorce is sometimes the only way to avoid a lifetime without love. Jesus did not deny that; it is implicit in his reply. While advocating the ideal marriage, he did not lose sight of human frailty and how hard it can sometimes be to forgive.

Among many other churches world-wide, The Uniting Church in Australia[61] has formulated its approach to marriage and divorce:

> *Marriage for Christians is the freely given consent and commitment in public and before God of a man and a woman to live together for life.*

Where divorce is concerned it says:

> *In cases of the irretrievable breakdown of marriage, the Church acknowledges that divorce may be the only creative and life giving direction to take.*

The Church has the responsibility:

> *to care for people, including children, through the trauma of the ending of a marriage;*
>
> *to help people, where appropriate, to grieve, repent, grow in self-understanding, receive affirmation, grace and forgiveness;*
>
> *to support them as they hear God's call to new life.*

Finally, The Uniting Church says:

> *The grace and healing of God are available to people who are divorced, which may free them to marry again.*

The Uniting Church is typical of many mainstream Protestant churches which believe that statements of this kind reflect Jesus' teachings about human imperfection, repentance, forgiveness and renewal.

An important question concerns whether the Bible has an opinion on what God might think about divorce. The Bible was written by people reflecting on their faith in God. It describes the relationship between God and humanity as a covenant – a two-way commitment, one to the other. Over and over, God is said to be totally faithful to this covenant. Therefore marriage is described in the Uniting Church as a covenant, or two-way contract. It represents what the church believes is God's ideal for mutually faithful and loving human relationships. Yet it is the very idea of a broken covenant, plus Jesus' statements about divorce, that some churches use to prohibit remarriage after divorce. The reason given is that divorced people have broken the vows they made before God. What is missing is the teaching of Jesus about forgiveness and new life.

There are many reasons for marriage break-up, and divorce is sometimes a painful necessity. It may be necessary because the marriage was ill-advised in the first place. It may be necessary because partners in marriage grow and change so profoundly that the original relationship no longer exists. It may be necessary because of the destruction of a loving relationship through physical and emotional abuse or sexual infidelity. In any case, divorce can separate families and destroy friendships. Yet while it is never an entirely good thing, divorce can be the lesser of two evils. It can release people living without love to find new and life-giving relationships.

Jesus' humane approach to the interpretation of scripture also indicates how his followers might regard people going through a marriage break-up. Other biblical ideals for human life may be broken in private or disregarded, but divorce is a very public process. I remember well a woman who returned to church after a difficult divorce. She said that she had never felt so lonely in all her life as she did standing alone after church among people she had thought were her friends. In the Sermon on the Mount Jesus gives his followers the ultimate ideals for their lives. Yet they could fail to carry out most of them and still hide that fact from others. It is not so with divorce. For that reason there is need of compassion and support for people going through the public trauma of marriage break-up and divorce. When people fail to sustain ideals for their relationships, those ideals should not be used as weapons against them. Instead, they can become the means to a new future.

Jesus did not advise people against marrying, as the Apostle Paul did in his expectation that God would soon intervene to bring the present world to an end (1 Cor. 7:8). Rather, Jesus advised people how to live the best possible way in their ongoing human relationships. Individual marriages may not be made in heaven, but Jesus' guidelines for life-giving relationships contain the possibility of forgiveness and new life whether marriages continue or not.

16
The Picture Broadens

You have heard that it was said, 'You shall love your neighbour and hate your enemy.' But I say to you, Love your enemies and pray for those who persecute you. (Matt. 5:43-44)

When a man runs for public office his supporters often describe him as a good family man. There is an unwritten rule about this; if you wish to present the candidate as ready to commit to responsibility, call him a good family man. It is widely believed that every office, from president of the local football club to President of the United States, will benefit if the nominee is a good family man. Another indicator of good character is said to be a love of animals. In newspaper advertisements targeting people looking for a partner, 'loves animals' usually gets a big tick. Yet Adolf Hitler was devoted to his mother; he carried her photo until the day he died. He also loved his Alsatian dog Blondi.

Jesus blows wide open all the assumptions about connections between love of family and good character with his comment: "If you greet only your brothers and sisters, what more are you doing than others?" He makes then what would have been for his fellow Jews an invidious comparison: "Do not even the Gentiles do the same?" It is often claimed that Jesus had little contact with Gentiles, which disregards the fact that throughout Jesus' lifetime the land of Israel was occupied by a foreign force. There were officials of the Roman Empire everywhere, and the Roman army included soldiers from all over Africa, Asia Minor and Europe. For that reason the Jewish people in Jesus' time would commonly have seen Gentiles from many different places and cultures. Gentiles were regarded then by Jews as rough and lacking in moral fibre, for which reason they were often used by Jewish teachers as examples of how not to behave.

However, Jesus' remark about greeting sisters and brothers (as the Gentiles do) does not single out Gentiles; it is directed to his listeners – his own people – as well. His comment points to an important truth about loving people outside the family circle; he says this is the kind of love that can be unlimited. An active love for humanity as a whole produces its own reward in the amount of love and peace received in return. Implicitly, Jesus is asking his listeners to think about how their own lives are diminished if they love only those people who love them. Yet even this would not have prepared them for what was to come.

This reading contains another instance where Jesus quotes from scripture (in this case, Leviticus) and then 'ups the ante': "You have heard that it was said, you shall love your neighbour and hate your enemy. But I say to you, love your enemies and pray for those who persecute you." There is a whole lot more at stake here than family love and devotion, love of people in one's own social circle, or even the general idea of loving humanity. This is where the picture widens, where the stakes are broadened to the utmost. The scope of traditional teaching about love of neighbour has suddenly become unlimited. Here Jesus is not setting aside biblical tradition, he is building on it. "Love your neighbour as yourself" is an integral part of the teaching of Jesus, originating in the Book of Leviticus (19:18). Jesus' own people were familiar with the idea of loving family, friends and neighbours – and oneself. Now there is a teaching about loving your enemy.

Luke says Jesus illustrated that with the story of the Good

Samaritan. For centuries Jews and Samaritans had been implacably opposed – mainly on religious and racial grounds, and with that story the old definition of neighbour is blown out of the water. Perhaps it now means anyone in need? Yet this teaching of Jesus in the Sermon on the Mount goes even further than the story of the Good Samaritan. It concerns loving those who are actively inflicting pain or suffering on others. It is about those who are actively persecuting or threatening people (including oneself) with persecution. The persecutors Jesus had in mind could have been Roman authorities, or they could have been representatives of King Herod. In either case ordinary people were imprisoned, flogged or sold into slavery because they could not pay taxes. Jesus is telling those same ordinary people to love people who inflict such things on them, their friends and relatives, or neighbours. This is where the radical nature of this teaching is revealed. Why does Jesus want his followers to love their enemies? How is it even possible?

We should identify what is meant here by 'love'. To love family and friends usually means to provide for their needs, encourage their development and relate to them with respect. It means treating members of our 'tribe' as we would want them to treat us. There is nothing new about that; everyone knows Jesus taught the Golden Rule. What is new is that with this teaching about loving enemies Jesus has ratcheted up the Golden Rule to another level. Even the opposite version of it – do nothing to anyone that you would not like done to you – does not equate with the significance of loving enemies.

Jesus acknowledges that. After instructing his followers to love their enemies and pray for people who persecute them, he gives them the reason. This is so that his followers will know they are part of the whole family of humanity, both good and bad. If your family includes everyone on earth, you are obliged to love them all; to treat them all as you would like to be treated. Jesus is inviting his hearers to take their notions about loving one another way beyond their usual thinking.

Then there comes a piece of Jesus' own mind. Here we begin to grasp the extent of his vision for humanity and see how far-reaching was his understanding. It is not for nothing that black civil rights champion Martin Luther King called Jesus "the most influential character that ever came into this world." Before Jesus, his people believed that God would reward the Israelites because they were inheritors of the covenant with Abraham. Because they were the 'chosen people', God would eventually reverse the wrongs inflicted on them, and their enemies would be defeated. The result was that many simply waited for the Messiah to appear.

Jesus begs to differ; he knows the answer is different and difficult. He has observed the suffering of his people and seen the prosperity of the rulers. He could hardly miss it; he grew up a short walk from the Greco-Roman-styled Jewish city of Sepphoris, built by Herod the Great.[62] Jesus' carpenter background may even have meant that he and his father were involved in its extensive rebuilding after the Galilean called Judas son of Ezekias led a disastrous rebellion against Herod's palace in Sepphoris. The Roman general Varus retaliated by burning the city to the ground in 4 BCE, but during Jesus' lifetime Herod Antipas rebuilt it and made it his capital.

It is therefore reasonable to assume that as a local carpenter, Jesus would have known Sepphoris. It is more than likely that he would have walked the streets of this city just five miles from his home village. He would have seen the marbled and mosaic-covered floors, beautiful drapes, magnificent amphitheatre, bejewelled women and all the other signs of wealth. He would have known that the riches came from exploitation by Herod and his Roman masters of poor workers in fields and vineyards and fishing boats. He would also have noted that this wealth was not taken away by God as their punishment for inflicting hardship on the people. Any notion he may have held in his youth about God intervening on behalf of the down-trodden would have been swept away by the reality of the times and place in which he matured into adulthood. It is hardly surprising that it was the Galilee from which Jewish rebels led by messianic aspirants came, convinced that freedom from tyranny could come only through violent uprisings.

The idea of loving the enemy indicates the conclusion Jesus reached on all of these things. He came to understand that nature gives the benefits of sun and rain – that is, good harvests, and the curse of too much sun and rain – that is, droughts and floods – to both deserving and undeserving alike (see Matthew 5:43-45). In other words, he understood that both good and evil are part of the natural world. He understood that the wealthy exploiters of his day still belonged to the human family, also receiving blessings from the Creator of all. Jesus understood this as an all-embracing, unconditional kind of love which his followers came to call grace. He then gave his listeners a goal to move toward. Through this teaching, he invited them to imagine what might happen if they embraced this kind of unconditional love and loved their enemies. Undoubtedly there would need to be a time of transition while people began to put this teaching into practice. We might ask how it is even possible to begin.

One way is to look for the good in the other person, even if it is hard to find because he is your 'enemy'. When Abraham Lincoln ran for President of the United States, a Democrat called Edwin MacMasters Stanton said a lot of unkind things about him. He even criticized Lincoln's looks: "You don't want a tall, lanky, ignorant man like this as president of the United States."[63] Stanton talked on and on like that and wrote at length his objections to Lincoln. Lincoln was duly elected President and began to choose a Cabinet. For Secretary of War, he chose Edwin Stanton. When his colleagues reminded him of what Stanton had been saying about him, Abraham Lincoln said: "Oh yes, I know about it; I've read about it; I've heard him myself. After looking over all the country, I find he is the best man for the job."

When Lincoln was assassinated, Stanton said: "Now he

belongs to the ages. There lies the most perfect ruler of men the world has ever seen." That may or may not be the case, but Stanton's change of heart would never have happened if Lincoln had repaid his hostility in kind. If Lincoln had not had the courage to look foolish in the eyes of his peers and give due respect (an integral part of love) to his enemy, Stanton would have gone on living with hatred in his heart for Lincoln. Significantly, Stanton's potential as a leader in the struggle against slavery might never have been realised. When an opportunity comes to get even with an enemy who has inflicted an injury, Jesus says here that his followers must not do it.

A further illustration is contained in a story from Martin Luther King. In a 1957 sermon he described how he and his brother were driving to Chattanooga one evening. Drivers were not dimming their lights as they passed, and his brother became angry about that. He stated that the next time it happened he would also refuse to dim his lights. Martin Luther King's response was to talk him out of it:

Somebody's got to have sense on this highway. That's the trouble. As all of the civilizations of the world have moved up the highway of history, so many, having looked at other civilizations that refused to dim the lights, they decided to refuse to dim theirs. Out of twenty-two civilizations that have risen up, all but seven have found themselves in the junk-heap of destruction.[64]

In twenty-first century Australia, loving the enemy would have many and varied consequences. In one respect it would mean flooding Afghanistan with goodwill and good things for all of its people. It would mean removing Australian combat troops. It would mean making friends with the Taliban – not with their ideology, but with their humanity.

Jesus did not say it would be easy. He had the courage to look in the eyes of those who hated him and love them. He had the courage to pray for them even as they did their very worst to him. Through love of his own enemies, he showed humanity the way to a non-violent world of peace.

17

The Responsive Heart

Beware of practising your piety before others in order to be seen by them; for then you have no reward from your Father in heaven. So whenever you give alms, do not sound a trumpet before you, as the hypocrites do in the synagogues and in the streets, so that they may be praised by others. Truly I tell you, they have received their reward. But when you give alms, do not let your left hand know what your right hand is doing, so that your alms may be done in secret; and your Father who sees in secret will reward you.
(Matt. 6:1-4)

We have noted that Jesus' teachings are profoundly interconnected and reliant upon each other, and that they are part of a whole system of human behaviour Jesus believed would bring about the best possible world. The next teaching concerns the spiritual life of his followers. Jesus wanted his hearers to realise the fundamental importance of spiritual resources. His teachings are very difficult to carry out and he knew his followers would need continuing encouragement and wisdom. For that reason he gave them instruction about their spiritual life. In summary, it teaches the followers to concentrate on aspects of worship such as giving to the poor and prayer. The emphasis should not be on unimportant questions like who is watching me, who has noticed how pious I am in prayer, or who is impressed by my level of giving.

I once visited the Parish Church of Kemberton in the United Kingdom. I was leaving the church when I spied a sign on the wall in the entrance porch. It was headed 'HINTS to those who worship GOD in this Church'. 'Hints' was in capital letters and clearly they were more like iron-clad rules than hints. The list was probably distributed to British Anglican churches in the early twentieth century. These are some of its hints about behaviour in church:

Be in Time.
Go straight into Church.
Kneel down on your Knees.
Do not look round every time the door opens.
Join in all the Prayers, and the Singing, and Amens.
Do not whisper to your neighbour.
Keep your thoughts fixed.
Make Almsgiving a regular part of your Worship.

When the choir and Clergy enter, or leave the Church, then stand up in a body. When they have passed by, kneel down in Prayer, for them and yourselves.

To twenty-first century church-goers that looks plainly dictatorial. The language is far from what they might use to persuade fellow church members to behave in a certain way. Even so, Jesus' followers these days would not be at odds with the aim of the hints. They are designed to focus the worshipper on the reason for being in worship in the first place. In this teaching about piety, Jesus is saying something with similar meaning, his point being that worrying about who will notice how holy I am can have consequences! He put it this way: "Beware of practising your piety before others in order to be seen by them; for then you have no reward from your Father in heaven."

In mentioning 'reward' Jesus is not talking about missing out on heaven, or some kind of afterlife. The reward in question is connected with the ultimate aim of his teachings. For him the ultimate reward for his followers is to belong to the Kingdom of heaven on earth. Clearly that membership will not be for free-loaders; those who enter this kind of world will be the people who helped to create it. Secondly, membership applies to the here and now, not to some future time when it has finally reached fulfilment. For Jesus, the best possible world is not a future state of affairs at the end of time when the Messiah (re)appears. His teachings indicate otherwise. Self-evidently he believed that as long as his followers are trying to put his teachings into practice, the potential for the best possible world is already present and growing among them. It will not happen in the twinkling of an eye; it will require ongoing dedication to the truths he taught. The reward is to take part in its creating.

It might be helpful to rephrase Jesus' saying like this: If you are preoccupied with what other people think of you instead of working to create the best possible world, you will miss out on its benefits now. This will not be punishment from God; it will be self-inflicted by your self-centred behaviour.

The rest of this teaching expands on its first sentence and it is useful to examine it in three parts. First there are instructions about donating to the poor. It sounds ludicrous that people had a trumpeter announcing their almsgiving ("So whenever you give alms, do not sound a trumpet before you, as the hypocrites do in the synagogues and in the streets" – Matthew 6:2). Perhaps it was not quite like that. Herod the Great's Temple in Jerusalem contained thirteen trumpet-shaped brass vessels into which the people would throw their donations to charity. As the coins were thrown in the brass would make a loud noise; in other words, it would 'sound'. Perhaps Jesus was thinking of that in his comments about the way some people gave to the poor in the synagogue and on the street. The noisy and ostentatious way they went about their giving was akin to making the brass 'trumpets' in the Temple 'sound'. It is likely that this is the origin of Paul's expression in 1 Corinthians 13 about a person without love: "I am become as sounding brass".

In any case, Jesus is obviously unimpressed by this and he points his followers to the higher motive for helping the poor.

People doing it to be noticed and well thought of, miss the point. If they make a public song and dance out of giving and receive the adulation of the masses for doing it, Jesus says that will be their sole reward. They simply do not understand the biblical reason for giving to the poor – to bring justice to people who have missed out on a fair share. They do not understand that having the right motive for giving will lead them closer to Jesus' vision for the world. They do not see the big picture as he did. They are denied the satisfaction of bringing Jesus' vision to reality.

Second comes this curious instruction: "when you give alms, do not let your left hand know what your right hand is doing." This is probably so that giving can be done in complete humility, so secret that one hand is unaware of the other's generosity. There is another possible inference here. In the Middle East both ancient and modern, there are cultural rules regarding the use of left and right hands. The left hand is widely regarded as unclean. In cultures where food is sometimes eaten by hand without utensils, the right hand is reserved for eating because the left hand is used for matters of personal hygiene. The right hand is therefore regarded as more pure than the left hand.

The Bible often refers to the right hand as the means by which God connects with humanity. An example is Psalm 73, where verse 23 has God holding the right hand of the psalmist. The writer of Ecclesiastes notes that "the heart of the wise inclines to the right, but the heart of a fool to the left." (10:2). It is clear that there is a lot more going on here than the giving of alms in secret. Jesus is referring to the inner life, the struggle between good and evil that goes on in every human being. The message is, do not allow your impure side, or the selfishness in your nature, to overcome your desire to be on the side of justice. Jesus is telling his hearers that giving with the correct or compassionate motive is an essential qualification for citizenship in what he called the Kingdom of heaven.

Thirdly, Jesus gives instructions about praying. Again there is the theme of being seen to be pious, or good. He says: "And whenever you pray, do not be like the hypocrites; for they love to stand and pray in the synagogues and at the street corners, so that they may be seen by others." I have already noted that giving to the poor to be seen as a good person goes against the spirit of Jesus' teaching. The same principle applies in the teaching about praying. Those who pray in order to be seen have also missed the point of prayer, and again Jesus calls people who try to attract attention to their piety, 'hypocrites'. It is often assumed that the word hypocrites here refers to the group caricatured in the gospels as adversaries of Jesus, the Pharisees. That is not necessarily the case; the word as used in this teaching does not refer to any particular group in Jesus' society. Hypocrite in English is derived from a Greek word which means an actor in Greek plays – someone who acts while hidden behind a mask. A hypocrite in the area of religious practice is any person pretending to be something or someone he or she is not.

Jesus also criticises the words used by people who pray loudly in public. Their prayers are full of pious-sounding but empty phrases. Apparently Jesus is encouraging his followers to 'get real' when they pray. I once visited the home of a clergy colleague in a country parish. When it came time for lunch his teenage daughter Becky was asked to say grace. This is what she said: "Hey God, thanks for this great day! Thanks for this yummy food, and for making Mum such a grouse cook! Catch you later. Amen." I was a bit surprised at the time, but when I thought about it I realised that Becky had it just right. She did not see the need for pious-sounding phrases; she was just being honest and intimate with the sacred as she understood it.

In all three of these instructions, Jesus is clearly encouraging his followers to focus on their openness to the spiritual resources of wisdom and encouragement. Followers of Jesus' vision need that openness every bit as much as he needed it, and private prayer, even silent prayer, is an opportunity to receive its benefits.

18
Treasure Worth Keeping

> *... store up for yourselves treasures in heaven, where neither moth nor rust consumes and where thieves do not break in and steal. For where your treasure is, there your heart will be also.*
> (Matt. 6:20-21)

Most interpretations of 'treasures' in this teaching identify a focus on the storing up of material possessions. The message usually is that this preoccupation rules out an intentional development of spiritual or moral treasures – those associated with heaven. I will discuss the subject of preoccupation with material goods in Chapter 20 ('Souls for Sale'), which concerns money. Given that, this chapter will interpret Jesus' teaching as applying to religious treasures. It certainly applies to churches, but it might just as well apply to the religious practices of other faiths such as Judaism, Buddhism, Islam, Hinduism. Immediately after giving blunt advice about keeping spiritual practices private – not using them for self-aggrandizement – Jesus goes on to talk about storing up 'treasures'. The treasures could be worldly goods, but given the proximity of this and the previous teaching, I will interpret 'treasures' as treasured religious rites and practice.

I begin by stating the obvious: Jesus was not a Christian! It is perfectly clear that Jesus never intended to start a new religion; he remained a Jew to the end of his life. In this teaching his aim is to free people from anything (including religious observances) not worth storing up, and focus their minds and hearts on ways to usher in the best possible world. The problem for some was that their religious observance had become the sole sign of their righteousness. Their religious rites had become their greatest treasures. Their particular way of practising their religious rites mattered more to them than the way they lived as human beings according to their belief in God.

For contemporary Christians there is nothing new about that. In the twenty-first century most of Jesus' followers have continued to define themselves through their performance of religious rites. Each Christian group usually considers its own way as the only way, or at least that their particular church is among those who have got it right! When I was a theological student some of the lectures in Ormond College at Melbourne University were held in what was called Room A. Room A has since been renovated, but in the early 1990s it was a time-warp – a piece of history preserved in its uncomfortable nineteenth-century wooden benches and desk-tops. Many past students had survived long lectures in Room A by decorating the desk tops with their initials. One did even better than initials; in large thick letters dug deep into the timber was one student's full name. (I was inspired by that to add my own initials!). When the United Faculty of Theology was established in Melbourne in 1969, Catholic, Presbyterian and Anglican ordinands began to be educated together. After the inauguration of the Uniting Church in 1977, jokes started circulating about the seating in Room A. If you were Uniting Church you would say, "The Catholic candidates are in the front rows, because they believe they stand for the first and only true church. The Uniting Church candidates are in the back rows because they believe they stand with the marginalized. The Anglican candidates are in the middle rows, because they don't know where they stand." There was the Catholic version and the Anglican version of the same joke.

Humour has always been used by Christians to express

criticism of other religious groups. Sometimes it reveals blindness to characteristics of the joke-teller's own group. A man in my own denomination told a story about the pastor of a large Pentecostal congregation showing a visitor from the Uniting Church around his church property. They toured the vast auditorium with its ear-splitting sound system, enormous plasma screens and plush seating. They stopped at the book shop and DVD centre and they drank mugguccinos in the church coffee shop. They took a buggy ride around the extensive grounds. They crossed acres of car park to the church's spacious signboard at the front entrance. The sign was gigantic, but it had to be! It said: Oak Road Bible-Believing, Hand Clapping, Foot Stomping, Chorus-Singing, Coffee-and-Donuts-after-church, Non-Denominational Church. "Why does your church have such a long name?" asked the visitor. "Well," said the pastor, "if you don't have any written theology, you have to squeeze an awful lot of doctrine into your name!"

The visitor laughed, but his own church notice board may well have read: "High Street Traditional Worship, Old-Hymns-Singing, Cuppa-After-Worship, Uniting Church". It is so easy to poke fun at other Christians while hoarding one's own religious treasures. Sometimes it is not clear what those religious treasures are until a new Minister arrives and tries to take them away! After all, the people in Jesus' time who treasured their own observance of religion were only following what they had been taught since childhood. The problem Jesus often identified was that for some the rules had become ends in themselves, until the outward signs of piety, like fasting, were all that was left. Observation of religious rules had sometimes obscured the sacred laws of love, justice and mercy that underpin the Torah.

Many times Jesus challenged this religious correctness. He knew that observing religious rules had become more important for some people than their personal spiritual growth. He saw that they had lost sight of religion which helps people live in harmony and in understanding of values which enhance that harmony. Jesus wanted to free them from faith in their religious 'treasures'. He wanted them to reclaim faith through good religion that would equip them to be creators of the best kind of world.

Good religion does not ridicule or vilify other believers on the basis of their particular observance. Nor does it laud those who practice their piety for all to see. Good religion focuses on the needs of human beings and frees people from obsession with adherence to religious rules and dogma. Good religion teaches the basic values for life that are enshrined in Jesus' teaching. In contemporary society good religion also encourages respect for people of other faith positions. There is no place in Jesus' vision of an inclusive humanity for efforts to convert someone else to 'my way' of being religious, or 'my way' of understanding the transcendent. Trying to make other people religious 'like me' is a sure way to frustration, anger and trouble.

One of the bishops of the early church was John Chrysostom. He was also called the 'golden mouth', because of his preachings about truth and love. He was even made a saint of the church. Yet John's ministry was contaminated and spoiled by his hatred of the Jews. John was the victim of a very human need for everyone to 'agree with me'; for everyone to be 'like me'. John's hatred stemmed from pure frustration; no matter how hard he tried he could not win over the Jews of Antioch to Christianity. Worse still, some of his congregation stayed friends with Jews and even continued to attend Jewish festivals. In response to that, he called the synagogue:

> ... the temple of demons, a den of thieves; a house of ill fame. Whatever name more horrible could be found, will never be worse than the synagogue deserves.[65]

Those words came from John's own heart. Unfortunately they were also planted in the hearts of his congregation. When he condemned the Jews to hell on earth for rejecting Christ, it is not surprising that some of his flock decided to make sure it happened – and it did. John Chrysostom would certainly be in breach of the Victorian state government's anti-vilification legislation, that outlaws statements about individuals or groups which inspire hatred of those people.[66] It certainly dissuades religious people from looking for things to hate or vilify in other religious groups. In that regard Jesus' own brother James wrote this to Jesus' followers: "let everyone be quick to listen, slow to speak, slow to anger; for your anger does not produce God's righteousness." (James 1:19)

It is easy for Christians to look on from the sidelines at divisions and quarrels in other churches and other faiths. They can feel exasperated with some Christians who believe it is God's will that Muslims and Jews become converted to Christianity. They can roll their eyes at Catholics who believe the Mass should be recited only in Latin. They can shrug their shoulders at Muslims who claim their faction is the only true descendant of Mohammed. They can laugh at a journalist's experience in a Greek Orthodox monastery. When he said he was a Catholic, the Orthodox priest quickly replied, "Oh, I'm so sorry." Where religious rivalry is based on different religious practices, there is invariably heat and passion on either side of the divide. Both sides are in danger of vilifying the human beings involved. As James the brother of Jesus wrote: "If any think they are religious, and do not bridle their tongues but deceive their hearts, their religion is worthless." The first Letter of John (4:20) puts it even more clearly: "Those who say, 'I love God', and hate their brothers and sisters, are liars." The twentieth century Roman Catholic theologian Romano Guardini noted that, "The church is the cross upon which Christ is crucified again and again."[67] After two thousand years it would be good if Christians could stop doing that.

The second century Gospel of Mary is claimed to have been written by Mary Magdalene. It does not have the status of scripture, but it ends with a saying very much in tune with the Jesus of the gospels. In chapter 4 there is a farewell scene between Jesus and his disciples. Jesus says, "Peace be with you! Acquire my peace within yourselves! … Go then, preach the good news about the Realm (or Kingdom) of God. Do not lay down any rule beyond what I determined for you, nor promulgate law like the lawgiver, or else you might be dominated by it."

Religion worth keeping is not about writing and observing rules or rites that become ends in themselves. Religion worth keeping helps its members to become fully human and is a blessing to all who come in contact with its followers. It is firmly based on the teachings of Jesus, whose faithful followers inspired others to say: "Behold how these Christians love each other", not, "Behold how they compete with each other."

Given that the best possible world would contain people practising different faiths but all focussed on harmonious relationship with the divine, this interpretation of Jesus' teaching emphases how essential it would be that no particular religious group regarded its particular spiritual 'treasures' as superior to those of any other group.

19

Through the Eyes of Jesus

The eye is the lamp of the body. So, if your eye is healthy, your whole body will be full of light; but if your eye is unhealthy, your whole body will be full of darkness. (Matt. 6:22)

Jesus had crucial insights to offer about the importance of seeing the world in a positive light. This teaching warns that it is not possible even to comprehend the human potential to create the best kind of world unless each person can see the good qualities in others. Here Jesus points out that it is not always easy to see the good in other people, or in the things other people do. In fact it is very easy to have a negative view of the world.

This obviously applies in the world of music. After the first performance of The Marriage of Figaro, the Emperor Ferdinand wrote a little note to the composer: "My dear Mozart, Far too noisy; far too many notes!" In 1837, the Boston music critic Philip Hale wrote in the Boston Globe: "If Beethoven's Seventh Symphony is not by some means abridged, it will soon fall into disuse." Not to be outdone was Peter Ilyich Tchaikovsky himself. Writing in his diary in 1886 he made the observation: "I played over the music of that scoundrel Brahms. What a giftless person! It annoys me greatly that this self-inflated mediocrity is hailed as a genius." We might say it is fortunate that other people did see Mozart, Beethoven and Brahms in a positive light!

Jesus' teaching about 'seeing' touches on the way each person views the world. Given the prevalence of untreated eye ailments and blindness among his contemporaries, this teaching would have been close to the bone. In all likelihood physical blindness then would have made its victims bitter and negative, with no hope, and no confidence or purpose in life. To explain his teaching Jesus again used the language of metaphor; he called the eye the "lamp of the body". The idea of the eye as a lamp is linked with what he named as a healthy eye. The Greek word (*aplous*) that Matthew uses carries the meaning that the NRSV translates as 'healthy'. Through a healthy eye the world is seen clearly and positively. For this to happen, the individual viewing the world must first of all be positive in his or her mind and heart.

When the voting finally confirmed that United States Senator Barack Obama was about to become President-Elect Obama, the vision of countless people for a better world seemed to be given positive life and light. As one commentator said, "The whole world took a deep breath, and smiled." There were of course mountainous challenges ahead of Barack Obama, as he well knew, but those who supported him believed he had seen a way forward. His positive vision enabled his supporters to see what he could see – a nation with a positive sense of its presence and influence in the world. Most importantly, the new President said this was to be accomplished by dialogue with others as the first initiative, instead of the last. In 2011 the vagaries of political and economic life are taking their toll on Barack Obama's vision, but his positive reception around the world in 2008 threw light on a better way of wielding power among the nations. In his 2006 book *The Audacity of Hope*, he wrote of the builders of the United States, including Abraham Lincoln and Martin Luther King. In addition he remembered:

> *All the faceless, nameless men and women, slaves and soldiers and tailors and butchers, constructing lives for themselves and their children and grandchildren, brick by brick, rail by rail,*

> *calloused hand by calloused hand, to fill in the landscape of our collective dreams. It is that process I wish to be a part of.*[68]

This vision contains echoes of the way Jesus saw the creation of the best possible world. In both cases there is reliance on the participation of every individual – particularly on what each individual sees of his or her current circumstances and of the future. Even if Barack Obama's dreams become bogged down under the weight of political manoeuvrings in the domestic and international spheres, his ascendancy has given humanity a glimpse of a positive way to view the world. It entails what Jesus calls a healthy eye.

Given all of that, no one would find it surprising that an unhealthy or negative view of the world closes off positive possibilities. Jesus' metaphor says an unhealthy eye or negative outlook means the individual does not have the means of seeing the positive in other people, either in the present or in the future. The word of warning here is that those who see only darkness and hopelessness in their own lives and in the world at large, are ill-equipped to be followers of Jesus. His vision sees a future in which all men, women and children are positively involved. Through his eyes every person, old or young, rich or poor, black or white, skilled or unskilled, strong or weak, is capable of creating his or her small part of the best possible world. The key is to follow the blueprint he outlines in his teaching. It becomes apparent, when we think along these lines, that Jesus would never have been able to develop his vision without a strongly positive view of humanity. His healthy eye reflected his positive heart and mind and enabled him to have faith in the ability of humanity to reach its full potential.

On the surface, this teaching looks relatively unimportant. In fact Jesus regarded it as an integral part of teachings worth dying for. Before other teachings can be put into practice, the follower of Jesus must learn to view the world through his eyes. He saw immense human deprivation and was neither indifferent to it nor defeated by the scale of the need. Instead, he was inspired to develop ways of addressing that need. It is hard even to imagine what a difference it would make if Jesus' followers could see the world as he did; if they could see other people as he saw them; if they could see the future as he imagined it.

Professor Graeme Clark, who developed the cochlear implant (or bionic ear) for deafness, saw a vision for helping the deaf to hear and speak. His vision stemmed from his awareness of the needs of people with hearing difficulties, beginning with his own father. Mr Clark was a pharmacist in a country town in the state of New South Wales (Australia). Because of his deafness customers had to shout their need to buy pharmaceutical products, including describing certain intimate commodities, something most people do not want to do publicly. Young Graeme was embarrassed for his father and embarrassed for the customers who were placed in this situation. He began to dream about developing the means of improving hearing in the hearing-impaired. Ultimately, he dreamed about restoring hearing to people who had gone totally deaf.

Graeme Clark persisted in that vision despite many setbacks and disappointments. He maintained his clear view of a hearing future for the deaf even when the obstacles looked too high. What sustained him was his awareness of the need, reaching back to his father's deafness. He also believed in the potential for doctors and scientists working together to bring sound where there had been silence. His positive view of others with whom he worked sustained him over many years and despite many negative viewpoints expressed about their work. His vision gave him the courage to go on and on. By 2010, two hundred thousand deaf people in one hundred countries had received a cochlear implant enabling them to hear, including my three-year-old granddaughter, Ashlee Neiwand-Thomas. In an interview Graeme Clark once said this about his goal:

> You have to be in it for the long haul, and to be willing to make that sort of long-term commitment when you start. It is not something in which you can just dabble.

The same applies to being a follower of Jesus. Obviously not everyone can be a Barack Obama or a Graeme Clark.[69] For most, opportunities to view the world positively concern the people and events close by.

That is precisely what Jesus meant. His followers do not have to be world-shakers with their own vision for immense change. Jesus had already dreamed the world-encompassing dream for his followers. He had seen the big picture and offered it to them with all its possibilities. Their role then and now is to catch his vision of a positive future, see it as he saw it, and take part in it as they are able. That includes seeing the good in everyone. When the 1950s-1960s Australian preacher Dr Gordon Powell was compiling his Famous Birthdays book, he wrote this in the introduction:

> *I have had to select some rough diamonds, but Christianity is founded on the conviction there is a diamond in every soul no matter how rough the exterior.*[70]

That may well be the case, but for many people there are questions about seeing the world positively. What if I'm a natural pessimist? What if I see the hole and not the doughnut? What if I see the weeds and not the flowers? In times of economic difficulty, when people lose jobs and homes and security, how can I look positively on the future? How can I begin to imagine the kind of world Jesus envisaged? Surely that's for fools or for people with their heads in the sand. On the other hand, what if I'm a natural optimist? What if I can't see the difficulties standing in the way of a world as Jesus imagined it? What if I am unrealistic, and even a bit naïve about what I can do?

All of those reasons for not taking up Jesus' challenge have been cited by people inside and outside of the church. They are reasons given for putting aside the teachings – because they are too hard. The church collectively has tended to maintain a negative outlook which does not allow it to see positively its vocation as follower of Jesus and full implementer of his teaching. Instead it has concentrated on converting people to belief in Jesus as the crucified Christ whose death saves them from their sins. There is no more effective disempowerment of

Jesus' followers than belief that Jesus has already defeated evil in that way and that God will soon send him back to reign triumphant when 'The Great Divine Cleanup'[71] has taken place.

In Jesus' own day there doubtless were people who regarded him as a wild, unrealistic dreamer. Many who dismissed his teaching would have described themselves as realistic or down-to-earth, only too aware of the world-changing effects his blueprint for the best possible world contains. For them, the opposition would have looked too great, too entrenched to change, and it would have been madness to try. In Mark's Gospel (3:20-21, 31-35) we see the response of Jesus' own family to the things he was saying. Given the large numbers of people following him around, his mother and brothers and sisters would naturally have been concerned for his safety. They were probably also embarrassed about his teaching, which made no sense to many. In a nutshell, his family thought he had gone crazy and their intention was to take him home, forcibly if necessary. They could have done that, because Mark (6:3) says he had four brothers, as well as several sisters. When he was told they had come for him, he nominated as his true 'brothers and sisters', the people who were taking him seriously.

It is to the people of Jesus' day, including his own family, and to those who have been tempted to give up following him or haven't really tried, that this teaching about seeing things positively is addressed. The answer for everyone is that Jesus' message contains both hope and realism. He knew life's ups and downs, difficulties, disappointments and dangers, as well as its excitement and joys. He also knew how entrenched are what are regarded as normal governing systems. For those reasons he knew how easy it would be for his followers to see the world through a negative eye – to give up hope of ever changing it.

Yet through his healthy eye he could also see humanity's good potential to create a better world, and his followers are called to see other people the way he did. The flip side of this teaching carries a stark warning: a negative view of others sees nothing but hopelessness.

20

Souls for Sale

No one can serve two masters; for a slave will either hate the one and love the other, or be devoted to the one and despise the other. You cannot serve God and wealth. (Matt. 6:24)

Here Jesus is speaking his mind about money (or wealth). There are several references in his sayings to the place of money in the lives of his followers. One reference is to the issue of paying taxes to the government – in Jesus' case, the government of Caesar. In his time the Roman emperor was Tiberias Caesar. No doubt Jesus recognized that no matter who was in power, taxes had to be paid to maintain the infrastructure of society. For that reason he instructed his hearers to give Caesar his due (in monetary terms), and at the same time to give ultimate loyalty to the things he understood to be of God.

The teaching about wealth is succinct, only thirty-four words. It is also completely unambiguous: if a worker tries to be loyal to two different bosses he will not succeed; he will hate one of them and love the other. The original saying is couched in the language of master and slave, yet in essence it means the same as dealings between employee and employer in our time. There is also a qualifier. When Jesus says someone working for two bosses will hate one and love the other, it is not the same as a person working as a hospital cleaner all week and a taxi driver at the weekend. Jesus means someone like an individual who works for an anti-gambling task force during the week, while his weekend job is card-dealer at a casino. Another example would be a weight-loss technician who also works a night shift selling junk food. Each form of employment or loyalty is at odds with the aims of the other.

Jesus then homes in on the particular bosses he had in mind all along. They are God and wealth. Not God and Caesar, but God and wealth. Significantly, he does not say, "You shall not serve God and wealth." It is not a command; it is much more forceful than a command, which can always be broken or ignored. Jesus' saying is a simple statement of fact: "You cannot serve God and wealth." This teaching is integrally related to Jesus' other teachings about bringing to reality the world according to his vision. For that reason a serious attempt should be made to understand it.

There are many senses in which being a slave to the accumulation of wealth is not a healthy way of life. This is what Jesus means. He is not saying that money itself is antithetical to the kind of world he imagined, or that to have money is to be anti-God. He is talking about the person who 'serves' wealth, whose every waking moment is devoted to accumulating more wealth. In the end, what does his or her life mean? A case in point was the American financier Jay Gould. In the nineteenth century he was the wealthiest man in the world. He had been born to poor farmers who could not afford to buy him a pair of shoes, so as he grew up he swore that he would protect himself from that kind of poverty by making as much money as he could. In time he accumulated more and more stocks and shares, particularly in railways. Eventually he became the owner of 10,000 miles of railways in the United States, including the Union Pacific. He also owned the Western Union Telegraph Company. As the years went by he became increasingly unscrupulous in his business dealings and he developed a reputation to match. From insider trading to hostile take-overs, he did it all. He was the quintessential example of a class of financiers known then as robber barons.

When Jay Gould died in 1892 at the age of 56, the Brooklyn Daily Eagle reported a comment from a business associate of his, C. P. Huntington. While being questioned about the probable effect that the death of Jay Gould might have on Wall Street, Huntington said he did not think it would make any appreciable difference: "Men are but individuals, and when they die their money remains and someone continues the care of it and business goes on as usual." The Eagle reported that there was no marked effect on the London Stock Exchange. Union Pacific shares sustained a fractional relapse, but recovered immediately afterward. On the one hand we can sympathise with the young boy whose bare feet were scratched by thistles on the farm. On the other hand we can see how the desire to protect himself from poverty ruled Jay Gould's life.

When he died he left seventy million dollars (today about seven billion) entirely to his own family. He made almost no bequest of any kind to the nation or society. The one exception was reported in the New York Times because of its novelty: "The Mayor has announced a contribution of five hundred dollars (today about fifty thousand out of seven billion) from Mr Jay Gould to the Mayor's Relief Fund." On his death, his doctor wrote:

> *Jay Gould had no organic trouble ... (but) it is the keeping of the fortune, not the making of it, that takes it out of a man. The worry of investing so much each year to advantage, together with the anxiety of seeing that the original capital did not depreciate, told heavily on him. He always had an ache of some kind. Chest-ache, face-ache, neuralgia and chronic indigestion played havoc with his physical happiness. The pressure of his millions finished him.*

In all of this we can see someone very good at accumulating a fortune, but who was, in effect, a slave to his own wealth.

There is no evidence that Jesus saw wealth as evil in itself and there is no doubt that wealth can be used ethically. The ethicist and Master of Ormond College at Melbourne University, the Rev Dr Rufus Black, makes that point:

> *I want to encourage people to realise that all the choices they*

> *make have got to be ethical choices. So I think all investing is ethical. Whatever investment you make you're making an ethical decision. The question is, is it a good one? Wealth is a communally created resource. You participate in its creation, and once a reasonable set of needs have been met I think everything beyond that you hold on trust for the good that should be done in the world. I think all wealthy people have a profound philanthropical obligation.*[72]

The problem Jesus points to is how wealth can exert a kind of mastery over otherwise well-meaning and generous-hearted human beings. It can take over the heart, mind and soul of the person who accumulates wealth, particularly at the expense of others.

Jesus encountered just such a person. This young man had heard Jesus teaching about what he called the Kingdom of heaven on earth and wanted to know how he could be a part of it. Jesus apparently knew how rich this individual was, and how hard it would be for him to free himself from his possessions and help create this kind of world. In the end, the rich young man knew it too. He walked away from the possibility of helping to bring Jesus' vision to reality. Matthew says he was very sad about it, which underlines the strength of the hold his wealth had over him.

Given the means by which most of the world's richest people have built their fortunes – by buying and selling companies, and in the process often discarding workers, it seems unlikely that the best possible world would feature many billionaires. Vast wealth creates its own slaves. Even the American multi-billionaire Warren Buffett seems to know that. In 2006 he announced that he would give one and a half billion dollars per year to the Bill and Melinda Gates Foundation. By 2010 the foundation had given hundreds of billions of dollars to charity. It is not for nothing that Bill Gates has distanced himself from the business world to concentrate on using the foundation to ease the ills of humanity.

Along with a philanthropic attitude toward his wealth, Warren Buffett has no intention of leaving the bulk of his billions to his children. He feels it would be more of a burden to them than a blessing. He once remarked, "I want to give my kids enough so that they feel they could do anything, but not so much that they could do nothing." It seems he knew that if they inherited it all, they would be able to do little else but look after the money. That echoes Jesus' saying about the rich young man: "It is easier for a camel to go through the eye of a needle than for someone who is rich to enter the Kingdom of heaven."

Having said all that about the super rich, it is also clear that Jesus' teachings about money are for everyone. They address the way ordinary people live and spend their money, so this is not a subject from which most can distance themselves. It is not a case of sitting back and thinking, "I'm not Jay Gould or Warren Buffett, so this doesn't apply to me." Not at all; the use of money in any amount is an integral part of being a citizen of the best possible world. When Jesus envisioned this world he imagined it on this earth, not in some faraway Utopia. Of course there would be money in the world as he saw it. Of course there would be the necessity to produce and sell and buy. Jesus' sayings about wealth are not condemnations of wealth as such. They are always about a fair and even distribution of the earth's wealth.

It is important to remember that this teaching does not condemn individuals simply because they have accumulated huge wealth. Many wealthy people give away huge amounts to alleviate poverty, eradicate disease and promote education. In June 2010 thirty six US billionaires responded to a program started by Warren Buffet and Bill and Melinda Gates, by promising to give at least half of their fortunes to charity. The program will probably draw about six hundred billion dollars US into non-profit charitable organizations. Some of the money would have been donated anyway, but the aim is to set a good example for others.

All of that sounds very positive, but the point is that in Jesus' vision that kind of individual wealth simply would not exist.

The triumph of justice would mean that all had enough for their needs, but not too much. Of course such a world would need money, but money would not have a hold over the hearts and minds of individuals. Jesus' aim is a world in which no one would have the heart or will to exploit or disadvantage others in order to become wealthy. Involvement in the establishment of that kind of justice would be easier for people of moderate means than for most holders of vast amounts of wealth. For people who are not wealthy it follows that there is little preoccupation with maintaining wealth for wealth's sake, which is precisely Jesus' point. A close associate said this about the cause of Jay Gould's death:

> *My opinion is that his system gave way under the great strain resulting from the consciousness of his great wealth. It was a tremendous burden and he was always weighed down with the anxiety of protecting his properties.*

In the Australian business world there is a close parallel. Paul Barry, the author of *Who wants to Be a Billionaire? The James Packer Story*, commented on the effect of the 2008-9 financial crisis on Australian billionaire James Packer:

> *The value of Mr Packer's assets dropped by $4 billion at the depth of the global financial crisis, prompting him to withdraw from public view, take up smoking, put on weight, and become depressed. Money was what drove him, what he lived for, what had always served as the scorecard of his success.*[73]

The last word comes from Jesus, and is as integral to the fulfilling of his vision as are any of his other teachings. In his saying about serving two masters, he stated that a person trying to do that will despise one master and be devoted to the other. Where God and wealth are concerned it is not hard to see why. Attempts at devotion to the service of values believed to be of God are inevitably undermined by service of wealth. On the other hand, attempts at devotion to the service of wealth are undermined by service to universal values such as justice, compassion and peace. It is clear why Jesus' last word is: "You cannot serve God and wealth."

21
What's the Use of Worrying?

> *Therefore I tell you, do not worry about your life, what you will eat or what you will drink, or about your body, what you will wear. Is not life more than food, and the body more than clothing? Look at the birds of the air; they neither sow nor reap nor gather into barns, and yet your heavenly Father feeds them. And why do you worry about clothing? Consider the lilies of the field, how they grow; they neither toil nor spin, yet I tell you, even Solomon in all his glory was not clothed like one of these. (Matt. 6:25, 26, 28)*

In times of economic downturn jobs disappear fast. Life is hard for the unemployed and it is not surprising if some in those circumstances remember the old saying, 'The Lord will provide.' Jesus alluded to that when he instructed his followers: "Do not worry, saying, 'What will we eat?' or 'What will we drink?' or 'What will we wear?'." Yet those questions will always remain. On an internet chat site an unemployed woman commented on the saying 'The Lord will provide', and then she wrote, "I really don't see how it's possible for the Lord to pay our bills. So how do you pay your bills and what exactly is the Lord providing in order for you to manage?" There were several replies, quoting such sayings as 'God helps those who help themselves.'

'The Lord will provide' and 'God helps those who help themselves' are often-quoted sayings in times of need, although neither is biblical. The one internet comment that came close to what Jesus meant by not worrying cited such things as social security and welfare. In Jesus' day Centrelink was about two thousand years in the future, yet there is a close connection between the idea of providing for social welfare and what he was saying about the meeting of needs. Again Jesus' sayings about provision of daily needs can be understood fully only within the context of his vision. The question then becomes, what does this teaching about clothing lilies and feeding birds have to do with the needs of all human beings? Why was Jesus able to say things about basic human requirements that look to us naïve, or even foolish?

Jesus includes two key pointers in this particular teaching. The first is that in the best possible world all people will have enough of what they need – not enough of what they want, but enough of what they need. Jesus describes those needs as items like food and clothing. Shelter from the elements is also a basic human requirement. The second key point is that therefore there is nothing to gain in worrying, about either the present or the future. What should a person do? Sit around and wait for things to get better? That happens to be the attitude of many Christians who see no need for action with regard to climate change. They believe that Jesus' vision for life on earth will be inaugurated in the blink of an eye by God's sudden and decisive intervention into the physical world. When that occurs the earth will be renewed anyway, so there is no point in worrying about or doing anything about climate change.

The Texas preacher Pastor John Hagee held that view. He once claimed that hurricanes in Florida, gay marriages and 9/11 all signify that the second coming of Christ is imminent. For him that means a final violent battle between God and the powers of evil. "Upon winning that battle", he said, "Christ will send all unbelievers into the pits of hellfire, re-green the planet, and reign on earth in peace with his followers for a millennium." Quite apart from its depiction of a violent, sadistic, exclusivist Christ, this scenario means that all who believe in Christ have only to wait for God to recreate the earth. So why worry about it? Why do anything about making it happen? Around 50 million Christians in the United States believe in a similar 'End of the world' scenario. Needless to say they are not interested in efforts by world leaders to find ways of limiting the effects of climate change. We can safely say that is not the reason Jesus told his followers not to worry.

Worry on its own is counter-productive; it ties up the worrier in worry-knots that lead nowhere and accomplish nothing. Instead of just worrying, Jesus advocated action about things that are worrisome. The first of two main points from him is that in his envisaged world there will be enough food, clothing and shelter for everyone. "God knows that you need all these things," he said. Then he went on to offer the crucial clue to understanding this teaching. If you work toward the establishment of a just world through your personal commitment, you will have everything you need – not everything you want, but everything you need.

The provision of enough food for everyone's needs has vast implications. It means that land given over to agriculture would be protected from warfare. It means people would be given adequate food by those who have it, when drought or flood or fire or insect plagues destroy crops. It means food-growing technology would be shared between all people. It means adequate payment to farmers for the produce of the land. It means being able to buy other food products for a fair price.

Enough food also means good nutrition, which is the major shield against illness. Most children in Ghana for instance, do not get the vitamins and minerals they need. In 2006 more than eighty per cent of Ghanaian children under the age of five suffered from anaemia. In 2007 an organization called Global Alliance for Improved Nutrition was established. It works with the Ghanaian government on a project called Flour Power. All wheat flour in Ghana is now fortified with eight different micronutrients, including iron. This is not accomplished through sitting around worrying that there is insufficient food to eat. Nor is it made reality by piously waiting for 'the Lord' to provide, or intervene. Instead, this is about the intentional development of a better world. The same good intention drives organizations developing vaccines against malaria and strategies against other major killers such as TB and HIV-AIDS. For most other people, this is about offering support to people on the ground giving their help and their resources.

Enough clothing means fair manufacturing process, primary producers paid a fair return for raw materials, and garment makers rewarded justly for their labour. When Australians think of exploited clothing workers they are inclined to associate that with clothing factories in South East Asia or India. The unfortunate fact is that they do not have to look that far. In 2006 the Federal Court of Australia fined an Australian clothing company one hundred and ten thousand dollars for failing to comply with the Clothing Trades Award. As he was imposing the penalty, Justice Marshall said:

> *Outworkers in the clothing industry are some of the most exploited people in the Australian workforce. They perform garment making work often at absurdly low rates in locations outside their employer's premises. This frequently occurs in the homes of outworkers.*

Enough clothing means the capacity of all people to buy suitable clothes for all climates. Adequate clothing not only means warmth in the cold or protection from the sun, it also means dignity and equality in society. Poor children in Australia and around the world are known to avoid school because they feel shame about their ragged clothing. Provision of adequate clothes for the poor helps them build confidence for the future.

Enough shelter means proper protection from heat and cold, sun, wind, snow and rain. Twenty-first century people understand that adequate and appropriate shelter also means housing that gives protection from insect-borne diseases. It means housing that provides clean water to prevent waterborne disease. It means adequate sanitation systems. In 2009 it was estimated that half of the population of the developing world – about two and a half billion people – do not have safe sanitation. Because this is an uncomfortable topic for most people in those areas, the problem has not received sufficient attention. In 2010 an organization called Total Sanitation Project was established. Its current aim is to provide sanitation for about four million people in Tanzania, Indonesia and India. It trains local workers to build a range of latrines affordable even by the poorest people in those communities. Enough shelter means protection against all manner of threats to life and health and well-being. People working in the area of the most basic of human health measures are actually helping to create the best possible world.[74]

Jesus' second main point comes at the end of this teaching. He says, "Do not worry about tomorrow, for tomorrow will bring worries of its own. Today's trouble is enough for today." This is not instruction to be a devout optimist, or to wait for the world as we know it to end in an Armageddon style scenario. Jesus' point is that building anything can be done only one step at a time, and that includes creating the world as he envisaged it. The goal cannot be accomplished quickly so there is no point in worrying that the process is happening too slowly. After all, each person can do only what he or she is capable of doing in one day, every day. None of this teaching about not worrying robs Jesus' vision of its urgency; it simply acknowledges the limits of human capability in its creation.

We cannot fully imagine the end result of that creating. Jesus obviously believed that its fulfilment is in the mind of God, made known to humanity through the clear vision he was given. His love for humanity helped him to see how human beings themselves could overcome the suffering around them. He inspired his followers to provide for other people's needs as they found them, and in that sense they did set up a kind of social security system in his name. It is not often recognised that the setting up of government welfare programs has followed the basic pattern of care of the poor carried out by the first followers of Jesus.

It is also fair to say that Jesus would be greatly heartened by efforts in today's world to wipe out hunger and suffering and the exploitation of the poor. The response of his followers is first to recognise that the best possible world is not yet fully in place. Secondly, it is for them to recognise that this world is actually being developed – all around them. Jesus' followers have the opportunity to be a part of that development, day by day. It is not for nothing that Jesus ended his teaching with the words: "But strive first for the Kingdom and its righteousness, and all these things will be given to you as well."

22

The Clear Sight of the Deliberately Humble

Why do you see the speck in your neighbour's eye, but do not notice the log in your own eye? (Matt. 7:3)

"Do not judge, so that you may not be judged." Does this mean that nobody can call anyone else to account? Does it mean no one can object if they see a person acting badly toward someone else? What does it mean to judge someone, anyway? Those are the kinds of questions that spring to mind when we look at a teaching about not judging. It is an essential part of the vision that inspired Jesus' message two thousand years ago and it still applies today. The word picture he created to explain it is striking, even quite jarring. There is also something unreal about it. It may be possible to see a speck in someone else's eye. It may even be possible that the person concerned is unaware of the speck. It is something else to disregard a large piece of wood in one's own eye (Jesus called it a 'log'). I once saw a stark photographic image of a man with a large nail protruding from his eye – the result of an accident with a nail gun. He was rushed off to emergency surgery but he lost the eye.

On the other hand, everyone can recall having a speck of grit in the eye. It hurts, it makes the eye water, it makes it hard to see properly. Even if the speck is very small there is a real urgency to get it out. We douse the eye with water or try to flick out the grit with a tissue. Once it is gone the relief is enormous and we can see clearly again. Even though it is obvious that Jesus is using metaphorical language about these obstructions to seeing, his meaning is not immediately clear.

There are several possibilities. The metaphor indicates that the speck and the log represent obstacles to clear sight. The speck's presence in a person's eye causes him or her to have a flawed view of the world. Somebody else notices that failing (the "speck in your neighbour's eye") and condemns it, or judges it. Jesus indicates how easy it is to do that. It is entirely possible to see other people's imperfections even with a metaphorical 'log' in one's own eye, he says. This log blinds, or thoroughly blocks, a clear view of the world. It actually represents blind prejudice, which is pre-judging without evidence. Prejudice forms an opinion about the other without sufficient knowledge of that person. It often uses erroneous, hostile stereotypes about a whole group of people in order to judge one member of that group.

To cite a particular prejudice which has plagued humanity – when someone automatically expects a Jewish person to be tight with money, his or her judgment is based on the hate-engendered stereotype 'all Jews love money'. This does not take into account the fact that in sixteenth-century CE Europe, when Christians were forbidden to lend money for interest,[75] the Christian monarchs actually appointed Jews as official money-lenders. The king even prescribed the rate of interest they were allowed to charge. The end result was that the Jewish people became associated with money in the minds of Christians who had to go to Jews to borrow from them. Later ignorance about the historical origin of this role led to the blind prejudicial belief that Jews were involved in money-lending because 'all Jews love money'.

The greatest danger of this log in the eye called blind prejudice is that the person in whose 'eye' it is can be completely unaware that it is blocking a clear view of the world. He or she can think or say terrible things about members of other groups with little or no awareness of the injustice in that judgment. We could say that when people are judged unfairly simply because they belong to a particular group, the person doing the judging is more deserving of judgment. As Jesus said, "Do not judge, so that you may not be judged."

The fresh insight Jesus brings to this teaching about prejudice comes from his understanding of human nature. Human beings can see quite clearly the wrongs other people commit, but when it comes to their own behaviour they are often blind. The cause of the blindness (the log) is widespread, including the way many people perceive the homeless. The Brazilian writer and acclaimed educator Paolo Freire wrote a book called *Pedagogy of the Oppressed*. In it he made this observation:

> To accept homelessness, or refuse to be moved by homelessness (or worse still, to remove the homeless), to accept the distortion of the humanity of others, is to fail to observe our own humanity.[76]

Paolo Freire himself grew up in impoverished circumstances. He knew personally that if the manner in which a person judges other people diminishes their humanity, the judge's own humanity is also diminished. In dismissing the other's positive human attributes, the persons judging expose a lack of those things in themselves.

In 2008 Melbourne was host city for the Homeless World Cup. Teams from 56 nations played soccer in a specially constructed walled pitch measuring 16 metres by 22, with four players per side. The action was entertaining, but each player in each match represented a story of despair and renewed hope, and the impact of this was not confined to the players. In an interview with BBC Sport, Mel Young, one of the Homeless Cup's founders, said:

> I think it just changes everybody. The homeless people involved change because they find inspiration, self-respect, and self esteem from the crowd applauding them. The public also change, as they usually have a stereotypical view of what constitutes a homeless person; he lives on the street, is dangerous, etc.

How many can say they have not avoided people picking

through rubbish bins for bottles, or sitting on railway station steps, or asking for hand-outs? Jesus knew that perceptions about people determine the way they are treated. There is a fundamental truth there about how the best possible world would operate. It is included in that most fundamental set of rules for human behaviour – the Ten Commandments.

The particular commandment which applies here is alluded to in the Letter of James. James was Jesus' own brother. He was obviously a member of Jesus' original group of followers, as it was he who took over as leader after Jesus' death, not Peter. (The evidence for that is in the Book of Acts, 21: 17-18). Nobody would have understood Jesus' teaching better than James and he also wrote about judging other people: "Never pull each other to pieces, my brothers (and sisters). If you do you are judging your brother (or your sister) and setting yourself up in the place of God's Law; you have become in fact a critic of the Law." James then goes on to say that a person who criticises the Law does not carry out the Law. There is plenty of reason to make the case that James was referring to the ninth commandment: "You shall not bear false witness against your neighbour." In other words, you shall not tell lies about your neighbour, or 'bad-mouth' him or her.

We know Jesus was a teacher of the Law but it is easy to forget that in his time the Hebrew Bible was already ancient. He obviously saw it as needing fresh interpretation, and he taught scripture (or the Law) according to the precepts of justice, compassion, mercy and peace. For him, scripture interpreted in that way would be a reliable guide to creating the best possible world.

The log in the eye called prejudice controls the way all kinds of people are regarded and treated. In Jesus' time the prejudice of his own people included belief that all Gentiles were corrupt heathens, that all Samaritans were tainted by intermarriage with Gentiles and irreverent in their attitude to God, that all women were inferior to men, that children were non-persons with no rights of their own. In twenty-first century Australian society the list of prejudices includes people with purely physical disabilities who are also regarded as mentally disabled, uneducated or poorly educated immigrants regarded as less intelligent than 'real' Australians, people who fled from persecution but are regarded as free-loaders with mercenary ulterior motives. The list also includes people of different religions. Muslims? They are all terrorists. Buddhists? They all shave their heads and wear yellow robes. Hindus? They all throw widows on funeral pyres. The log in the eye even controls the way Christian denominations view each other. Catholics? They all have too many children. Uniting? They are all social justice freaks. Anglicans? They are all snooty royalists.

The log in the eye has often determined how different school systems view each other. Prejudice about the state education system in Australia includes such views as: the government schools have no proper discipline; they have second-rate teachers and inferior facilities; the students are not as bright as private school children; the parents don't care about their children's education. While those statements are true in some cases, they are by no means true of all state education. Prejudicial stereotypes from the state sector toward students in the private sector include: They are all snobby, selfish, spoilt brats; they are spoon-fed by teachers to get them into university; they think they are born to rule. While that is true in some cases, it is by no means true of all private school children. Prejudice pre-judges without taking the trouble to know and understand the other.

This kind of negative outcome can occur even when people are trying to accomplish something good. From time to time aid workers in Africa and the Middle East have been subjected to forms of violence. When local people are asked why this is so, two primary reasons emerge. The first is that aid organizations are seen as linked with the local government, which in turn is seen as linked with the US or the UK, or the UN. The aid workers are therefore politicised and sometimes regarded as enemy combatants. The second reason is the attitude of some well-meaning aid workers. According to an Afghani farmer struggling to make ends meet on the outskirts of Kabul, "They come, they look, they talk to each other, and they go away. They send things we don't need. They don't send things we do need."

Clearly, the aid workers concerned had pre-judged the people. They had not sat down with them and listened to their stories. They had pre-judged them as incapable of knowing what is best for their own welfare. Even if aid workers were there with good intentions, the log of prejudice had obscured their sight. As they had judged, they were also being judged. Again it is clear that those who are deliberately humble are best placed to see clearly the worth and point of view of others. They are not burdened by a sense of their own importance which blocks the view of the other.

23

Ask for What?

Ask, and it will be given you; search, and you will find; knock, and the door will be opened for you. (Matt.7:7)

Every now and then the media report that the president of a council of churches, or an archbishop, or an evangelical pastor, is praying for rain. All of them seem convinced that they should remind God how badly rain is needed. The reports also indicate that some Christians believe a lack of rain is God's way of rapping humanity over the knuckles. After a huge deluge on Sydney in 2006 various church leaders read that as God's approval of their prayers for rain. They also saw a lack of rain elsewhere as a sign of God's disapproval. This is belief in a God who says, "If you don't talk to me, I'll turn off the tap!" Where does this kind of belief come from? Some might even say it comes from Jesus; after all it was he who said: "Ask and it will be given you; search and you will find; knock and the door will be opened for you." That seems to give credence to belief in a necessity to pray for rain and that rain will be given to those who ask for it. If Jesus' saying does not mean that, what does it mean? For what things is it appropriate to ask? For what things is it appropriate to search? At what doors is it appropriate to knock?

Several times I have made the point that each of Jesus' teachings is compatible with the rest. Given that, it seems appropriate to look for the answer to this question about asking, searching and knocking, in other parts of his teaching. The obvious place is in the prayer he gave his followers. In it Jesus is not instructing his followers to talk to the emperor, or to the high priest, or even to parents or friends, about their needs. They are to talk about their daily requirements with God. Surely the prayer Jesus taught his followers will offer clues about what he considered it appropriate to ask of God.

Before searching the Lord's Prayer for clues it is worth pausing to look at the 'add-on' Jesus gives to this teaching about asking, searching and knocking. He makes this same point several times in his teachings: if you who are imperfect, even evil, know how to do good, how much more does God do good things? Specifically, if you know how to give good things to your own children, you can be sure God (the 'parent' of all) will give much better things to those who ask for them. Jesus clearly believed that humanity can expect to receive good things from God. The question is, what kinds of good things? After all, prayers ought not to be regarded as tools for manipulating the transcendent. They ought not to be specific requests for particular things. One young boy had yet to learn that. He and his brother were spending the night at their grandparents' home. At bedtime, when the two boys knelt beside their beds to say their prayers, the younger brother began to pray at the top of his lungs: 'I PRAY FOR A NEW BIKE! I PRAY FOR A NEW PLAY STATION! I PRAY FOR A NEW PAIR OF GYM SHOES!" His older brother leaned over and nudged him: "Why are you shouting your prayers? God isn't deaf." "No", said the little brother, "but Grandpa is!"

In the Lord's Prayer Jesus says it is right to express desire for the coming of the "Kingdom of heaven" on earth – "Your kingdom come!" It is right to pray that God's name will be respected – "Hallowed be your name". It is right to pray that the world will operate according to the ultimate values attributed to God – "Your will be done on earth, as in heaven". It is right to pray about sufficient nourishment for the day – "Give us today our daily bread". It is right to pray about a need for forgiveness, and for the strength to forgive others – "Forgive us our sins, as we forgive those who sin against us". Finally, it is right to express the desire that given the ongoing existence of evil, even when the best kind of world becomes reality, humanity would be able to avoid association with evil – "deliver us from evil".

That list of appropriate prayers is just as helpful in pointing out what not to look for, or to wish to have opened up for the petitioner. According to Jesus it is not right to pray: God, grant me everything I need, all the days of my life! The Lord's Prayer says it is enough to express a need for sufficient 'bread' (or necessities of life) in the short term.[77] It is right that each person should have enough of that for each day. On the other hand, there is plenty of evidence that a strong long-term focus on personal needs distracts attention from awareness of other people's short-term needs.

In 1953 a group of farmers in Victoria's Mallee district decided to take other people's needs into account as they went about making their own living. Through study of the teachings of Jesus in their local church they felt led to establish the Berriwillock Wheat Scheme. For fifty-eight years they have given the proceeds from sixty hectares of wheat crop to good causes in Australia and overseas – up to thirty-five thousand dollars (AUS) per year. The Mallee area has had three prolonged droughts in a row and the 2008 crop failed, but these wheat farmers still intended to give away a large amount of money. Among many other causes, they have helped doctors working in Africa and indigenous students and refugees living in Swan Hill (in the north of the state of Victoria). In 2009 they gave micro-loans to farmers in West Timor. They do not stop work and pray for rain; they accept the cycles and seasons of Planet Earth and the associated hardships. What they do ask God for is the encouragement to help other people make it through hard times. What they ask for, they receive.

Jesus also implies that it is not right to pray, "God help me to defeat my enemies." Jesus' prayer includes the line, "Forgive us our sins, [or our debts] as we forgive those who sin against us [or have debts owed to us]. Jesus' prayer also clearly indicates that it is not right to ask God to help wreak vengeance on enemies; if anyone asked God for that, they would not receive it. According to the Lord's Prayer there is one way for an individual to deal with people who offend against him or her; it is called forgiveness. Every person offends against another person from time to time. Sometimes the offence is trivial; sometimes it is downright damaging and hurtful. Jesus' prayer says that when people are genuinely sorry for offences against others, God will forgive them and so encourage in them the capacity to be forgiving toward others. This line of the Lord's Prayer encapsulates a hugely complex psychological and theological issue, yet the message is simple: "Ask (for forgiveness) and it will be given you." The implication here is that the act of admitting sincerely a need for forgiveness opens up the possibility of being forgiven.

The next complex psychological and theological issue embedded in the Lord's Prayer comes in the words: "deliver us from evil". You will notice that Jesus did not say, "God, please abolish evil from the face of the earth". The request is, help me to steer clear of it. That is both practical and real. There are bad things, evil things, in this world and Jesus says it is right for human beings to ask God to help them avoid involvement in evil. "Ask, and it will be given you; search and you will find."

Many people are searching for ways to defeat evil in today's world. Both sides of the Israeli-Palestinian conflict have contributed to the pain, shock, sadness, disability, hardship and violent death experienced by people in Israel and the Palestinian territories. Every peace proposal in high or low-level talks, in books or opinion pieces in the press, or in interviews on radio and TV, has been dismissed. Is it not legitimate to ask what answer Jesus might give to this apparently hopeless situation? Is it not legitimate to ask what Jesus would pray for in these circumstances? His followers do not have to search very far or for very long to find the answer.

Non-violent resistance to entrenched systems of oppression in America, India and South Africa has overwhelmingly been proven to work. Sadly, where there is ongoing reliance on violence, even when violence has been proven to be totally counter-productive, there is still widespread blindness to its destructiveness.

In 2002 the Palestinian Christian writer Mubarak Awad became the director of Nonviolence International, an organization dedicated to educating oppressed peoples about the legitimacy and effectiveness of non-violent resistance to power. In an article about the Israeli-Palestinian impasse, Mubarak Awad and the Palestinian lawyer Jonathan Kuttab set out the difficulties of achieving a large-scale non-violent resistance to the Israeli occupation:

> In the early 1980s, Mubarak Awad was able to convince many Palestinians as well as other Arabs and Muslims that non-violence can work and that it is more powerful than any other weapon we have. Because of his work, the Israelis considered him dangerous and he was arrested and subsequently deported. Nonetheless, there continues to be a great interest in non-violence. What is lacking is an overall strategy and commitment to do it on a massive scale. People are still trapped in the rhetoric of armed struggle, and many, especially abroad, would rather applaud the armed struggle from afar than actively engage in non-violent struggle and take responsibility for the future.[78]

The work of non-violence in the Palestinian territory is continued by Sami Awad, co-founder and director of the Holy Land Trust. In an interview filmed by the Globaloneness Project in 2009, he described non-violent resistance as empowering because it equips people to deal with and threaten structures of injustice. He sees non-violence as going beyond resistance and creating a foundation for mutually enriching relationships. This understanding of "Deliver us from evil" is congruent with Jesus' other teachings about repudiating violence.

On January 20th 2009, America installed its first black President. This new start for America can be traced back to the non-violent resistance of civil rights protesters. They put their own frail bodies between the forces of violence and the crying need of down-trodden, despised people. On November 4th 2008, black and white people all over America cried with joy that Martin Luther King's dream of freedom for black Americans had been so profoundly fulfilled. When civil rights protesters in the 1960's put aside fear of violent authority and murderous racists and simply stood up and said "Enough!" that dream began to live. When those protesters prayed for courage to overcome evil, they received it. When they searched for the means to do it, they found it. When they knocked on the door to equality, self-respect and freedom, it opened for them.

I have left the first part of Jesus' prayer until last: "Your kingdom come!" The saying about asking, finding and entering relates to creating what Jesus called the Kingdom of heaven in this world. All of the capabilities listed in the Lord's Prayer will be given to creators of this world, if only they ask. Those capabilities are designed to equip individuals committed to making a difference. Sometimes they can be used to encourage others to maintain their own commitment.

A striking example of this is the white woman who stood up to the worst of South Africa's Apartheid government. Helen Suzman, daughter of Lithuanian Jews, was the only Progressive MP in the South African parliament. For 6 years she was the only woman among 165 men. She described them as "narrow-minded, prejudiced bullies" and supported Nelson Mandela during his imprisonment in the face of enormous criticism. For thirty-six years she opposed all legislation that discriminated against black and coloured people in South Africa. When asked how she maintained this 'fire in the belly' against the evil of apartheid, she gave credit to a nun in the Catholic convent where she was educated. "When I shirk something I know I ought to do, the ghost of Sister Columba whispers in my ear, 'Do it child', and I do."

24

The Rule to End All Rules

> *In everything do to others as you would have them do to you; for this is the law and the prophets. (Matt. 7:12)*

When politicians sum up an argument they often use clichés like, "At the end of the day", "all things considered", "making all possible allowances" and "not to put too fine a point on it", "the bottom line" is that "the government has decided to institute an enquiry into, 'blah-blah'." As Sir Humphrey Appleby once told Minister Jim Hacker:

> *It is axiomatic in government that hornets' nests should be left unstirred, cans of worms should remain unopened, and cats should be left in bags and not set among the pigeons. Ministers should also leave boats unrocked, nettles ungrasped, refrain from taking bulls by the horns, and resolutely turn their backs to the music.*[79]

Jesus was not a politician; he was a teacher. His teaching about 'doing unto others' comes in remarkably few words yet it sums up his whole argument - his whole vision. "In everything do to others as you would have them do to you; for this is the Law and the prophets." Those few words have the potential to cause mind-blowing, earth-shattering effect and yet they have not. The problem is largely their familiarity. Because of that their full meaning is either forgotten or never actually understood.

This piece of Jesus' teaching is not original to him, but it is doubtless incorporated for the very good reason that Jesus repeated it often and wanted his followers to take it seriously. The idea that it somehow includes all of the teachings contained in the Law and prophets is not original to Jesus either. There is a well-known story about the great Pharisee Hillel, a leading exponent of liberal Jewish thought from around 30 years before the Common Era until about 10 years into the Common Era (at which point Jesus was about 14). At the same time the leading conservative Jewish scholar was the Pharisee Shammai. The story says that both Hillel and Shammai were approached by a Gentile who wished to convert to Judaism. The Gentile first approached Shammai and said to him: "Teach me the whole of the Torah while I stand on one foot." Shammai pushed him away with a stick. The same person approached Hillel, who said: "That which is despicable to you, do not do to your fellow. This is the whole of the Law and the rest is commentary. Go and study it." Jesus knew the truth of that.

There are several different versions of the so-called Golden Rule. It occurs in all major religions of the world, including Baha'i, Buddhism, Christianity, Confucianism, Hinduism, Islam, Judaism, Sikhism, Taoism and Zoroastrianism. The Golden Rule was first articulated in the sixth century BCE by the Chinese philosopher Confucius. He was one of the first to make a clear connection between piety and altruism. One day a student called Zigong asked Confucius whether there was any single saying that could be referred to every day as the basis for human behaviour. Confucius said, "Never do to others what you would not like them to do to you."[80] In the search for ultimate truth, this rule has been discovered independently by people all over the world. The implication is that if humanity could ask God, "Please tell us your rule for human life while we stand on one leg", God would say something like: "Treat other people the way you would like them to treat you."

In 1995 the Swiss theologian Hans Küng wrote about the need for a global ethic. It is hardly surprising that for humanity's common ethical foundation he chose the Golden

Rule. He argued not for the idea of one global religion, but of one common ethic:

> *My personal experience is that even people who didn't agree on questions of faith, dogma, and so on, can agree on certain attitudes and behaviours. And so my formula is, we do not need one religion. We do not need one religion but we need one global ethic.*[81]

The Parliament of the World's Religions held in Melbourne in December 2009 produced a continuous and strongly held message from religious leaders to world leaders. The message was that in view of the growing understanding and cooperation between religions, they ought no longer to be thought of as part of the world's problems, but as part of the solution to the world's problems. There is no better foundation for such a development than the Golden Rule, when embraced and taught by all.

Jesus' version of the Golden Rule indicates that his followers are not meant to be left to their own wisdom in carrying it out. Like Hillel's, Jesus' version is followed by the words, "this is the Law and the prophets". If the essence of teachings in all of the Books of the Law and the Books of the Prophets could be encapsulated in one rule, that makes a mighty claim about their purpose. If they are all sufficiently consistent to be contained in a single thought, their goal is absolutely clear. They are all intended to lead humanity to harmony, unity and peace. They all concern healing wounds, reconciling the alienated, lifting up the poor or despised, bringing justice where injustice has prevailed and making peace.

Jesus and Hillel both saw the Golden Rule as encapsulating their own scripture. For Christians it necessarily includes everything that Jesus himself taught. All of Jesus' teachings must also be contained in the idea of treating other people as you would like them to treat you. If teachings ascribed to him in the gospels do not conform to that rule, then questions must be asked about their origin. The same question must be asked of all New Testament writings, including Paul's superb summary of the character of love (1 Cor. 13:1-8a). We do not have to think long before we recognize that it is entirely consistent with the Golden Rule. I ought not be impatient, unkind, envious, boastful, arrogant, rude, bullying, irritable, resentful, or wish bad things for other people. Why not? Because I would not want other people to treat me like that.

It is no coincidence that when Jesus is asked which of the biblical commandments is the greatest, he quotes the one about loving God with heart, soul, mind and strength and then adds a quote from Leviticus (19:18): "You shall love your neighbour as yourself." What else is that but another way of stating the Golden Rule? When Jesus included this principle for life in his teaching, he laid the foundation for future harmony between his followers and people of all faiths and backgrounds. This is indeed the most universal of religious teaching. It has the potential to overcome all the religious differences and squabbles that ever were. It can bring human beings face to face with themselves and with each other.

Because of the breath-taking dimensions of the Golden Rule, this chapter can do little more than sketch the possibilities if humanity actually kept this ultimate principle for life. I can point out only some of these possibilities and leave the reader to go on filling in the gaps. Here are three potential scenarios in a world guided by the Golden Rule:

1. **A world without war.** *I want you to allow me to live in peace. Therefore I will not inflict war on you. I will not covet your land and its resources, I will not despise you for the colour of your skin or for your religion, politics or culture.*

    In a world without war there would be no need for armies and their military hardware. There would be no casualties of war. Resources saved could be invested in safeguards against natural threats like earthquakes, droughts, floods, bushfires, cyclones, tsunamis.

2. **A world without crime.** *I want you to respect me and my property. Therefore I will not be disrespectful of your person or your possessions.*

In a world without crime there would be no need for police, court-houses or jails. There would be no need for security guards, or locked houses and cars. There would be no losses from shop-lifting or vandalism. There would be no victims of domestic violence, including children. The resources saved could be invested in first class schools, hospitals and community facilities for everyone. No one would damage them.

3. **A world without hunger and sickness.** *I want you to ensure that I am well fed and in good health. Therefore I will not allow you to be hungry or ill.*

In a world without hunger, there would be equal sharing of food, with no one having too much or too little. No one would suffer from either malnutrition or obesity. The resources saved could be invested in the eradication of disease.

They are just three glimpses of a world which obeys the Golden Rule. Even through those brief observations we can begin to imagine the mind-blowing possibilities for a changed world. In many ways the foundations of such a world are now being laid. In the wake of the 2010 devastating floods in Pakistan, advances that have already been made in weather forecasting led leading climate scientists to pledge to use long-term predictions about severe weather events for the benefit of vulnerable societies.[82] The next step is to persuade local governments to match the science with a commitment to preparedness for natural disasters in their own as well as in other countries. Tim Flannery is hopeful that a world-wide system will alert humanity to impending disaster:

> *I can imagine the day when our surveillance of the atmosphere, the oceans, the land and the heavens is so complete that we will be able to anticipate most natural disasters. Such a system would also give us fair warning of when human intervention is required to disperse malign trends.*[83]

In case we should become too carried away, it is essential also to recognize that before actually applying the Golden Rule careful preparation is needed; there are prerequisites for putting it into action. For instance, treating other people the way you would like to be treated implies a positive knowledge of the self. If I do not understand what is good for me then I do not understand what is good for anyone else. That takes maturity, the ability to discern between real needs and superficial wants. It also takes empathy, understanding of how other people feel. Finally, it takes self-respect, wanting for others what is also actually good for me.

People who know how to put the Golden Rule into practice understand the impact of their actions on other people. I do not like being hurt, physically or emotionally, therefore I know how that feels for other people. The role of empathy in applying the Golden Rule sounds familiar. We have come across it before in exploring Jesus' teachings. Could it be that applying the Golden Rule first depends on Jesus' followers embracing his other teachings? Could it be that the place of the Golden Rule toward the end of the Sermon on the Mount is not accidental, but deliberate? With the benefit of his earlier teaching in mind, his followers are now ready to understand his vision of the world. Contained within this one rule is the essence of the wisdom Jesus formulated and taught and for which he lived and died.

25

No Turning Back

> *Enter through the narrow gate; for the gate is wide and the road is easy that leads to destruction, and there are many who take it. For the gate is narrow and the road is hard that leads to life, and there are few who find it. (Matt. 7:13-14)*

This exploration of Jesus' teachings in the Sermon on the Mount is almost complete. We have noted the enormous potential of the universal Golden Rule for overturning the usual norms of society and creating a world in which the ultimate values for life apply. We have also noted that most people treat the Golden Rule as a familiar saying, but too hard. That difficulty is the reason for the teaching we will explore in this chapter. It concerns 'narrow roads' and 'wide roads'.

When my husband and I were in Wales we travelled on a few eight-lane motorways, but mostly on narrow two-way country roads. They are not the wide two-lane highways familiar to Australians; instead they go on for miles with barely enough room for two cars to pass. There is no road verge, just hedgerows or dry stone walls right beside the bitumen. Driving on roads of this kind needs a lot of concentration and there is nowhere to park by the side of the road. I soon realised that the frequently-seen sign in Welsh, *Dim Parcio* ('No Parking') meant what it said!

There was one road with no signs at all; it had stone walls

on both sides and it wound around to the top of a fair-sized mountain. Our hotel was up there so we had no choice but to travel on this road. The problem was that it was as wide as one car, not two. "What if we meet someone coming from the other direction?" The thought was too awful to dwell on so we just kept going, willing the next bend in the road to be empty. Fortunately it was, because there was simply no room to turn around. I am quite sure I could not have reversed the car all the way down the mountain. Once on that road there was no turning back!

On reaching this point in the book, readers may be thinking that Jesus' teachings are too hard even to try. Yet Jesus was realistic. He knew his teaching could lead humanity to the best possible world; he also knew how hard it would be to make that world reality. For that reason, after the teaching about creating the Kingdom is complete, the final three sections of the Sermon on the Mount are addressed to people actually committed to carrying out Jesus' instructions. This teaching outlines what it really would be like to follow him. The metaphors he uses are a narrow gate and a wide gate and an easy road and a hard road. He speaks also about people who might distract travellers on the roads.

Traditional people of faith will tell you that understanding this teaching is simple – the narrow road leads to heaven and the wide road leads to hell. The two possible outcomes there are clear; they are personal reward or personal punishment. It is more than slightly incongruous that people who call themselves Jesus' followers should ignore his teachings about the earthly life and concentrate only on what might happen after death. There are also two possible outcomes for those who genuinely follow Jesus; given his teachings it is not surprising that these outcomes both concern life in the here and now.

The narrow gate opens the way to a goal he calls 'life'. In this case the word life is shorthand for 'the best that life can be'. To go through this gate is to accept that Jesus' way is the way to life as he believed God would wish it. The road to this goal is both narrow and hard. Just as it was on that mountain road in Wales, once Jesus' follower starts off up the road to the best that life can be, there is no turning back and there are no turn-offs to an easier road. The only way to continue is to keep an eye on the figure striding out in front. The author of Hebrews got it right when he/she wrote about following Jesus like this: "let us run with perseverance the race that is set before us, looking to Jesus the pioneer and perfecter of our faith" (Hebrews 12:1).

On the other hand there is the wide gate. It opens the way to what Jesus calls 'destruction', understood by many Christians as hell. In fact, the word in both Greek (*apolaian*) and Hebrew/Aramaic (*avadon*) means destruction of several different kinds, depending on the context in which the word is used. In essence, the Hebrew (and Aramaic) word *avad* means to become lost, or to go astray, when courage fails and all hope is destroyed. In the context of Jesus' teachings we can be sure it refers to the destruction of hope – the destruction of efforts to build the world according to God. There is a strong warning there for all who try to follow Jesus. Many of the people going through the wide gate have perfectly good intentions about following him and ironically, the road beyond the wide gate looks like an easy one. Yet the resting places and diversions along the way are traps where the unwary may become completely lost. It has enticing turn-offs that can take the traveller completely off the road. It is wide enough to do a U-turn – to turn around, go back and leave the road altogether.

For faithful Christians, the distractions from following Jesus may even seem appropriate. They may concern the maintenance of a church institution, or the observance of doctrine and tradition. Other distractions may come from outside of religious institutions and stem from the busyness of ordinary life. This is not to say that such persons on the wide road are evil, but simply that other aspects of life and religion have blocked their view of Jesus and his vision for humanity. The danger is that this can happen so easily, as family, career, recreation and social obligations can combine to preoccupy the person on the wide road. Paradoxically, the would-be follower of Jesus on the wide or easy road is less likely to succeed in following him, less likely to help create the best that life can be. The distractions of the wide road can weaken or even destroy inspiration that flows into individual lives from Jesus' teaching.

Then there is a further warning to the followers on the wide road. They may encounter people who entice them to take their eyes off Jesus. Jesus calls them false prophets. They say they speak in the name of Jesus, but they peddle what the twentieth century German theologian Dietrich Bonhoeffer called cheap grace.

Cheap grace means understanding the Christian faith in terms like these: "Of course you have sinned, but now everything is forgiven, so you can just stay as you are and enjoy the consolations of forgiveness." A proclamation like that is wholly self-centred, with no demand for following Jesus. In clear contrast to that is what Bonhoeffer called costly grace:

> *Costly grace confronts us as a gracious call to follow Jesus. It is costly because it compels a person to submit to the yoke of Christ and follow him; it is grace because Jesus says: "My yoke is easy and my burden is light."*[84]

Therein lies the key that opens up the narrow road. Without belief in grace, the power of unconditional love, following Jesus' teachings would indeed be too hard. The key to travelling the narrow road is to be sustained and encouraged through Jesus' love of humanity. In the context of wartime Germany, Bonhoeffer also made this timeless observation about the German church:

> *The price we are having to pay today in the collapse of the organised church is only the inevitable consequence of our policy of making grace available to all at too low a cost. We gave away the word and sacraments wholesale, we baptised, confirmed, and absolved a whole nation without condition. Our humanitarian sentiment made us give that which was holy to the scornful and unbelieving. But the call to follow Jesus in the narrow way was hardly ever heard.*[85]

Bonhoeffer wrote those words in very difficult historical circumstances, yet he could have written them yesterday. He did pursue that narrow way himself. He followed Jesus willingly, even to his death at thirty-nine for participating in a plan to rid the world of Adolf Hitler.

In the end, people on either the narrow or wide road are identified by what they accomplish for a good purpose. As Jesus put it: "You will know them by their fruits" (Matt. 7:16). Some will keep their eyes fixed on Jesus and put into practice what he says. Others will be satisfied with the gospel of cheap grace: "I am baptised with a baptism for the forgiveness of sins. I will give money to good causes and otherwise mind my own business. Changing the world is for other people, like those social justice freaks who keep reminding us of people starving in Africa, or treated unjustly, or suffering from war." The fruit of people on the wide and easy road is often indifference – indifference to the teaching of Jesus. Indifference rules out making a personal difference in his name. It is also deceptive for others; it persuades onlookers that being a Christian does not have to include following the hard or narrow way of Jesus. Social justice activists are not saints either, but many are trying to walk that narrow road. It is just as hard for them as for anyone else, but they draw their strength from the same source which inspired Jesus. The fruit they bear is called compassion, justice, freedom and peace.

If he is taken seriously, Jesus is a very disturbing figure. Yet following him on the narrow road is not only about changing the world in a big way. It is not only about generating whole social movements, or freeing slaves, or overturning governments. It is not only about encouraging people who can make a difference on a grand scale. Following Jesus on the narrow road also concerns ordinary relationships in local communities. The universal values of compassion, justice, freedom and peace apply equally to daily life. There are constant opportunities to spread their influence in the home, the neighbourhood, the shopping mall, the workplace, the school, the church. Wherever they are applied, they can help make life the best it can be.

Many years ago I knew a woman in her eighties called Florence. Florence was deeply involved in her church's mission activities. If people commented on her enthusiasm, she always said the same thing: "I do it because I'm a big fan of Jesus!" One day I saw her leaving the home of a single mother called Jan who lived down the street. Florence and I said "Hello" as we went past each other. On my way back, Jan was at her front gate. "Excuse me, do you know Florence?" she asked. "Yes. I know her through the church". "She's a saint!" said Jan. "I met her a few weeks ago in the supermarket. I had my two little kids with me, and she saw how tired I was. She helped me carry home my groceries and she's been coming back every week to do my ironing. She won't take anything for it. She just says, "I do it because I'm a big fan of Jesus!" Precisely.

26

Not in My Name!

> *On that day many will say to me, 'Lord, Lord, did we not prophesy in your name, and cast out demons in your name, and do many deeds of power in your name?' Then I will declare to them, 'I never knew you; go away from me, you evildoers'.*
> (Matt. 7:22-23)

In March 2008 the Washington Post writer Monica Hesse addressed her readers as 'Worshippers of Consumption', particularly of so-called organic products. She began her article like this:

> *Congregation of the Church of the Holy Organic, let us buy. Let us buy Luxury Organics Turkish towels at $58 US apiece. Let us purge our closets of those sinful synthetics, purify ourselves in the flame of the soy candle at the altar of the immaculate Earth Weave rug, and let us buy, buy, buy, until we are whipped into a beatific froth of free-range fulfilment. And let us never consider the other organic option – not buying – because the new green consumer wants to consume."*

Monica called this organic consumption simple greed in the name of 'green'; greed disguised as care of Planet Earth. To that, true defenders of Mother Earth would rightly say, "Not in the name of all that's green. Not in my name!"

"Not in my name!" That message comes loud and clear from this particular teaching of Jesus: you may regard yourself as religious; you may think you speak and act in my name, but I don't even know who you are! In Jesus' time there were people who thought they understood him, but actually got him terribly wrong. In fact anyone takes a risk by presuming to speak in someone else's name. There is a huge responsibility to get it right, particularly if a person is speaking in the name of Jesus, or even more so, in the name of God. It is not surprising that the third commandment of those first ten is: "You will not take the name of the Lord your God in vain"! In other words: do not invoke the divine name to justify what you want to do!

Speaking in Jesus' name is definitely risky, not least because different groups of Christians understand him differently. This teaching is addressed to eager-beaver followers who are quite certain they have got it right and are anxious to proclaim their version of Jesus. But the teaching itself carries a warning; the Jesus who appeals to us may be far removed from the real Jesus. When most Christians now over fifty years of age were in Sunday School, the Jesus they heard about was the soft-eyed, fair-haired, gentle Jesus, meek and mild. He gathered children around him and carried little lambs in his arms. He smiled at people, healed them, told them to love each other and that God was their 'father in heaven'. As the children grew older they were taught about the Jesus who told puzzling stories called parables. Mostly they were about being good to each other. So far, so good. Then there was Easter. Generations of Christian children have tried to make sense of Easter. Why did the loving father God require his son to be nailed to a piece of wood until he died?

Somehow it was about the individual child, and things he or she had done wrong. It made each of them fearful about death and dying. If they did not believe Jesus died like that to save them from their sins, they would not be forgiven and they would not go to heaven. They would go instead to an obscenely sadistic place of fire and punishment called 'hell'. They would never be released; they would be in excruciating agony for eternity. Somehow, Christian children had to put all of that beside gentle Jesus and his loving father God.

Through the ages most ordinary faithful Christians accepted the authority of clergy to pass on these ideas, and were simply grateful that Jesus had saved them from hell. The medieval church imposed its own hell when brave souls dared to challenge its dogma and were burned to death at the stake. Needless to say, that was the action of an institution which had buried the teachings of Jesus under its fearful doctrine of a judgmental God. Is it any wonder that whole generations of well educated adults in the twenty-first century have simply ditched it all? People still within the church know who those well-read adults are; they are often members of their own families and social circles.

In the past twenty years Christians in mainstream churches have been asking again what Jesus was actually saying. The tragedy is that most of the generations who left the church will not come back, which means they will have little opportunity to hear the real teachings of the real Jesus. Many church members grieve that their children have not followed them into the life of the church, but it may be up to them to tell their children about the church's old/new way of understanding Jesus and his purpose. In this teaching about speaking in his name, Jesus is pointing out to some would-be followers that they simply do not get it; they do not speak in his name. More than that, he says they actually promote acceptance of evil: "I never knew you; go away from me, you evildoers." The evildoers include prophets, yet we thought prophets were the good guys. Surely they are those who warn their societies about the consequences of injustice.

A true or false prophet may be known by the message he proclaims. In recent years so-called prophets have warned that God will destroy people who offend against a particular moral code. For example, in early 1990 the US evangelist Benny Hinn said:

> *The Lord tells me to tell you that in the mid 90's, about '94-95, no later than that, God will destroy the homosexual community of America. He will destroy it with fire, and many*

will turn and be saved and many will rebel and be destroyed. Another evangelist, the late Jerry Falwell, was certain he spoke for God when he blamed 9/11 on abortionists, feminists, gays and lesbians. Apparently his God was a terrorist who recruited other terrorists to carry out divine punishment, killing bystanders along the way. There are several ways in which these kinds of mindless 'prophecies' have evil consequences. They promote hatred of homosexual people. They put down women's right to equality. They condemn every woman who has ever had an abortion, for whatever reason. Their God is a crusading vigilante they expect to strike down all who offend against their particular moral code. These 'prophecies' bear no relation to the kind of God in whom Jesus had such faith.

There are many such examples of false prophecy in the third millennium. What did Jesus mean in his time, when he described some who were speaking and acting in his name as evil-doers? As we have so often found, the question is best asked in the context of his vision of the best possible world. Invariably that produces the key to understanding. In this case the answer involves the translation of Matthew's Gospel from Greek. The word translated into English as 'evil-doers' has an alternate meaning in Greek. It can mean 'doers of evil', but literally it means 'doers of lawlessness'. Western Christians who read the word lawlessness think of criminals – people who break the laws of the land. Jesus was referring to the Law of Moses. His teachings are a reinterpretation of the Law and here he says that some who claim to speak and act in his name actually disregard his teaching. Specifically, as these people do not follow the basic tenets of the Law that Jesus teaches, they have never really known him. They have placed on him their own interpretation of his significance and spoken and acted according to that view. Their interpretation of him has been defamatory of him and destructive of his cause.

That takes many people (particularly Protestants) back to their Sunday School understanding of Easter. The traditional view of Jesus and his death downgraded the importance and urgency of his teachings about the best possible world. It made them secondary to his sacrificial role as set out in the doctrine of substitutionary atonement. This idea, discussed in the fourth century by Augustine of Hippo,[86] removed from Jesus' death his willingness to die for his vision of an enlightened humanity in the best possible world. It disregarded the fact that it was by this means that his death had become sacred – his life freely given for others. It turned Jesus into a robotic, obedient human sacrifice for human sin, demanded by a God with no idea of the meaning of grace or unconditional love.[87] It was formulated by people who largely disregarded Jesus' teaching and adopted triumphalist religious ideas about him, shaped to become foundational doctrine in the state religion of the Roman Empire.

The result was a Christianity whose triumphalism validated the Roman state and sanctioned state-sponsored violence in the name of Jesus. Without question Jesus would have said to the formulators of these doctrines: "Not in my name!" The same condemnation by Jesus would apply to new attempts to preserve the doctrine of substitutionary atonement. Well-meaning scholars are reinterpreting its portrayal of a violent God, hoping to prove that where Jesus' death is concerned, violence is now loving, evil is now good, black is now white. This penultimate teaching in the Sermon on the Mount is a powerful warning to all who call themselves Jesus' followers. Unless they understand his purpose, even the most enthusiastic can lose sight of him and do more harm than good.

Tens of millions of words have already been written and spoken about US President Barack Obama; many millions more will be written and spoken about him in the future. In the days following his inauguration there was concern that so much hope had been placed on his shoulders for a better America and a better world. Many noted that he is not the new Messiah, but most importantly for world peace and harmony, he does not believe that himself. It is worth consulting his own words about his vision for the world. In his book *The Audacity of Hope*, in a chapter he calls 'Faith', there is an honest attempt to explain his 'progressive' faith in God and his understanding of Jesus. Here are just three of his insights:

1. In making a case for the separation of church and state, Obama acknowledges the socially subversive gospel of Jesus like this:

   Let's assume that we had only Christians within our borders. Whose Christianity would we teach in the schools? Should we just stick with the Sermon on the Mount – a passage so radical that it's doubtful our Defense Department would survive its application?

2. Where the moral values of conservative Christians are concerned, he says:

   As a general rule I am more prone to listen to those who are as outraged by the indecency of homelessness as they are by the indecency of music videos.

3. There is room for doubt in the new President's beliefs, as well as certainty. He does not regard the Bible as trapped in a time warp and irrelevant to the twenty-first century. Obama says:

   When I read the Bible I do so with the belief that it is not a static text but the Living Word. Things I am absolutely sure about are 'the Golden Rule', the need to battle cruelty in all its forms, the value of love and charity, humility and grace.[88]

Barak Obama says he is open to listening and learning with humility. The world can only hope he will succeed.

Discerning the truth of God and helping to build the best world through a change of heart and mind both require continuous learning from Jesus. Honest attempts to see what he has really been saying to his followers over two millennia will ensure that he will not have to say to well-meaning Christians: "Not in my name!" The danger is that certainty about God's will is likely to lead Jesus' followers astray. They may well construct a God very different from the God of Jesus.

27

Founded on Rock

Everyone then who hears these words of mine and acts on them will be like a wise man who built his house on rock.
(Matt. 7:24)

This chapter summarizes these explorations of teachings in the Sermon on the Mount. Given that in the gospels they are primarily a collection of sayings, it is highly unlikely that Jesus stood up and said them one after the other. For one thing they are often cryptic, requiring explanation. It is hard to believe that Jesus would not have followed each individual saying with an appropriate question and answer discussion, which was standard teaching methodology in those times.[89] There is also good reason to believe that if someone said, "Teacher, what would it be like in the Kingdom of heaven on earth?" in the manner of teachers in his day Jesus would have answered the question with one of his parables. In the Sermon on the Mount we have only his sayings, probably because he repeated them to different groups of people wherever he went. After all, they contain the greatest treasure Jesus had to pass on; together they amount to no less than directions to the best possible world. We have seen that there is a strong case for arguing that the order in which they appear in Matthew enhances their coherence.

The last saying in the Sermon on the Mount contains what we might call the final words of Jesus. They are not whatever he may or may not have said as he died being crucified; they are the climax of what we know to be his own teaching. These final words appear in both Luke's and Matthew's gospels, lending them credibility as authentic Jesus-speak. After he concludes teaching designed to bring out the best of hopes and the highest level of humanity in his hearers, Jesus indicates what it would be like if the teachings are actually embraced. Specifically he says, "Everyone then who hears these words of mine and acts on them will be like a wise man who built his house on rock."

There is an indisputable connection here between the hearing and the doing, as neither is sufficient alone. The previous chapter discussed followers of Jesus who do not first of all take the trouble to understand his teachings before acting on them. They often lose sight of the real Jesus and the God who inspired him. Significantly, this last saying contains another of Jesus' metaphors for God. The 'rock' upon which life is to be built is, unmistakably, faith in and faithfulness to the ideals Jesus believed originated in God. Given that Jesus is encouraging his followers to build their lives on such a rock, what does the Sermon on the Mount say about God?

Jesus does not set out to say that God is this or that or the other. What he does is to give his hearers guidance to become particular kinds of human beings. They are to be forgiving, not condemning. They are to be compassionate, not unfeeling. They are to be just, not unjust. They are to be peaceful, not violent. Jesus is encouraging humanity to bring about a reversal of the ways things are. If that happens there will be a complete transformation of life for the poor and hungry. The transformation will entail the rich and powerful giving up their power and riches. Their reward would be that they become rich in their humanity and powerful in their loving. Jesus taught that this would be a sign of a world which runs according to the nature, wishes and intention of God. Christians of all persuasions accept that.

Yet the often-asked questions are heard. Why doesn't God intervene? Why doesn't God ensure that the world is the way

Jesus envisioned it? Jesus' answer rings loud and clear through his teaching and his own life: God wants to bring this about – but in partnership with humanity. As St Augustine is said to have put it: "God without us will not; and we without God cannot."[90] For believers there is a real sense of mutuality there, a real working out of the ancient covenant: "I will walk among you, and be your God, and you shall be my people."(Lev.26:12). What this amounts to for the biblical writers is their understanding of an empowerment of humanity, even in a world where bad things do happen to good people. In spite of the ways the world can and does inflict pain on its unsuspecting creatures, it is still possible to believe that God created out of love and intends goodness for all who live. To bring about the best possible world, even one which includes evil both natural and moral, what is needed is humanity's profound commitment to a practical expression of love.

That is why Jesus died. His teaching was in large part political; it was definitely socially subversive. Jesus felt called to kick-start a process that would overturn social systems that suited the unjust, violent, unfeeling and unforgiving elites of his time. The people who stopped long enough to listen to him loved what he said; they could not get enough of it! The gospels say again and again that the crowds followed him everywhere he went, hungry and eager for more. To gain a little respite from their demands and excitement, he had to escape into boats on the Sea of Galilee or to the tops of mountains. Readers of the gospels often note the excitement of the crowds, but ascribe that to miraculous messianic healings as portrayed by the gospel writers.[91] In fact he had opened the people's eyes to what could be and through him they saw the heavens opened. Through him they saw love and compassion incarnate. They were willing to take hold of his dream and follow him to the end of the earth.

There is no doubt that all of this also made Jesus hugely unpopular. None of it would have escaped the notice of people in power. Naturally they would have wanted to be rid of Jesus before his followers challenged their entrenched power. In *The Rise of Christianity*,[92] Rodney Stark set out fundamental ways in which the teachings of Jesus threatened the Empire. Among them is his contention that Christianity brought a new dimension of humanity to a world saturated with cruelty. In particular, Jesus' teachings regarded mercy as a virtue, not as a pathological emotion or defect of character as commonly thought. Christianity's humane imperative turned on its head the belief that pity was excusable only in children or the unwise and called into question the cruelty used to oppress captive populations. Jesus decisively challenged the common understanding of the means by which the powerful were entitled to exercise power.

In Jesus' time there were three levels of powerful people in the Roman province of Judea. The lower level included ecclesiastical power-brokers such as the High Priest and other ruling clergy. They relied on the goodwill of Rome to maintain their religious authority over the people. The middle level included the hated Roman-appointed 'puppet-king' of the Jews called Herod Antipas. He was half Jew and half Edomite (the Greek name is Idumaean), and relied on Rome's goodwill to remain in power. At the upper level the Roman governor called Pontius Pilate represented the Emperor of Rome. Jesus' teachings about a transformation of the world threatened them all. They had collaborated to defeat various messianic aspirants and now they collaborated to rid themselves of this man Jesus, who inspired people to believe they could create a better world. He knew the ruling elite would feel that way about him, yet he could do no other. He had to pass on what he knew was the truth about life for humankind. In that sense, he died 'for our sake'.

Here we return to his final words to all humanity. "Everyone then who hears these words of mine and acts on them will be like a wise man who built his house on rock. The rain fell, the floods came, and the winds blew and beat on that house, but it did not fall, because it had been founded on rock." The reverse is true of people who build their houses on the shifting sands of political, religious or secular ideology and traditions. When life's challenges come, their houses will not stand. No matter where one's house is built, or on what foundation it stands, the same will apply; the rain will fall, the floods will come, the winds will blow and beat on the house. In other words, natural disasters and moral evils will continue to happen and the follower of Jesus will have difficult times like everyone else. It is not a matter of whether difficult things will happen, but when and to what extent. As Henry Wadsworth Longfellow wrote:

Be still sad heart and cease repining;
behind the clouds the sun is shining,
thy fate is the common fate of all,
into each life a little rain must fall,
some days must be dark and dreary.[93]

Sometimes there seem to be no answers to the worries that surround and beat upon the soul. What difference does it make then, to be a follower of Jesus? What difference will it make if the world he imagined becomes reality?

This exploration of Jesus' message reveals that his followers have the qualities for bringing into being the world he imagined. We first came across these qualities in the nine teachings known as the beatitudes. Their over-arching characteristic is that they can create connecting bridges between people. They can create mutually supportive relationships that bring strength and resilience when the rains come and the winds blow. These qualities are variously called forgiveness, compassion and selflessness. They draw people closer together; they enable the healing of hurts without violence; they bring an end to sorrow; they build strength into commitment to the poor and the hungry. These qualities are not designed for super-humans. They are not designed for especially pious or perfect people; they are designed for whoever has the desire to embrace them.

SECTION III: THE TEACHINGS

When life is founded on the teachings of Jesus it is founded on what he called the rock of God. Jesus' God is not a managing, punishing deity who places conditions on forgiveness and grace. Jesus based his life on his belief that God is the source of all human compassion, forgiveness and commitment to the well-being of others. There is an assurance here that followers of Jesus will find the strength and inner peace to overcome storms that occur in personal life and in the process of developing the world of his vision. As a global community unlimited by ethnic, geographical or religious borders, they will find the impetus and energy to create the best possible world. To all of them Jesus once said, "The Kingdom of heaven is within you!"

28
Why Parables?

He told them another parable: "The kingdom of heaven is like yeast that a woman took and mixed in with three measures of flour until all of it was leavened." Jesus told the crowds all these things in parables; without a parable he told them nothing.
(Matt. 13: 33-34)

Parables are partners of the teachings of Jesus included in the Sermon on the Mount. As Matthew's Gospel notes, Jesus often used parables to illuminate his teachings, perhaps during question and answer sessions. One major reason for this is that parables offer the listener a different perspective on the old familiar world. Parables are like cryptic crosswords; they offer metaphorical clues and invite the hearer to discover hidden shades of meaning. Because they are stories about 'other people', they place the hearer in the role of an onlooker who comes to recognize himself or herself in the story. The onlooker is then pointed back to his or her life situation with a challenge to change it. We know that parables were a common teaching method in the time of Jesus, as attested in the rabbinic writings of early Judaism which contain over two thousand parables. For that reason, parables were the natural partners of Jesus' explicit teachings. It is apparent that the gospel writers were also authors of parables. The greater part of the gospels is stories written about Jesus that would appropriately be called parables.

An old rabbinic legend highlights the common appeal of parables. It happened that Rabbi Judah ha-Nasi[94] failed to invite his disciple Rabbi Bar Kappara to his son's wedding, although all of the other rabbis had been invited. It was a mistake, an oversight, but the embarrassed host organized another banquet purely so that he could invite Rabbi Kappara. Something strange happened during the banquet. The host, who was supervising things in the kitchen, noticed that although the waiters took sumptuous courses of food out to the guests, when they eventually brought back the plates the food was untouched. The waiters explained that there was an old man at the table who, whenever a new course arrived, told three hundred parables. This so fascinated the guests that they forgot to eat. We can guess the identity of the old man, but the story says more about the power of parables.

Parables invite comparisons. In his own parables Jesus compares his vision of the Kingdom of heaven with ordinary things and events. The hearer can draw on a wealth of personal experience in comparing this vision with the reality of life. Parables concern everyday activities such as growing things in fields. They refer to natural substances like salt. They use metaphors like fruit and light.

Most importantly, Jesus' parables reveal his purpose. They throw light on what he is trying to teach his listeners. Time and again when he was asked a question about the purpose of his teaching he responded with a parable. The people of his time did not need a detailed explanation of the purpose of parables; they knew parables concerned their world with all of its cultural, religious, geographical and historical features. The timelessness of parables is proven when people of the twenty-first century can see beyond the historical details to the central truth the parable reveals. When the hearers recognize themselves and hear the story as an individual call to action, any similarity with a cryptic crossword ends and the message of the parable becomes personal. Legitimate responses to parables are, "How do my actions compare with that?" "How should I act in the future?"

Significantly, Jesus' parables offer a subversive view of life in his own society. The land owner, or king, or other metaphor for God, acts in ways opposite to conventional wisdom. For instance, in the ears of the hearers the vineyard owner sounds ridiculously generous in offering equal pay to all workers, regardless of how long they have worked (Matthew 20). Jesus knew this had the potential to help bring about an equal share of resources for all, but it sounded like nonsense to people working within the parameters of business codes. In short, the new code of ethics contained in Jesus' teaching and parables looked like foolishness to those who were well off. To the disadvantaged it sounded like heaven on earth.

Other subversive ideas in the parables concern the issue of unearned forgiveness. Only a fool would 'forgive' debts owed to, or offences committed against, him or her. In Jesus' time, to be merciful was to be regarded as a fool, particularly in the ruling Greco-Roman culture. There are similar ideas still current in the twenty-first century world of business and politics. The details of the parables may be from another time and place, but their central meaning remains relevant for ever.

The gospels also contain explanations of parables. Chapter 13 of Matthew contains seven parables about the Kingdom of heaven. It also contains explanations of the parable of the sower and the parable of the weeds. These explanations are almost certainly from Matthew, offering an interpretation for the followers in his own time. The parables as Jesus told them stand on their own as revealers of the mysterious Kingdom of heaven. Their wisdom concerning how the world he imagined might look did not need explanation then. Neither does it need explanation now.

In the 1970's Richard Bach wrote a best-selling book called *Jonathan Livingston Seagull*.[95] The leading character is a young seagull named Jonathan who finds that ordinary life in the flock is restricting his desire to be the best he can be – in his case, the best flyer he can be. So he begins to break out of the limits set by the flock and look for his own limit. As he learns to overcome fear and fly further and faster and higher, Jonathan realises he is becoming more completely himself – more completely the way he was born to be. Encouraged by heavenly seagulls he meets in the higher realms, he returns to the flock to become a teacher and encourager of others. He simply tells them how to follow him in the way that he himself has gone. Richard Bach's story is a modern parable. It needs no further explanation.

Jesus' parables are also clearly a call to action, yet they are intentionally non-directive. They are framed deliberately to prompt the hearer to examine his or her own life and respond individually to examples of compassionately subversive behaviour. They are definitive answers to the individual's question: "Teacher, where is the Kingdom of heaven?" The answer is the same for everyone: it is in your own heart, or it is nowhere.

QUESTIONS FOR DISCUSSION CONCERNING ISSUES RAISED IN SECTION III

1. Do you think belief in God is a necessary pre-requisite for following Jesus' teachings?

2. Do you know of any teachings of other faiths that parallel the teachings of Jesus?

3. Name some of the ways the world would have to change to be called the Kingdom of heaven or 'best possible world'.

SECTION IV

The Vision of Jesus and the Events of Easter

29
Taking a Stand

"When he entered Jerusalem, the whole city was in turmoil, asking, "Who is this?" The crowds were saying, "This is the prophet Jesus from Nazareth in Galilee." (Matt. 21:10-11)

This chapter and the two following are interrelated. There are three titles but there is one theme: why did Jesus die? I have stated several times that Jesus' teachings are worth dying for. I believe he knew that beyond doubt, which empowered him to endure every torment his enemies could inflict on him. These three sections contain an alternative view of the events and meaning of Easter which makes sense of all that occurred in Jesus' life. It is also a view that liberates Jesus' followers from the vengeful God of Christian doctrine.

This first of the three chapters focussed on Easter examines the events on what the church calls Palm Sunday. There is no denying that Jesus did not have to go to Jerusalem; he could have stayed up in the hills in the Galilee. He could have wandered around obscure little villages telling his parables. He could have gone on dreaming of a world he called the Kingdom of heaven on earth. He could have hoped that someone else would get the message and take a stand to defend it. He could have hoped that someone else would confront the powers of empire and show them how different things could be. He could have left it for someone else to take the risk. He did not. Taking a stand is precisely what Jesus was doing when he rode a donkey into the heart of earthly power.

In our time, challenging the powers could perhaps mean being ordered out of the public gallery in Parliament House, or being moved along from demonstrating outside the Town Hall. It could mean being fined for holding up the traffic, or at worst, being jailed for contempt of court. In Jesus' day anyone who stood up to oppose the hegemony of Caesar and Herod found themselves in a very different situation; they were usually condemned to death. In their time execution was not carried out by means of a gallows or gas chamber or electric chair or lethal injection. Barbaric and morally repugnant as those methods are, at least they are relatively quick. Jesus knew he risked being killed by one of the slowest and most agonizing forms of execution ever devised. Historical records tell us that Pontius Pilate, the Roman governor portrayed in the gospels as a philosopher and a gentleman, was actually so cruel and perverse he was recalled from his post by Rome. That really is saying something; in those days cruel, uncaring treatment of the masses by rulers was the norm. There was almost no recognition of the rights of an individual, particularly someone from the lower, or peasant classes. Jesus came from a poor village in a remote district of a remote province of the Roman Empire. He would have been of absolutely no account to the Romans. The only reason he attracted the notice of the Roman establishment was that it came to regard him as a threat to its authority in Judea.

It is probable that by the time Jesus came to Jerusalem he had quite a large following. The gospel writers are unclear about the numbers, but his activities were obviously known to the ruling powers and he knew that fact would put him at risk of a charge of insurrection. He knew the penalty for that was crucifixion, and he also knew that insurrectionist leaders from the Galilee had been crucified by the Romans. At the time of his trial the Galilean rebel leader Barabbas was in prison in Jerusalem. The fact that Jesus was a Galilean would have further counted against him, but still he went to Jerusalem.

Before we consider what compelled him to take such an

extraordinarily risky step, it is worth reflecting on what would have happened had he stayed at home in Nazareth. The obvious first answer is that the world would never have heard of Jesus, and the history of the world for the past two thousand years would have been unimaginably different. Almost all of the large movements in history over that time have been inspired by, or have occurred as a result of, the existence of Christianity. Some of those movements have not been positive, but many Christian rulers have shaped their basic law-making by reference to the ethics taught by Jesus. Over the course of two thousand years those ethics have enabled huge steps to be taken in improving human rights and even animal rights. Many peaceful and orderly societies have been created which owe their foundations to the teacher from the Galilee.

If Jesus had not entered Jerusalem that day the world would never have heard a single Christmas carol, or Handel's Messiah. It would never have heard of Martin Luther, or John Wesley, or Mother Teresa. The New Testament would not have been written. No-one would have heard of a 'good Samaritan', or a 'prodigal son', or a 'lost sheep', or of any other theme from Jesus' parables. Crucially, the world would not have heard about 'turning the other cheek', meaning non-violent resistance to brutality and oppression. For that reason it would not have known Mohandas Gandhi, Martin Luther King or Nelson Mandela. Judaism is not a missionary religion, so the rest of humanity might not have come to know Jesus' own scriptures, including the Psalms. The list could go on *ad infinitum*, detailing how different the world would be if Jesus had not taken a stand for what he believed. So we should examine more fully that fateful day when he did arrive in Jerusalem.

The gospels tell us he did not slink in incognito, hoping to avoid trouble. He came in the 'front gate', accompanied by a crowd of his followers shouting to announce his arrival. People in the streets were naturally curious and they lined up to see who was entering the city. What they saw was a man on a donkey, and many would have understood that this symbolized a text from their scriptures. Zechariah 9:9 says, "Rejoice greatly, O daughter Zion! Shout aloud, O daughter Jerusalem! Lo, your king comes to you; triumphant and victorious is he, humble and riding on a donkey." To the downtrodden Jewish people the meaning would have been clear; this man was coming as their leader. He was presenting himself as humble, hence the donkey, but he was nonetheless a leader. Given the scriptural reference, the natural title they gave him was 'king'. In the end, it was a title that proved fatal to Jesus.

Yet he had not come to Jerusalem to claim superior status for himself, like an earthly king. He had come with something to say to the people about their ultimate loyalty. He had come to point them to a power higher than Caesar's. He had not come in his own name; he believed he had come in the name of God. The people received him gladly and they shouted another quotation from scripture: "Blessed is the one who comes in the name of the Lord"! (Psalm 118:26) There is no reason to think that Jesus was intentionally carrying out a kind of altruistic suicide mission. Yet he certainly would have known the terrible risk he was taking to bring his vision for the best kind of world to his people.

To certain people watching from the sidelines, he would have looked like a threat. It was obvious that he had touched the hearts of the people, so much so that if he had chosen to, he could have rallied them to rebellion against the ruling powers. He could have threatened the fragile agreement between Herod, the Temple leaders and Rome. As long as the Jewish leadership maintained law and order they could remain in power and the people could practice their religion. Several leaders before Jesus had claimed to be the Messiah, or God's chosen representative. They had all incited their followers to violent rebellion and the result had been brutal Roman reprisals against them and the ordinary people. To the Jewish leadership it probably seemed like 'here we go again', which is why they wanted to nip this movement in the bud. They wanted Jesus out of the way before he incited another such violent uprising. They did not understand that this was not his purpose, so they assumed it was.[96] The High Priest Caiaphas no doubt spoke for many of the leadership when he said to them, "It is better for you to have one man die for the people than to have the whole nation destroyed." (John 11:50). It was precisely that kind of reaction to his popular reception that Jesus knew he risked. The question is, knowing the risk, why did he take a stand in this way? It was hardly likely that he and his band of followers could prevail against the whole Roman army. Or was it? Perhaps that is precisely what he had in mind, all along.

How did Jesus see the coming of the best possible world? He was certainly no wild-eyed fanatic, but he had a dream that could change the world – even the brutal world of the Roman Empire. One of the foundations of this was his passion for non-violent resistance to moral evil, or injustice. As we have seen, this belief resonates in his teachings from beginning to end. It is expressed clearly in Matthew 5: 38: "You have heard that it was said, 'An eye for an eye and a tooth for a tooth.' But I say to you, do not resist one who is evil (who could be a slave master or a member of the Herodian or Roman military), but if anyone strikes you on the right cheek, turn to him the other also."

Many have dismissed this as a passive, Christian 'doormat' approach but nothing could be further from the truth. This kind of teaching can cause shivers down the spines of the powerful. A modern example occurred in the 1970s in Alagamar, Brazil, when peasant land was seized by international corporations with the help of corrupt local officials. The farmers organized protests against this injustice and some were arrested and jailed. Hundreds of their fellow farmers marched to town and peacefully occupied the judge's house. They demanded that they all be jailed with the arrested ones. The judge had no choice but to send them home, including the prisoners.

One of the worst examples of systemic evil in human history

was the regime of Adolf Hitler. Yet even he could be beaten when the vision of Jesus actually was put into practice. In occupied Denmark during World War II the Nazis ordered that all Jews should wear a yellow armband with a Star of David on it (so they could be recognized and taken away to be murdered). King Christian X of Denmark, the current Crown Prince Frederik's great-grandfather, responded to the Nazi order by attending a synagogue wearing the yellow armband. The Danish church affirmed his stand and almost the entire population of Copenhagen took to wearing the armbands. The effectiveness of this non-violent resistance to tyranny meant the Nazis had to rescind the order. One can only wonder what effect there might have been on Nazi aspirations had whole populations in other countries resisted Hitler in similar ways, and stood in solidarity with Europe's Jews. Jesus knew he had the key to disarming evil. Nothing demoralizes those who use violence more than a lack of submission combined with a lack of violent resistance. When people peacefully refuse to obey or to submit to brute force they rob the would-be conqueror of a subservient population. In the end, this was the reason the British in India had to pack up and leave.

Underlying all of this is the teaching of the man from Nazareth that the first shall be last, and the last, first. In his sayings there is his firm conviction that all people are equally precious in the eyes of God. Jesus aimed to save humanity from its own brutality and establish a world in which the inequality underpinning the hierarchies of empires is eliminated. He foresaw a world in which all people have an equal say in the way they live and the way they work. He knew it would be a society based on the rule of love.

It is no wonder that the supporters of empire did not understand him. It is no wonder that they thought he would play the game according to their own rules of violence and death. It is also no wonder that he knew he had to defend his vision for humanity, even at the risk of his own death. That is why he came to Jerusalem.

30

Facing the Consequences

*Then Pilate said to him, "Do you not hear how many
accusations they make against you?" But he gave him no
answer, not even to a single charge, so that the governor was
greatly amazed. (Matt. 27: 13-14)*

We have seen how threatening to the powerful of his day was Jesus' formula for the non-violent defeat of evil. Here the story of his confrontation with the kingdoms of this world continues. For him the consequences were very clear, but the key to our understanding of what happened to Jesus in Jerusalem is his own teaching. When he taught his followers to turn the other cheek to an aggressor, he meant it. He was not paying lip service to this idea; he intended to live by it, if necessary to the bitter end. Before considering his trial and execution it would be helpful to look more fully at one aspect of his teaching. In Matthew's gospel the saying is: "You have heard that it was said, 'An eye for an eye and a tooth for a tooth.' But I say to you, do not resist an evildoer. If anyone strikes you on the right cheek, turn the other also." As with all of Jesus' teachings, it is important to look at the historical context of this saying. It would have been immediately obvious to people listening to him, but twenty-first century people need to know the background.

In Jesus' time slavery was widespread, which means his audience would often have included slaves. The brutal fact is that the relationship between a slave and his or her master is not an equal one. A slave in the first century was traditionally reprimanded by a backhanded blow with the right hand to the right cheek. That kind of action is dismissive, contemptuous violence. On the other hand, if you were to hit an equal you would probably punch him with your right fist, so that the blow would land naturally on the left side of his face. In effect, Jesus was teaching slaves how to respond to violence from their owners. Do not just let him hit you on the right cheek; face up to him so he has to treat you as an equal, and hit you on the left cheek. He may realise then what he is doing, begin to respect you and change his behaviour toward you.

The slave's non-violent resistance in this scenario is not submission to brutality; it signifies his or her claim to equality with the slave owner and all of humanity. In effect, the slave is loving the slave owner by forcing him to face up to his own brutality and acknowledge the pain he has caused. The same teaching of Jesus called on his followers to resist non-violently the common brutality of the ruling authorities and military toward the people of the Galilee and Judea: "Love your enemies and pray for those who persecute you". This is the foundation of Jesus' commitment to the best possible way of living. This is the foundation of his ability to forgive those who ridiculed, tortured and eventually murdered him. That foundational idea is revealed more fully if we examine the events on the night before and the day of the crucifixion. There are three scenes: the garden, the trial, the crucifixion.

First, the garden scene. After a meal together Jesus and his group went to a garden, where Jesus prayed. The city leadership would not allow him to remain at large for very long, so he knew they would soon arrest him. Although the gospels say otherwise, no one knows how he prayed that night. No one was recording his words as his friends slept. All we need to know is that he was a human being with a natural fear of the obscenely violent death likely to happen to him. The words we have are those of gospel writers. Matthew, Luke and John follow the lead of Mark, who has Jesus express understandable reluctance to fall into the hands of the authorities. Jesus was humanly vulnerable and reluctant in the face of unimaginable cruelty. Yet the subsequent events bear witness that no matter what happened, he remained determined to stay true to his vision for the best possible world. He clearly believed that what he saw in that vision was God-inspired and he was committed to defending it, not only through his words but through his actions.

Eventually the Herodian/Roman arrest party arrived, under cover of darkness so as not to stir up the people, who were largely supportive of Jesus. One of those with Jesus could not believe he was not actively resisting arrest. This man drew his sword and struck a slave of the High Priest. Jesus was obviously dismayed, and with good cause because the violence was completely contrary to the reason he was in that situation in the first place. The man was ordered by Jesus to sheath his sword, and Matthew's gospel has Jesus make another key statement: "Put your sword back into its place; for all who take the sword will perish by the sword."

Secondly, the trial scene. Several leaders questioned Jesus, who maintained his dignity and restraint. We note that he was slapped, presumably in the face, but in effect he turned the other cheek. Various people tried to get a response from him and their taunting was relentless. The high priest told him that he had been blaspheming against God. The governor Pilate tried to get him to admit to being the king of the Jews. Jesus merely turned it back: "You say so." Then came the key to understanding why Jesus was behaving this way. He told Pilate that his kingdom was not a kingdom of this world. If that were the case, his followers would be defending him in the usual earthly way, that is, with violence. Pilate did not understand: "So you are a king?" Jesus replied that his mission was to tell the truth, meaning his understanding of ultimate truth for life. Pilate even tried to reason with him, telling Jesus that he had the power to order his release. The gospel accounts say that Jesus was given the chance to escape the consequences of his commitment, but he refused the opportunity. He knew it would have meant his surrender to the abusers of power; he would have allowed their violence to defeat him. It would become known that he preferred his own welfare to bringing his vision for the world to reality. Eventually Pilate was defeated by Jesus' courage and faithfulness and he handed him over to be crucified.

Third, the crucifixion scene. Jesus' final words from the cross are different in each of the gospels, yet there is a distinct thread connecting them. In Mark and Matthew the emphasis is on the full outcome of Jesus' loving faithfulness. The excruciating agony of crucifixion causes him to feel abandoned – even by God: "My God, my God, why have you forsaken me?" Only a being who was more than human would not feel abandoned while being crucified. The gospel writers Mark and Matthew remind their readers that in his dying moments Jesus reached the limit of his endurance. Luke's account introduces a conversation involving two insurrectionists crucified with Jesus. The first made the mistake of thinking Jesus was a violent revolutionary, as they were. The other understood; perhaps he had heard Jesus talk about non-violent resistance to evil. He asked Jesus to remember him when the "Kingdom of heaven" on earth became reality.

As already noted, this chapter on Good Friday and those immediately before and following, address one question: why did Jesus die? In the events of Good Friday we see the consequences for Jesus of entering Jerusalem. If he had not been prepared to die in defence of his vision, the world would not have heard of it or of him. The consequences for him were dire, but what were and are the consequences of Good Friday for his followers? I have left the final words from the cross in Luke's gospel until last. Before considering their full impact, it is important to remember the purpose of Jesus' self-giving, even to death. His sayings about responding to violence with non-violence point each of his followers to his ultimate aim – to change the world by loving one's enemy. The wisdom of the world is turned upside down when the persecutor is met with non-violent resistance. It should be clear that this is not a passive acceptance of evil; it is definite resistance to evil and commitment to the defeat of it, but without the use of violence.

Just one example of this has had huge repercussions for

humanity. I have mentioned that Jesus' stance on non-violence was the underlying cause of the British colonial government's withdrawal from India. By the 1920's Mohandas Gandhi had become more and more despairing about the exploitation of Indians under British rule. In 1930 he led a campaign of civil disobedience in which hundreds of thousands of ordinary people refused to pay tax imposed on salt, an essential part of their diet. Also in that year, Gandhi's follower Sarojini Naidu led two thousand five hundred people in a peaceful march on the Dharasana Salt Works. There they were viciously beaten with wooden rods by hundreds of British-led police. Many protestors were killed, but they did not retaliate against their tormenters with violence.

After that, British leaders acknowledged Gandhi as a force they could neither suppress nor ignore, and India's independence was finally granted in 1947. Its underlying cause was inspired by Jesus' Sermon on the Mount, which profoundly and directly influenced the thoughts and actions of Gandhi. He wrote:

> *The example of Jesus' suffering is a factor in the composition of my un-dying faith in non-violence. The lives of all have, in some greater or lesser degree, been changed by his presence, his actions, and the words spoken by his divine voice ... I believe that he belongs not solely to Christianity, but to the entire world; to all races and people.*[97]

Jesus' commitment to non-violence, even to death, was designed to help the violent as well as their victims. It was intended to help them contrast their behaviour with that of people who resist violence with non-violence. Its aim was to bring about repentance and a profound change of attitude to others. The ultimate expression of love for enemies is to forgive them when they do their worst to you and to advocate for their forgiveness by God. In Luke's gospel Jesus' dying words from the cross are entirely in keeping with the way he lived: "Father, forgive them, for they know not what they do."[98] It is essential that the cross be re-interpreted as the cause of Jesus' death, not as the purpose of his life.

31

Understanding the Meaning

He has been raised from the dead, and indeed he is going ahead of you to Galilee; there you will see him. (Matt. 28:7)

We have pondered what it would mean for the world if Jesus had not gone to Jerusalem. We have wondered at Jesus' own response to violence with non-violence. We have seen that it led him to the cross. We have also seen that out of his death a seed of hope was planted in the human heart. Two thousand years later, alongside modern examples of violence as a means of solving difference, a great tree of peace grows from that hope.

No one knows for how long after the crucifixion Jesus' friends were scattered and demoralized. Even those who understood him and his vision could not then see how his death had advanced his cause. He was dead and his teachings appeared dead, too. Perhaps it had all been a wonderful dream and nothing more. His followers knew that if they even met together, let alone repeated his teachings, they might also be arrested. So they were scattered and afraid. There is good reason to believe that some went home to the Galilee, from which many had first set out to follow Jesus. No one knows how long it was before they remembered things which germinated that seed of hope Jesus had planted, but in the decade following the crucifixion something decisive and powerful took root. It continued to sustain the committed followers through times of trial and turmoil.

In the midst of persecutions and exile from the land following the destruction of Jerusalem, the followers still holding on were in need of a coherent and inspirational account of Jesus' potential impact on the world. By the time the gospels were written the seed of hope he planted was growing and spreading. This was in spite of the massive suffering, social and religious upheaval and displacement associated with the Jewish War of 66-70CE. The gospels were written by people who had already experienced the ongoing encouragement of his teachings. They knew what it meant to say, "Jesus lives!" They had caught his vision and were seeing the world through his eyes. He was still with them in their hearts and minds as they endeavoured to follow him.

Out of that experience come the resurrection narratives. They are different in each gospel, yet the situation of Jesus' followers forty to fifty years after the crucifixion can be seen between the lines. The stories address their circumstances and give them directions for the future. The writers crafted their resurrection stories about Jesus to help those who were then trying to follow him. In all gospels we see people whose first instinct was to look for Jesus among the dead. They were looking backwards to the past, to the time when he was still with them, instead of forward to the future. They were doing what bereaved people have always done – lingering with sadness and regret at a graveside. They were longing for the past when the loved one was still with them. Then comes the resoundingly clear message – this is not for you! This is not the place for you to be; this is not the direction to be looking.

The gospel writers had all discovered this in their own ways and had come to believe they had received this message from God. Naturally they wanted to pass it on to their readers. Each story therefore features an angelic presence at the graveside, bearing a message from heaven. The instructions are always in three parts: Jesus is not among the dead; go and tell that to others; Jesus will be with you. The resurrection stories are designed to carry a message of hope that Jesus' vision for the world would live on. None of these stories requires belief in a literally resuscitated corpse. There is something else they do not rule out. They may at least in part have been inspired by an experience of Jesus' presence by his closest friends. It is well known that many bereaved persons report experiencing the presence of a loved one in the days following his or her death. In any case, the resurrection stories are included to remind readers of the gospels that they are still called to follow Jesus.

Matthew and Mark addressed followers living outside of Jerusalem in the countryside, so they are told in those gospels that Jesus will meet them in the Galilee. Luke also addressed followers around Jerusalem, so they are told Jesus will meet them there. In any case, the message is that wherever they found Jesus in the first place, they will find him there again. His teachings will apply to the way they live both then and into the future, wherever that might be. They are to look for Jesus among the people with whom they live and work and in those ordinary settings the seed of hope he planted will grow. It will give them courage to put into practice his vision of humanity at peace.

The Book of Acts was written around the same time as the gospels. It clearly depicts Jesus' followers moving on from preoccupation with the past. Most importantly, Acts shows Peter, James and John facing up to the authorities as followers of Jesus. Luke the writer of Acts depicts them as renewed, reinvigorated and reinstated as bearers of Jesus' vision for the best possible world. They have done it unarmed, knowing full well what happened to Jesus. They are jailed, flogged and generally persecuted, but crucially for the readers of Acts, their non-violent resistance to official violence begins to bear fruit. The powerful begin to take notice. Gamaliel, one of the leading Pharisees, becomes uneasy about these resisters of their authority. He points out that two other men had claimed leadership of the people through armed uprisings. Both had been killed by the Romans and their followers dispersed. With that knowledge Gamaliel makes the wise point that if this Jesus movement also attacks the Romans and is wiped out, it will not have been from God. If it is from God, it will not be able to be wiped out. Gamaliel then advises the ruling Council that they should wait and see what happens to the Jesus group, otherwise they may find they are fighting against God. With that in mind they decide not to imprison or execute Peter and his friends.

Yet even though they were flogged and ordered not to speak in Jesus' name, his followers resisted the powerful by going on doing just that. They knew the inspiration of Jesus was with them in their efforts to follow him. Eventually they too were killed by nervous power-brokers, but their influence had touched the lives of countless more followers.

That was the situation of people who followed Jesus two thousand years ago – very different from the lives of followers in recent years. Or is it? On Sunday March 7, 1965, six hundred people began a fifty-four mile march from Selma, Alabama, to the state capital, Montgomery. They were protesting against the denial of voting rights for African Americans. After the marchers crossed the Edmund Pettus Bridge on the outskirts of Selma, they were brutally assaulted by heavily armed state troopers. They resisted non-violently, bravely facing up to their attackers. They were led by John Lewis and Hosea Williams, leaders of the Student Non-Violent Coordinating Committee. It was based in the African Methodist Episcopal Church, which had been born out of protests against slavery.

That very night, the American Broadcasting Company (ABC) telecast a Nazi war crimes documentary, Judgment in Nuremberg. It illustrated in stark detail the depraved humanity that can result from the acceptance of blind prejudice as truth. The ABC interrupted it to show footage of the violence being done to the Selma protestors in the name of prejudice against black Americans. In the combination of these two images on their TV screens, the American nation saw a powerfully disturbing metaphor of its own prejudice and violence toward a downtrodden minority.

Within forty-eight hours, demonstrations supporting the Selma marchers were held in eighty cities. They involved thousands of black and white religious and lay leaders, including Martin Luther King. A Federal Judge ruled that the demonstrators be permitted to assemble and on March 17, twenty-five thousand of them stood peacefully outside the state capital, Montgomery. As a direct result, the US Congress passed the Voting Rights Act of 1965, guaranteeing every adult American the right to vote. Thirty five years later, on March 7, 2000, John Lewis and Hosea Williams crossed the Pettus Bridge again, this time accompanied by President Bill Clinton. John Lewis said, "This time when I looked there were black faces among the troopers. This time when we faced them, they saluted."

That story gathers together the power of non-violent resistance to evil and the contemporary world of the twentieth and twenty-first centuries. Yet even that example can seem far removed from individual lives. It can reinforce the idea that the vision of Jesus is about big, momentous events, out of the experience or influence of ordinary people. That is not necessarily so; even in big events it always comes down to personal encounters between someone using violence to wield power and the intended victim. There are varying degrees and forms of violence and there are various ways of turning the other cheek. In the 1960s when fruit crops were made worthless by Victorian state legislation, farmers reacted peacefully but powerfully by dumping their unwanted fruit on the steps of Parliament House.

Humour and irony also have their place as resistance to oppression. In Johannesburg in the 1990s, a black woman was walking on a street with her children when a passing white man spat in her face. She stopped and said, "Thank you for that, and now for the children." The man was so nonplussed he could do nothing but walk away. South African Anglican

Archbishop Desmond Tutu was once walking by a construction site on a temporary footpath only the width of one person. A white man appeared at the other end, walked up to Tutu, and said, "I don't give way to gorillas." Tutu stepped aside, made a deep sweeping bow and said, "Ah yes, but I do." So too, satire has the power to demoralize and disempower state-sanctioned bullies. Chinese students forbidden to demonstrate against government policy sometimes put on masks of the communist leadership and carry signs like, "Support martial law"; "Support Dictatorship"; "Support Inflation".

In all incidents of non-violent resistance large and small, the aim is to give the violent one the opportunity to recognize evil in his or her own behaviour. Even on the home front, social workers agree that the most loving thing a battered wife can do is to have her husband arrested. This is non-violent resistance as tough love. She is freed from his violence and he is forced to face up to it and seek help to regain his humanity. In such ways the tree of peace grows and grows.

The reader may wonder why the recurring focus in this book on Jesus' teaching about non-violence is included in an examination of the events of Easter Day. The reason is that this teaching lies at the heart of an enlightened humanity in the best possible world. All other teaching of Jesus is linked to this central idea: "love your enemies". The genius of this teaching is that not only does it express the peaceful nature of the world Jesus imagined, it also shows humanity how to attain it. In Matthew the third beatitude is: "Blessed are the meek, for they shall inherit the earth". We have noted that 'meek' does not mean a weak, submissive person, lacking in courage. A much better understanding is that the meek are the deliberately humble, the non-violent, the gentle strong. It is they who will inherit the earth.

There is no limit to the potential of this teaching. It is not inspirational for Easter Day only or for any one day of any year. It is not limited by the size or future of the church. It does not require those who put it into practice to sign up as Christians. It is equally accessible and applicable to people of all races and religions and cultures. Its ethical values apply also to those of no religion and no belief in God. Jesus' vision has the potential to unite all people in the name of peace.

In that sense he belongs not to the church or to any religion; he belongs to the whole of humanity. He must therefore be set free from church tradition and its flawed interpretations of his meaning. He is the teacher of an enlightened humanity and the implementation of his vision depends on humanity's free acceptance of what he offers.

QUESTIONS FOR DISCUSSION CONCERNING ISSUES RAISED IN SECTION IV

1. Why do you think Jesus died? Did he have any control over what happened?
2. What difference does this version of why Jesus died make to your view of God?

SECTION V

Where To From Here?

32

What Jesus Left Behind

And Jesus came and said to them, "go therefore and make disciples of all nations ... teaching them to obey everything that I have commanded you." (Matt. 28:18, 20)

The last chapter of this book before the conclusion concerns what Jesus left behind. Here we are addressing the non-material things each person leaves behind when he or she dies. As we all will, when Jesus died he left behind a legacy for the future. We would probably wish that what we leave behind will be valuable and useful for our family and friends. What he left behind was essential wisdom for the whole of humanity.

One of the good outcomes from contemporary study of Jesus is that increasing numbers of Jews are discovering him. Some Jewish scholars interested in the period in which Jesus lived have come to realise that he really was a Jewish man of his own time and place. They have been able to reach back before the beginnings of Christianity and find a fellow Jew with a message for all humanity. Julie Galambush is one such Jew. She was originally a Christian – an ordained minister in the American Baptist Church. She is now an associate professor of religious studies at William and Mary College in Virginia and has written a book called *Christianity's Forgotten Jews*[99]. She makes the point that many Christians do not know, or have forgotten, that the New Testament is Jewish literature, written by Jews exploring the teachings of Jesus the Jew. At the time, the hostility between Jews who believed Jesus was the long-awaited Messiah and Jews who did not believe that, became so great that there had to be a parting of the ways. It was a painful parting, as Julie Galambush points out:

> *Difficult as it is to affirm today, the New Testament authors wrote out of a deeply grounded love of the heritage entrusted to them, the tree of life that was and is Judaism. For both Jews and Christians, the task of taking the New Testament authors seriously as Jews is demanding, often even threatening. And yet, however challenging it is, in the twenty-first century it is important that we pause to consider our shared roots as well as our distinctiveness – in short, how reluctant the parting of Jew and Christian really was.*

What Jesus left behind is universal and not limited by its relevance to Christianity, or to any other religion. In fact Jesus left behind two legacies crucial to the spread of his teaching. The first is 'authority'. Before thinking about the kind of authority Jesus left behind, it is important to remember the kind of authority he did not leave behind:

Jesus did not leave behind the authority of a religious institution. He is not the founder of Christianity; it was initiated by the apostle Paul.

Jesus did not leave behind the authority of hierarchies. He said the first would be last, and the last, first.

Jesus did not leave behind the authority of a book to be followed literally. He did not read scripture literally himself.

Jesus did not leave behind the authority of doctrinal formulations concerning himself – as 'second person of the Trinity', or 'God incarnate', or 'Saviour of the world'.

In short, Jesus did not focus on himself but on the God who informed and inspired him. The authority Jesus did leave behind is the authority of universal wisdom for life.

Of paramount importance for the subsequent history of Christianity is the fact that many of Jesus' followers have sidestepped the imperative to pass on his teachings about the best possible world in favour of converting people of other faiths to Christianity. Their authority comes from the missionary imperative or Great Commission at the end of Matthew's Gospel. Given Matthew's careful record of Jesus' teachings, the original intent of chapter 28 verses 18-20 would most likely have been to inspire followers of Jesus to observe those teachings. As Matthew's gospel was written around 70 CE and includes the core teachings, the original version of this passage most probably had Jesus saying: "Go and make disciples, teaching them to obey everything that I have commanded you." Jesus is not otherwise recorded as authorizing his followers to baptize. He did not claim "all authority in heaven and on earth" in his teachings.

In particular Jesus did not claim to be the Messiah; that is the claim of the New Testament writers. In the gospels, each in their own way, the writers make a case for Jesus as Messiah. Significantly, the great commission in Matthew 28 is included in resurrection sayings that claim to record words of Jesus after his death. They are intended to promote missionary activity among readers of the gospels, but ultimately they represent the hopes and beliefs of the gospel writers concerning their view of Jesus as the Messiah. Even so, it is not likely that Matthew actually wrote the trinitarian formula included in later versions of chapter 28:19. The 'Great Commission' itself is likely to have been added in the second or third century CE, during the 'christological debates' which continued on until well after the Council of Nicea in 325 CE. The New Testament scholar F. C. Conybeare found eighteen citations of Matthew 28:19 in the writings of Eusebius of Caesarea (270-340 CE). They were all devoid of the Trinitarian formula:

> *I have, after a moderate search in these works of Eusebius, found eighteen citations of Matthew 28:19, and always in the following form: 'Go ye and make disciples of all the nations in my name, teaching them to observe all things whatsoever I commanded you.'*[100]

In religious terms, what Jesus left behind was the authority of ultimate truth, what many regard as God's truth. What he said about this wisdom for life is that it is, as John the gospel writer puts it, like 'light': "the true light, which enlightens everyone". When Jesus said "love your neighbour as yourself", "forgive one another seventy times seven", "turn the other cheek" and "love your enemy", he understood his authority as coming from God. When Jesus said, "first be reconciled to your brother and sister" (and then worship God), he understood his authority as from God. Most of those teachings are encapsulated in the Sermon on the Mount, about which the fourth century theologian St Augustine wrote:

> *If any one will piously and soberly consider the sermon which our Lord Jesus Christ spoke on the mount, as we read it in the Gospel according to Matthew, I think that he will find in it, so far as regards the highest morals, a perfect standard of the Christian life[101].*

That sounds clear and compelling enough, but for many Christians the idea of the Sermon on the Mount as a perfect standard of the Christian life has created massive misunderstanding and resistance. How could anyone carry out such teaching? Perhaps it is meant to be an ideal that Christians can only try to carry out – a kind of holy dream. For that reason the Sermon on the Mount has often been regarded as meant only for the most pious and saintly of Christians. The Russian Christian writer Leo Tolstoy opposed that kind of thinking in the strongest of terms:

> *I accepted the fact that Christ meant exactly what he said. Christ did not consider his teaching as some high ideal of what mankind should be, but cannot attain to ... he considered his teaching as work, a work which is to save mankind. His suffering on the cross was no dream; he groaned in agony and died for his teaching[102].*

After the Protestant Reformation Jesus' teachings became more and more separated from the life of the state. From the nineteenth century onward, churches concentrated on the 'work of Christ' on the cross to save humanity. The idea of actually following Jesus' teachings to redeem the world even became presumptuous, given the church's understanding that Jesus had already made atonement for redemption from sin.

SECTION V: WHERE TO FROM HERE?

The Christian's duty, therefore, was simply to believe and await the second coming of Jesus. This would bring to completion his atoning sacrifice on the cross.

As we have noted, Dietrich Bonhoeffer was so strongly opposed to that kind of distortion of Jesus' purpose that he could hardly find words strong enough to express his feelings. Addressing his fellow Lutherans in the 1940s, he let his feelings be fully known:

> *We Lutherans have gathered like eagles around the carcass of cheap grace, and there we have drunk of the poison which has killed the life of following Christ. The word of cheap grace has been the ruin of more Christians than any commandment of works*[103].

Jesus believed that the authority for the teaching he left behind, the ultimate wisdom for life, came from God.

There is something else that Jesus left behind – his followers. Jesus' followers today may be surprised to realise that they are not different from James and John and Peter and Mary Magdalene and Andrew and all the rest of Jesus' first disciples. There is distance in time and technological development between the followers now and the first followers, but other than that today's followers are the same; they also have heard Jesus' teachings! When Jesus first passed them on he expected them to be carried out, and the same is still true. If Jesus' followers today met him, do they really think he would say, "I meant all of that for the people I was talking to then; it has nothing to do with you." If it were not true now, what he said would also have been utterly irrelevant back then. Jesus' words of authority have been passed on all the way from his first disciples to those who call themselves his followers now. His words are there for his followers to pick up, carry out and pass on.

In 2008 Krister Stendahl, the former Dean of Harvard Divinity School and Bishop of Stockholm, died at the age of 86. During one of his last interviews, he chose to talk about the problem of authority. What he meant was Christians who fail to pick up the authority Jesus left them. He referred to the reluctance of many Christians to take a stand, to make a noise, to be 'out front' with the teachings of Jesus. The fact is that many Christians grow up with the idea that being a Christian means being a quiet, unassuming servant of others. To that, Krister Stendahl said:

> *The idea of "servant leadership" sounds good and aims at fostering humility rather than arrogance. The pope is called "the servant of servants". This ideal can become an excuse for not taking firm and necessary decisions. It is misplaced humility to claim "I am not an authority figure" when, in fact you are.*[104]

Neither Stendahl nor I are talking about authority as given when someone becomes a 'chair' of this or secretary of that. This is about authority as left behind by Jesus. When Christians, or people of other faiths, or even atheists[105] listen to his teachings, they receive the authority to carry them out and pass them on. Krister Stendahl reminded us that this is not a short cut to arrogance. He said that "doing something for Jesus is a very safe way to humility". As soon as someone actually tries to carry out Jesus' teachings, there are plenty who will endeavour to cut him or her down to size: "How dare you tell church leaders or even the government, what to do!"

Jesus left behind the priceless gift of his authority. Ultimately, whoever claims the authority of Jesus' teaching is obliged to leave it behind in working order for those who come after. There is no higher aim than that. There is no greater legacy than that. There is no other way this world can become the best possible world.

Conclusion

A reclaiming of Jesus' foundational teachings will compel Christianity to re-examine its origins. Such an examination will reveal a profound inconsistency between the characteristics and message of a church institution built over millennia and the nature of Christianity's earliest foundations in Jesus of Nazareth. For many Christians this process of reclaiming Jesus has already begun in earnest. In the twenty-first century a new kind of Christianity is emerging, although ironically it is based on the oldest foundation of the faith. It calls the faithful to return to the vision of the world seen by Jesus of Nazareth and his original followers. This old/new interpretation of Christianity is known by different names (such as the progressive or emerging church), but whatever it may be called, a return to the original basis of Christianity involves a profoundly new Reformation of the church's teachings and traditions about both Jesus and God.

Whereas the original Protestant Reformation created a schism in the church over accusations that those who claimed ultimate authority had departed from the norms of scripture, this new Reformation is destined to create a schism infinitely more far-reaching. While many Christians regard the emerging church negatively, as destructive of ancient church traditions precious to them, many others welcome it as the doorway to a meaningful faith for the third millennium.

It is undoubtedly a new Reformation. The acceptance of an emerging or progressive church as normative Christianity for the twenty-first century would entail a profound re-thinking of the faith. There will be no room for neo-orthodox half measures which try valiantly to stretch old doctrines and traditional ideas into new shapes. There will be far-reaching implications for the form and content of the church's liturgies, including a necessary complete rewriting of its sacraments and creeds. Jesus' life, and particularly his death, will need to be restated in accordance with contemporary understandings of God.

In the process there is the real possibility of a renewed faith in God as 'Ground of Being' which does not set Christians against people of other faiths. Instead, the way will have been opened for a reformed Christianity which can build bridges with other peoples and faiths on the basis of Jesus' teachings. The potential of such a renewed Christianity for the healing of the world's ancient feuds and hatreds cannot be overstated. The potential for an outbreak of compassion on a global scale is world-shaking in its implications. Followers of Jesus understand that no faith has exclusive and exhaustive knowledge of God, that no faith is the single source or repository of all positive human values. Rather, they understand that each faith has come independently to its own knowledge of the universal sacred values of compassion, justice, freedom, acceptance of others and peace. On that shared ethical foundation people of different faiths can meet with a rich anticipation of respect, cooperation and peace.

We cannot doubt that Jesus would approve heartily of such a sharing of values. At the same time it is hard to over-estimate the impact that the growth of Christian dogma may have had on him, had he known it. He would have been horrified beyond measure to find his legacy of inclusiveness in the transforming of the world had been changed beyond recognition. Instead he had become the symbol of triumphalism and exclusivism unparalleled among religions. In his book, *Einstein's God*, Robert N. Goldman quotes Albert Einstein the Jew's response to a Catholic science student concerned about Einstein's soul. He wrote to Einstein, begging him to pray to Christ and the Virgin Mary, and to see a

Catholic priest immediately. Einstein replied:
If I would follow your advice and Jesus could perceive it, he, as a Jewish teacher, surely would not approve of such behaviour.[106]
I can only agree with Einstein. The same would apply to Jesus' undoubted disapproval should he discover he had became known as 'Christ' (the Messiah). Innumerable generations of Christians have struggled with the church's confusion in speaking of Jesus variously as Jesus of Nazareth, or as Christ. (Or, having a bet both ways, as Jesus Christ). Preachers and teachers have profoundly confused their congregations by referring to something done by the historical Jesus as 'Christ' did it, as in: "Christ talked to his disciples". Or where something expected of the mythical Christ is related to the historical Jesus, such as "the second coming of Jesus".

The name Jesus and the title Christ have been taken for granted as interchangeable, whereas the former is simply the name of a historical human being and the latter names a mythical Messiah. For that reason countless Christian sermons have muddied perfectly good interpretations of Jesus' parables by adding a mandatory dash of Pauline or even Anselmian christology.[107] Christians have been obliged to integrate two totally different founding figures, often incorporating two very different theologies, into one mystifying and often contradictory religion called Christianity.

In the process of a new Reformation of the church there is an urgent task to be accomplished. It involves Christians agreeing to release their christological stranglehold on Jesus. It includes Christians ceasing to dress him in the robes of a heavenly potentate, or a mythical mediator between heaven and earth. It involves Christians relinquishing a view of the crucifixion where Jesus' death means universal salvation from sin on condition that humanity acknowledges him as Saviour of the world. In short, the effect of the new Reformation will allow Jesus to step down from the realms of exclusivist mythology and resume his rightful place among human beings. Fundamentally, it requires Christians to acknowledge that Jesus is not the property of the church. It requires recognition that his wisdom about life belongs to the world. It requires acceptance that this wisdom calls humanity from its preoccupation with the self to an unselfish embrace of the other. It involves recognition that Jesus' teachings have the potential to heal the wounds of egotistical human interaction and create an enlightened humanity.

The implications for the church touch every part of its life. Unlike Christian dogma based on the mythical Saviour Christ, the teachings of the real, original Jesus are not triumphalist. They do not divide; they unite. They do not discriminate; they include. They are the necessary foundation stone of any emerging church which may develop during the twenty-first century. The necessary quality that can make them the basis of a united planetary community is their universality. The ethics undergirding Jesus' teachings are already known and accepted by people of other faiths and even by those with no belief in someone or something they could call God.

This was starkly illustrated in January 2010, in the midst of one of the worst natural disasters yet recorded. Given that the dreadful devastation and huge death toll caused by the earthquake in Haiti was caused by a natural movement of the earth's crust, this signals again that even in the best possible world such disasters would continue to happen. The essential equipment needed to restore the lives of people involved in such tragic occurrences is not confined to doctors and aid workers, bricks and mortar. The populations of devastated areas need a unity of purpose that disregards religious difference and builds a community based on love and compassion.

Father Hans Alexander, a Catholic priest in Haiti during the disaster, noted that religious differences had come crashing down. "Catholics and Protestants and other religions are praying together now," he said. "We are saying, 'We love Jesus; we don't care about religions.'" Father Alexander had tried for years to change the minds of people in his parish who believed that their religion was better or truer than others. The disaster also confirmed for him the essential goodness in people he observed giving themselves to help the survivors. This self-giving on a vast scale ruled out for him any doctrine of original sin. In the face of huge suffering caused by natural forces, it reinforced his belief that "God created us for good."[108] Father Alexander points here to sublime aspects of the church's interaction with the world.

Before I set out ways in which the church has strayed far from the call of its Teacher, the following is a sample of the ways it has been a force for good in its historical journey.

The church has been a force for good, in:
- providing help and healing for the ill and injured
- educating children in the world's worst slums
- caring for orphans and disabled children
- feeding and assisting the frail aged in their homes
- assisting poor farmers in improving their food crops
- accommodating the aged in a caring environment
- offering free food and clothing to the poor
- freeing slaves from their bondage to others
- bringing food and shelter to disaster-affected families
- giving supportive community to the lonely and marginalised
- transforming warring tribes into peaceful societies
- calling the nations to relinquish their reliance on war

There is no denying that in the foregoing and in all cases where the church has been a force for good, this has happened because the church remembered the call of its Teacher, Jesus of Nazareth. When the early church began to regard Jesus' teaching as too difficult, it placed its reliance on a Greco-Roman religion of personal salvation, based on a mythological Christ and a literal reading of scripture. The church's about-turn from the foundation laid by Jesus led it to involvement in social injustice on a gigantic scale, reliance on war, complicity with the hierarchical structures and policies of the state, and enthronement of the Bible as literal 'Word of God'. This last was obviously not adhered to by Jesus himself, whose scriptural interpretations often ran counter to literal readings.

The following are many ways in which traditional Christianity's distortion of Jesus' teachings and life has denied the church its sacred vocation and allied it with the same evil influences that Jesus stood against.

The church has lost its vocation as follower of Jesus:
- by turning Jesus into the mythical Christ, a God-man who 'came down from heaven'
- by failing substantially to follow Jesus' teaching about the best kind of world
- by teaching that all human beings are born evil and in need of divine forgiveness
- by claiming that God's forgiveness is conditional on belief in Jesus' death as penalty for human wrong-doing
- by promoting the ideas of heaven and hell as reward for goodness and punishment for sin
- by depicting God as eternal torturer of wrong-doers
- by distorting Jesus' teaching about a forgiving God into a religion of fear
- by characterising the Jewish people as 'killers of Christ', the catalyst for Christian antisemitism underpinning the Holocaust
- by appointing church leaders according to the patriarchal power structures of empire
- by regarding the Bible as an idol to be worshipped and followed literally
- by using scripture as warrant for colonial exploitation of the earth's resources and disregard for the rights of indigenous peoples
- by claiming scriptural warrant to justify racism and the enslavement of human beings
- by rejecting the claims of science about the reality of the universe
- by excluding homosexual people from leadership and equality in church and society
- by dismissing the equality of women in church, family and society and encouraging their domination by the male sex

- by teaching fear and rejection of human sexuality
- by denying the right of parents to decide the size of their family
- by assisting the spread of HIV-AIDS by forbidding the use of condoms
- by accepting war as the way to peace
- by rejecting other faiths as viable ways to relationship with the divine
- by judging all non-Christians as needing conversion to Christianity

All of the foregoing leads to the question: what would a church of the twenty-first century based on Jesus' teachings look like? Clearly a viable compelling religion needs a foundational story about an inspirational pioneer figure, from whom a clear set of values or principles is given, to be passed on by followers. It also needs a coherent idea for the twenty-first century about the divinity to which it pledges its ultimate allegiance. The story of Jesus' life, teachings, and death in defence of those teachings, clearly holds the power to satisfy the human capacity for good and its need of a grand and compelling vision to follow and celebrate. A religion based purely on those pre-requisites has the potential to become the most positively world-changing force that humanity has ever known. Jesus' teachings also hold potential for the development of an acceptable contemporary view of the divine.

I have several times made the point that followers of Jesus the Teacher can be Christian, or adherents of other faiths, or people of no religion at all. Accordingly, an idea of the divine which is not defined by the strictures of any particular faith would have most resonance with an international community of Jesus' followers. It could also incorporate the many millions of formerly religious people who call themselves agnostic, plus those who have never considered themselves religious – the atheists.

Jesus did not leave his followers with theological treatises on the nature of the divine. What he did leave with them is a clear view of his own spiritual understanding. The nature of the God of whom he spoke can be seen in his references to the many facets of love. Jesus was a man of his times with its primitive understanding of cosmology. Because of that he probably saw God as somewhere 'above the clouds' although at the same time accessible to the hearts of human beings. If he were living and teaching in the twenty-first century, Jesus' view of God as a loving and forgiving presence (which some have called the 'Ground of Being') would coalesce with the view of the divine espoused by many agnostics and people of all earth's major faiths.

In 1997 Marcus Borg edited a book called *Jesus and Buddha: the Parallel Sayings*. Its introduction was written by the Buddhist monk and writer, Jack Cornfield. He describes the time when he was visiting a Buddhist monastery in the Mekong Delta of Vietnam, during the Vietnam War. The monastery was built on an island by a master of peace known as the Coconut Monk and it was filled with monks during the war years. The monks explained to Jack Cornfield the teaching of non-violence and forgiveness on which they staked their lives. After eating, they went for a walk:

> *They took me to the end of the island, where on top of a hill, there was an enormous fifty-foot tall statue of a standing Buddha. Next to Buddha stood an equally tall statue of Jesus. They had their arms around each others' shoulders, smiling. While helicopter gunships flew by overhead and the war raged around us, Buddha and Jesus stood there like brothers, expressing compassion and healing for all who would follow their way.*[109]

On the other hand, traditional Christian doctrine has divided and separated humanity for two thousand years.

A church of the third millennium focussed on Jesus as guide to the best way of living and the best understanding of the divine, could bring together humanity's best hopes and best potential for the best possible world. Such a church could be a catalyst for interfaith harmony and a foundation of the world according to Jesus. The world has never been more in need of it.

SECTION V: WHERE TO FROM HERE?

The best news comes last, and ensues from all that has been written in this book. The church which truly follows Jesus in a post-doctrinal age is equipped to carry out his teaching in a way never before known, or possible. His followers in this age have been freed from the impossible call to follow Jesus the Christ. They have freed Jesus himself from the moribund trappings of christology. They now recognize that Jesus' teachings come from an imperfect human being whose ideas are specifically formulated for imperfect human beings.

Jesus' followers now know that it is eminently possible to put into practice his blueprint for the best possible world. They do not have to despair that G. K. Chesterton and Leo Tolstoy will always be right – that Christianity is too hard and for that reason will never really be implemented. Jesus' followers cannot now make the excuse that they are incapable of emulating a divine 'Son of God'. They can follow Jesus – the man for others – the man from Nazareth.

QUESTIONS FOR DISCUSSION CONCERNING ISSUES RAISED IN SECTION V

1. Having read this book, do you now think it is possible for Jesus' followers to find unity and harmony with people of different faiths and cultures, or of no faith? What might stand in the way of that?

2. Do you think it is possible for human beings to bring the best possible world to reality? How much would they have to change to make that possible?

3. What changes would have to take place in the church to enable this to happen?

Appendix I

THE JESUS CREED
A NEW CREED FOR FOLLOWERS OF JESUS.

PREAMBLE

For increasing numbers of Christians the ancient creeds of the church have lost any real credibility. They are no longer regarded by Christians inside and outside of the church as genuinely credal ('I believe') statements. In the church of the future any attempt to formulate a creed will of necessity include a profoundly different content from that of the christologically-framed Apostles' and Nicene creeds. Such a creed will emphasise the ideals which encourage unity with people of all faiths; it will not focus on differences which create barriers to understanding and cooperation.

Contemporary Christians asked to evaluate the traditional creeds almost invariably point to the hole at the heart of those confessions. They rightly identify the fact that although the creeds begin with belief in God, they move from the birth of Jesus immediately to belief in his 'salvific' death. There is no mention of the teachings which undergirded his passion to establish what he called the 'Kingdom of heaven' on earth and whose universal integrity was the reason he died in their defence. This curious omission flies in the face of overwhelming biblical evidence for Jesus' belief in a God who did not require his unthinking acquiescence to (man-made) religious codes, no matter how venerable, but who encouraged him to live profoundly for others. The sayings of Jesus are a clear guide to the thinking of one who found all he needed to know about God as he put into practice the ethic of love for others. For all of those reasons, any new creed for Jesus' followers ought of necessity to have as its foundation the ethical imperatives of the Sermon on the Mount.

It is long past the time for the traditional creeds to be removed from contemporary Christian liturgies. They are products of their own time and place and their ideas about God and the meaning of Jesus no longer possess credence in the world-view of the twenty-first century. They are long overdue for consignment to the archives of history alongside other time-bound documents such as the Magna Carta and the US Declaration of Independence. Humanity of necessity continues to develop new ideas for its understanding of a changing world. In a multi-cultural, multi-faith world, religion will be an ongoing part of human experience only if its foundational statements encapsulate and express credible and acceptable guidelines to a positive, functional and inclusive planetary community.

Given that this book has outlined Jesus' vision for an enlightened humanity, it seems appropriate that a new creed for those who follow him and create the best possible world will be based on what are known as the beatitudes. The following suggestion ('The Jesus Creed') is an example of what such a creed might include. Of necessity it is non-christological, and as such it has potential to be accepted by people of other faiths or even of no faith, who acknowledge Jesus as Teacher of humanity.

THE JESUS CREED
(Based on the Beatitudes in Matthew 5: 3-9)

All: I believe in Jesus' vision of the best kind of world, made known to us in his teaching.

L: Jesus said:
Fortunate are the humble-minded;
P: they will live in the best possible world.
L: Fortunate are the mournful;
P: they will face the future with strength.
L: Fortunate are the non-violent;
P: they will govern the earth.
L: Fortunate are those whose passion is for justice;
P: they will receive justice.
L: Fortunate are the compassionate;
P: they will receive compassion.
L: Fortunate are the undivided in heart;
P: they will commit to the way of Jesus.
L: Fortunate are the peacemakers;
P: they will forgive and reconcile humanity.
L: Fortunate are those in danger for living Jesus' way;
P: they will be freed from fear to follow him.

All: I believe that all who follow him
will create a world according to Jesus.

Appendix II

This sermon was written and delivered on the first Sunday following the attack on the World Trade Centre, on September 11, 2001. It illustrates both the sublime truth and the difficult love which undergird the teachings of Jesus.

'LOST ON THE WRONG ROAD'
Luke 15. 1-10

The neighbourhood I live in is fairly typical of Melbourne. People from several cultural and religious backgrounds live in my street. There are Anglo-Celts, who I presume are at least nominal Christians, there are several Greek Orthodox and Italian Catholic households, there are Jewish families all around and opposite me lives a family from India or Pakistan. They may be Hindu, or perhaps Muslim, but in any case, one of their frequent visitors wears the turban of a Sikh. A family of Middle Eastern origin runs the local 'Chicken and Chippery'. Australia is not becoming a multicultural society. It already is a multicultural society. An enormous amount has happened to change our nation in the past twenty years or so.

Even so, we meet this morning in a world that seems dramatically different from this time last week. Even though the terrible events in New York and Washington happened half a world away, they have changed our expectations of safety and security forever. Images that previously belonged in Hollywood disaster movies have been shown again and again on our TV screens, until the truth has finally sunk in. Now we know it does not necessarily take a declaration of war or an invading army for innocent civilians to be killed. We know people can be horribly slaughtered and injured in the heart of their own peaceful homeland, in the midst of their ordinary lives. We also know that many of our fellow Australians have been counted among the dead, injured, and missing. Last Friday's fall of one of our great Australian icons, Ansett airlines, and our sympathy for those affected by that, has added to our growing sense of insecurity.

In the face of all these things we continue to express our deepest and most heartfelt sympathy to those directly involved in the events of September 11 – to the families and friends of all who have been killed, injured and traumatized. Our hearts go out to grieving people searching in vain for their loved ones. During the past few days our personal reactions have fluctuated between disbelief and sadness at the scale of death and destruction, incredulity that human beings could plan and execute such cold-blooded murder of the innocent, and mounting concern about the way America's response might be expressed. It is that final concern that I believe we should discuss this morning.

Christians are unambiguously committed to the good news from Jesus. Christians look to his teachings as our guide. Without those teachings, in a rapidly changing world we have nothing to use as our yardstick for understanding and hope. Today we read a portion from Luke's Gospel which I believe speaks plainly and unequivocally to this week's events. In short, it is a word about the lost. On the face of it, it is about finding something as ordinary as a sheep or a coin. The shepherd finds the lost sheep. The woman finds the lost coin. But it ends with a statement about the return of a sinner. So there is much more going on here than first meets the eye. In both stories the thing lost is separated from others of its kind. We will concentrate on the story of the lost sheep.

The scene is typical of the Judean wilderness - a shepherd

leading his flock to sources of food and water. For some reason one sheep has become separated from its fellows. When it looks around, the shepherd and the rest of the flock have vanished. Without its guide the sheep is left to its own resources, its own choices, its own wisdom. The shepherd and the flock are not far away, but because it is separated from them the sheep takes a wrong turn. With every step it wanders further and further from where it belongs and soon it is hopelessly lost. The dye was cast when it first took that wrong turn. Now it is lost on the wrong road, completely in the dark about where it is going. There are many and varied consequences of taking a wrong turn and getting lost. Let's look at some of them.

Firstly, the sheep lost on the wrong road is NOT IN ITS RIGHTFUL PLACE. It is separated from the flock. When that happens it quickly loses its sense of direction and every step takes it further from where it belongs. After all, to be lost is to be lost from somewhere or something. The lost are locked out from where they belong. Any child rejected by his or her playmates knows very well the agony and sadness of rejection, of being locked out of its group. That kind of sadness can turn to anger and resentment and destructive revenge.

Terrorism does not always result in devastation on the scale of the past week. Smaller acts of terrorism happen all the time around the world. Obvious examples are the car bombings in Israel. The Palestinians responsible feel locked out of the place where they believe they belong. The boys who murdered fellow students at Columbine High School in the US had been rejected as different and felt locked out of the larger community in their school. The lost understand themselves as abandoned and denied their rightful place. Sometimes they visit terrible vengeance on those who reject them.

Secondly, the lost sheep is IN THE DARK. It has entered unfamiliar territory where there are none of the old familiar landmarks to guide it. From now on it must make its own way. If it is lost in the dark because it feels rejected, its guide through the darkness may well be hatred. We can put all of this in the context of events during the past few days. Time and again we've seen images of people identified as enemies of Western society. They have a distinctively Middle-Eastern appearance, with different clothing and the dark hair and beard of the classic stage villain. Their very appearance speaks to Western eyes of Muslims whose grievances against the West have led them first to religious fundamentalism and then to terrorism. They are easily identified as different, and are therefore to be hated and feared.

One of their leaders is known to have been behind various acts of terrorism and those acts cannot be allowed to continue. People who kill and maim the innocent must be brought to justice. Yet therein lies the dilemma for the President of the United States. Two days ago he revealed the inner struggle between his basic decency and his role as protector of the American people. He said, "I'm a loving guy, but I'm also someone with a job to do."

Everyone understands the need to prevent further acts of terrorism. Yet we know that retaliation by means of war will only bring more death and destruction to the innocent. War has never brought any decisive end to cycles of hatred, vengeance and violence. The Australian Queen's Counsel Geoffrey Robertson has suggested that the perpetrators be captured and tried in an international court for crimes against humanity. This would be an appropriate focus for the righteous anger of the world. It would also prevent more destruction of the innocent. The problem is that for many in the Western world terrorists who use religious fundamentalism as their guide represent the entire face of Islam. The inevitable result is fear and hatred of all Muslims. They are all understood to represent a threat to security and the western way of life. Therefore they must all be kept at a distance – in other words, rejected.

Already there are signs of this fearful rejection of Australian Muslims. Fire bombs have been thrown at a Mosque in

Brisbane, and Muslim leaders all over Australia are receiving bomb threats and messages of hate by telephone and email. As I have already said, the rejected soon learn to hate their tormentors, and the whole cycle goes around and around. The question is, how can this cycle of rejection and hatred be broken? How can the lost sheep ON BOTH SIDES OF THE FENCE come in from the dark?

The Book of the Prophet Isaiah contains some of the most magnificent poetry in scripture, but the grandeur of verses 2 and 6 in chapter 9 outshines them all. "The people who walked in darkness have seen a great light; those who lived in a land of deep darkness - on them light has shined. For a child has been born for us, a son given to us; authority rests on his shoulders; and he is named Wonderful Counsellor, Mighty God, Everlasting Father, Prince of Peace." Christians recognize in Jesus the characteristics about which Isaiah wrote. Christians say they follow the one who sheds light in the darkness – the teachings of Jesus are their guide and light. If so, what does he say to us in these terrible days?

Jesus' own people were powerless and poor, locked out from the structures of power. They were rejected by the powerful and well fed, and they longed to strike back against the occupation of their country by the Romans – the super-power of their day. Some formed themselves into what we would call terrorist groups. They included people called Sicarii, named for the curved dagger or sica that they carried. Jesus understood their pain, but he utterly rejected their way; he refused to be drawn with them into the darkness of envy and revenge. Instead he called on the power of love and forbearance. He knew it was immensely more powerful and creative than force of arms. So he told the story of the lost sheep, and the shepherd who actually went out and brought it back home. And remember that the story clearly indicates the repentance of a sinner. But is the sinner necessarily the lost sheep? Hold on to that question as we look at a third consequence of taking a wrong turn.

Thirdly, the lost sheep in our time also need to be FOUND, AND BROUGHT HOME. The teachings of Jesus do not encourage us to judge others. They challenge us to look in the mirror at ourselves. Jesus' stories about other people lit up imperfections in the lives of his hearers. So who is the sinner who repents in Jesus' story? Is it the lost sheep, or is it the shepherd? Is it the one who has been allowed to stray, or actually forced from the flock? Or is it those who have rejected it as different who now repent, and go out to bring it back home?

During this past week the news from America has almost totally overshadowed the plight of asylum-seekers aboard an Australian warship. We have hardly even heard about another group whose boat barely made it to Ashmore Reef. What is happening to them? We have been so engrossed in the attack on America that we have forgotten the lost sheep on our own doorstep. The result is that these people are in danger of being rejected a second time. Certainly we need to protect the security of our nation – no one argues with that. But among the asylum-seekers are people who actually refused to join the cycle of hate and vengeance being played out in the Middle East. They have been forced out of their homeland because they protested against those things and in their despair they heard about Australia. They were told that this is a land where acceptance and forebearance rule, where religious differences do not force people into warring factions. They have often fled with just their lives and very few possessions. They have come here trusting that in this country they will find acceptance and new hope. The questions for us in these dark times are urgent ones: Will they once again be rejected? Will they continue to be lost? Will they be pushed back into darkness, where despair breeds hatred and violence? Will we actually contribute to the kind of despair that gives birth to terrorism?

These past few days have brought the painful events of the world into our own living rooms. We have been constantly confronted with images of death, pain, destruction and despair. If these images have done nothing else they have pushed Christians right back onto the foundations of their faith. People are looking to their faith for understanding and hope. Yet a newspaper report clearly illustrates the confusion among Christians at this time: A young man hidden in the crowd at Columbia University hesitantly described his stab at taking a stand. He had, he said, hung a poster on his door that said: "Forgive". But, he added, when he told his parents about the poster, they demanded that he take it down, saying the attacks were "an act of war" that could not be forgiven. The young man paused, then added in a frightened voice, "I just want to say that for the first time in my life, I'm utterly, completely confused."

It is vital to understand that if we ignore the teachings of Jesus in these times we do it at our own peril. We also do it at the peril of those who look to us for help. That much is clear, yet we should never think Jesus' teachings are the easy option. Make no mistake – if we are faithful followers of Jesus, he will lead us to the very limits of our love. He lived in a time when violence and intolerance bred despair and revenge. He taught God's law of love in the face of a cruel and ruthless empire. He remained faithful to the imperative of love even when it meant losing his own life. He willingly risked his life to shed light on the lost sheep of the world. Even as he died, he asked forgiveness on those still lost in the dark cycle of violence: "Father, forgive them. They don't know what they're doing."

A sermon preached by the Rev Dr Lorraine Parkinson at St Aidan's Uniting Church North Balwyn, on September 16, 2001.

Endnotes

SECTION I:

1. Luke's shorter compilation of Jesus' core sayings (The Sermon on the Plain) is at Luke 6:17-49.
2. For example, W. D. Davies, *The Setting of the Sermon on the Mount*, Cambridge: Cambridge University Press, 1964.
3. "Blessed are those who are persecuted for righteousness' sake, for theirs is the kingdom of heaven. Blessed are you when people revile you and persecute you and utter all kinds of evil against you falsely on my account."
4. H. D. Betz, "The Sermon on the Mount: Its Literary Genre and Function", in JR59 (1979), 285-97. Betz sees the Sermon on the Mount as "a carefully crafted epitome of Jesus' teachings".
5. The scriptural quotations in this book are from the New Revised Standard Version, HarperCollins*Publishers, 1998.*
6. Albert Einstein, *The World as I See It*, Philosophical Library, New York, 1949, pp.111-112.
7. The jury is still out as to whether Matthew wrote his gospel originally in Aramaic which was translated into Greek, but outside of Jesus' sayings in the Sermon on the Mount, a Greek writer/translator has used the Greek word for God (*Theos*).
8. David Aune, *Prophecy in Early Christianity and the Ancient Mediterranean World*, W. B. Eerdmanns Publishing Company, Grand Rapids, Michigan, 1983, p. 121.
9. E. P. Sanders, in *Jesus and Judaism*, Fortress Press, Philadelphia, 1985, listed things he believed to be 'certain or virtually certain' about Jesus' purpose. The final point in his list is that while Jesus and his disciples did not believe the kingdom would be established by force of arms, they did look to God for an eschatological miracle, a world brought about not by human endeavour, but by intervention of God.
10. John Dominic Crossan, *The Essential Jesus: Original Sayings and Earliest Images*, HarperSanFrancisco, NY, 1988, p.8.

11 Jason Koutsoukis, "Bulldozers Return to the West Bank", in *The Age* newspaper, September 28, 2010, p.8.
12 Marcus Borg, *The Heart of Christianity: Rediscovering a Life of Faith*, HarperSanFrancisco, 2003.
13 BCE means 'before the Common Era', i.e., the era 'common' to both Jews and Christians.
14 Epicurus, in *De Rerum Natura*, by Lucretius, reprinted by Oxford University Press, 1947.
15 Luke's gospel espouses an apocalyptic eschatology, in accordance with a Pauline view of Jesus as the Christ who will return at the End-time when God intervenes to defeat evil.
16 John Hick, *Evil and the God of Love*, Macmillan/Palgrave Press, London, 2007.
17 See chapter 7 ('The Undivided Heart') for a fuller explanation of integrity as a goal and consequence of following Jesus. The 'Holiness Code' of Leviticus (esp. chapter 18) understands God as undivided and uncorrupted and hence as wholly complete and good.

SECTION II:

18 The story in which the manifesto is quoted was created by Luke for his own purposes, but given Jesus' teachings in the Sermon on the Mount, there can be little doubt that the quotation from Isaiah had definitive significance for Jesus' own understanding of his purpose.
19 E.g. the voice of God at the time of Jesus' Baptism, as stated in Luke 3:22: "You are my Son, the Beloved; with you I am well pleased." This is a paraphrase of Isaiah 42:1: "Here is my servant, whom I uphold, my chosen, in whom my soul delights …". The inference in Luke is that Jesus is the fulfilment of the prophetic witness of Isaiah concerning the one who will bring justice to the nations (or "judgment to the Gentiles" [Septuagint].)
20 Wilhelmina Stitch, *Then Joy Stepped In*, in A. L. Alexander (Comp.), *Poems That Touch the Heart*, Doubleday, New York, 1986 (New Enlarged Edition). Wilhelmina Stitch is the pseudonym of Ruth Collie (1888-1936), a British poet.
21 *The Macquarie Concise Dictionary*, A Delbridge and J.R.L. Bernard (General Editors), Third Edition, The Macquarie Library Pty Ltd., Macquarie University, Sydney, NSW, 1998.
22 Gandhi, Mohandas, in Thomas Merton, *Gandhi on Non-Violence: Selections from the Writings of Mahatma Gandhi*, New Directions, New York, 1965, p.36.
23 M. Fethullah Gülen, *Pearls of Wisdom*, The Light, Inc., New Jersey, 2005 (chapter headed 'Social Interaction').

24 Melbourne youth worker Les Twentyman is to meet the Dalai Lama in June 2011. Commenting on this Twentyman said, "People follow the Dalai Lama because of the passion he showed about turning the other cheek after the terrible things that happened to him and his people." (*The Age*, 18/8/2010).

25 Walter Wink, *Engaging the Powers: Discernment and Resistance in a World of Domination*, Minneapolis, Augsburg Press, 1992, p.217.

26 Pacifism is often understood in a way interchangeable with the principle of non-violent resistance. However, by its nature, pacifism is not pro-active resistance to violence but is 'passive' when faced with violence, such as in the case of conscientious objectors to military service.

27 John Dominic Crossan, *God & Empire: Jesus against Rome, then and now*, HarperSanFrancisco, 2007, p.23

28 John Dominic Crossan, *Victory and Peace or Justice and Peace?* Lecture published on DVD by 'Living the Questions', 2005.

29 Martin Luther King, in an address delivered on August 28, 1963, at the Lincoln Memorial in Washington, DC.

30 M. Fethullah Gülen, *Pearls of Wisdom*, op. cit.

31 Walter Wink, *Engaging the Powers*, op. cit.

32 Again we are confronted with one of the basic meanings of the Aramaic word translated into English as *blessed*. *Ashar* means happy and strong, or fortunate.

33 This concept of justice is not confined to the theory of distributive justice, which concerns the just allocation of goods in society. It also encompasses the theory of restorative justice, where offenders are encouraged to take responsibility for their actions; e.g. by apology and returning stolen goods.

34 Wesley J. Wildman, "What's Radical about Christian Ethics?", in *Focus*, Boston University School of Theology's Alumni Magazine, Fall, 2007.

35 Horace Miner, "Body Ritual Among the Nacirema", in *The American Anthropologist*, vol 58 (1956), pp. 503-507.

36 Wesley J. Wildman, op. cit.

37 Tim Flannery, *Here on Earth: An Argument for Hope*, Text Publishing, Melbourne, 2010, p.216

38 The crowds who watched people thrown to wild animals in Roman arenas regarded the showing of mercy as a weakness of character. For that reason they lacked empathy with the victims.

39 Frank Mason North is the author of the hymn about poor workers: 'Where Cross the Crowded Ways of Life'.

40 In 1824 the SPCA was founded by William Wilberforce, Richard Martin and the Rev Arthur Broome. In 1840 Queen Victoria granted it royal status.

41 Albert Schweitzer, "The Ethics of Reverence for Life", in *Christendom* (1 [1936]), pp.225-39.
42 Reinhold Niebuhr, *Moral Man and Immoral Society*, Charles Scribner's Sons, New York, 1932, p.xi-xii.
43 John Stuart Mill, *On Liberty*, in *India: its Administration and Progress*, Sir John Strachey, pp. 496, 502.
44 G. K. Chesterton, *What's Wrong with the World*, London, 1910.
45 The most commonly used version of the Lord's Prayer is from Matthew. However, in the line regarding forgiveness it is the Lucan emphasis on forgiveness of 'sin' that is included in the prayer (not the foregoing of debts). Luke's emphasis on sin is what Australian church-goers pray about in the Lord's Prayer each week.
46 There are no recorded historical examples of this actually happening, which underlines how difficult it is to 'forgive' debt in this way.
47 See Appendix II for 'Lost on the Wrong Road', written by this author for the Sunday following 9/11.
48 Toyohiko Kagawa, *Love The Law of Life*, SCM Press, London, 1934, p.256.
49 Flavius Josephus, *Antiquities* 17. 10. 10
50 Historical extra-New Testament references to Jesus as Messiah are from the second century, when the Jesus movement had developed a messianic view of him. The Roman writer Tacitus (*Annales* 15.44) described 'Christus' (or Chrestus) as a person convicted by Pontius Pilate during the reign of Tiberias (14-37CE). Tacitus wrote this c.116CE. The earliest New Testament references to Jesus as Messiah are from a period at least a quarter of a century after his death.

SECTION III:

51 In Luke the references to Jesus in prayer are: Luke 3:21; 5:16; 6:12; 9:18; 9: 28-29.
52 Richard Dawkins, *The Greatest Show on Earth: The Evidence for Evolution*, Bantam Press, London, 2009, p.422.
53 Rodney Stark, *The Rise of Christianity*, Princeton University Press, 1996, p.161.
54 Phillips Brooks, *Phillips Brooks Year Book: Selections from the Writings of the Rt Rev Phillips Brooks*, Boston, 2005.
55 Union for Progressive Judaism, Melbourne, Victoria, 2010.
56 Torah can be equated with the first 5 books of the Hebrew Scriptures, but it is usually related to all books of the Hebrew Scriptures. Its meaning is that it constitutes God's way of life for humanity. Its ideals if carried out encourage justice, freedom, compassion and peace.

57 Lawrence Kushner, in the Foreword to *Our Lives as Torah: finding God in our own stories,* Carol Ochs, Jossey-Bass, San Francisco, 2001, xi.
58 David Wright-Neville and Anna Halafoff (Eds.), *Terrorism and Social Exclusion: Misplaced Risk – Common Security,* Monash Studies in Global Movements series, Edward Elgar Publishing, Cheltenham UK, 2010.
59 Somerset Corry Lowry, *A Man There Lived in Galilee,* The Australian Hymn Book, Collins Liturgical Australia, Blackburn, 1978, No. 176.
60 Paul Trudinger, *Honest to Jesus,* Frye Publishing, Winnipeg, Canada, 1983, p.63.
61 The Uniting Church in Australia is a Protestant church, formed in 1977 by a union of most people from the existing Methodist, Congregational and Presbyterian churches.
62 Mark Chancey and Eric M. Meyers make a convincing case for Sepphoris as a primarily Jewish city with Hellenistic overtones in "How Jewish was Sepphoris in Jesus' Time", 2009 Biblical Archaeology Society publication *Israel: An Archaeological Journey,* Washington, 2009.
63 Abraham Lincoln was 6'4" (or 193cm), very tall for the time.
64 Martin Luther King, *"Loving your Enemies",* 17th November, 1957
65 John Chrysostom, *Homilies Against the Jews,* 1.3, 2.3, 4.3.
66 *Racial and Religious Tolerance Act 2001,* State of Victoria, Australia.
67 Romano Guardini, in "Proclaiming the Sacred in a Modern World", Robert A. Krieg (Ed.), *Liturgy Training Publications,* September, 1995.
68 Barack Obama, *The Audacity of Hope: Thoughts on Reclaiming the American Dream,* Crown Publishers, New York, 2006, p.362.
69 In September 2010 at Melbourne University, Distinguished Professor Graeme Clark was awarded the world's most prestigious medal for surgery, the Royal Society's Lister Medal.
70 Gordon Powell, *Famous Birthdays,* Joint Board of Christian Education, Melbourne, 1988.
71 John Dominic Crossan, *God and Empire,* op. cit., pp.78-82, calls the theory of God's eschatological intervention 'The Great Divine Cleanup of the World'.
72 Rufus Black, interviewed by Peter Thompson for *UCA Funds Management News,* Melbourne, April 2010.
73 Paul Barry, *Who wants to Be a Billionaire? The James Packer Story,* Allen & Unwin, Crows Nest, NSW, 2009, quoted in "Packer took money too seriously", by Elisabeth Sexton, in *The Age,* October 9, 2009.
74 On March 22, 2010, organizations such as End Water Poverty and Freshwater Action Network organized an attempt on a Guinness

World Record called 'The World's Longest Toilet Queue'. Its aim was to raise money for water and sanitary projects in developing nations.
75 Christians were banned from charging interest on loans by the Fifth Lateran Council of 1515.
76 Paolo Freire, *Pedagogy of the Oppressed*, English Tr., Continuum Publishing Company, New York, 1970.
77 I believe it is not appropriate to 'ask God' for anything, but simply to express in prayer the hopes and joys and needs and sorrows of everyday living. Through that kind of spiritual engagement, the means of addressing life's vagaries is often given strength and encouragement. I do not attempt to explain how that might be so, but simply to note it here.
78 Jonathan Kuttab and Mubarak Awad, "Non-violent Resistance in Palestine: Pursuing Alternative Strategies", in *Information Brief* No. 90, 29 March, 2002.
79 *Yes, Minister*, 'A Public Inquiry', BBC, 1980.
80 Confucius, *The Analects of Confucius*, Arthur Waley, (Ed. And Tr.), First Vintage Books Edition, Random House Inc., New York, 1989, 15:23.
81 Hans Küng, "One Global Ethic" in *A Parliament of Souls: Conversations with 28 Spiritual leaders from Around the World*, Michael Tobias, Jane Morrison and Bettina Gray (Eds.), KQED Books, San Francisco, 1995, p.125.
82 The World Meteorological Organization's Ghassem Asrar said the researchers had modelled the atmospheric currents that brought the rains to Pakistan weeks before they arrived. They "clearly flagged this formation and kept track of it". Jo Chandler, "Lost amid the deluge", *The Age*, August 21, 2010.
83 Tim Flannery, *Here on Earth*, op cit., p.242.
84 Dietrich Bonhoeffer, *The Cost of Discipleship*, Macmillan, New York, 1966.
85 Op. cit.
86 The doctrine of substitutionary atonement was fully developed by St Anselm in the eleventh century.
87 Augustine of Hippo: "By His death, that one most true sacrifice offered on our behalf, He purged, abolished and extinguished whatever guilt we had. By it God's wrath was appeased, and we were reconciled to him". In J. N. D. Kelly, *Early Christian Doctrines*, Second Edition, Adam and Charles Black, London, 1960, p.393.
88 Barack Obama, *The Audacity of Hope*, op. cit., pp.218-224.
89 I do not include the parables in this. The only 'explanation' of parables themselves in the gospels is clearly from gospel writers. See Chapter 28 for an explanation of the importance of Jesus' parables.

90   St Augustine of Hippo, Sermons, *Nature and Grace* (415), cited in Michael Marshall, *The Restless Heart: The Life and Influence of St Augustine*, Grand Rapids, Eerdmans, 1987, p.135.

91   Jesus probably did perform exorcisms for healing, in accordance with beliefs which linked physical ailments with the presence of evil (or wrong-doing) in the sufferers. For that reason he associated healings with faith in the God who forgives ("Your faith has made you whole" Matt.9:22). The gospel writers' eschatological beliefs understood such healings as signs that Jesus was the Messiah, whose 'End time' return when God intervened would defeat evil, including illness, and create a perfect world. This is entirely at odds with Jesus' teachings, where humanity takes responsibility for building the best possible world.

92   Rodney Stark, *Op Cit.*

93   Henry Wadsworth Longfellow, *The Rainy Day*, 1842.

94   Also known as Judah the Prince (died c.188CE), the editor of *The Mishnah* in its final form.

95   Richard Bach, *Jonathan Livingston Seagull*, Avon Books, An Imprint of HarperCollinsPublishers, New York, 1970.

SECTION V:

96   Many have cited Jesus 'cleansing' the Temple as proof that Jesus was capable of violent action when it suited his purpose. In fact the gospels say that in this prophetic or symbolic action Jesus overturned some tables and let some birds and animals out of cages. No one was attacked or hurt. Given the size of the Temple area, his action would have involved a small number of the people selling sacrificial animals and changing money.

97   Mohandas Gandhi, in *Mahatma Gandhi: Essays and Reflections*, Jaico Publishing House, Mumbai, 1957.

98   The NRSV translators acknowledge that these words are a later addition to Luke's gospel and that they are retained in the text because of their congruence with the recorded life and teaching of Jesus.

99   Julie Galambush, *Christianity's Forgotten Jews*, HarperCollins, San Francisco, 2005.

100 Fred. Cornwallis Conybeare, *Myth, Magic and Morals: A Study of Christian Origins*, Watts & Co., London, 1910.

101 Philip Schaff (Ed.), *Nicene and Post-Nicene Fathers*, Vol. 6, William Findlay (Tr.), Buffalo, NY, Christian Literature Publishing Company, 1888.

102 Leo Tolstoy, *The Kingdom of God is Within You: Christianity not as a Mystic Religion but as a New Theory of Life,* University of Nebraska Press, 1984, Reprint from 1894 edition.
103 Dietrich Bonhoeffer, *The Cost of Discipleship,* op. cit
104 Krister Stendahl, *An Interview with Krister Stendahl,* Yehezkel Landau (interviewer and writer), Harvard Divinity School Bulletin, Vol. 35, No. 1, Winter 2007.
105 The well-publicized British evolutionary biologist and atheist Richard Dawkins wrote an article in 2006 called 'Atheists for Jesus', in which he advocated following Jesus' teachings as a means to "kick start the meme of super niceness in a post-Christian society. If we play our cards right – could we lead society away from the nether regions of its Darwinian origins into kinder and more compassionate uplands of post-singularity enlightenment?"
106 Robert N. Goldman, *Einstein's God,* Jason Aronson, Northvale NJ, 1977, p.88
107 Anselm of Canterbury (1033-1109 CE) was a Benedictine monk who developed 1st to 4th century theories of Jesus' death as substitutionary atonement for human sin.
108 Quoted by Manuel Roig-Franzia, "United by loss, worshippers find new meaning in a shared, open-air faith", in Washington Post, January 18, 2010.
109 Jack Cornfield (Introduction) in Marcus Borg (Ed.), *Jesus and Buddha: The Parallel sayings,* Ulysees press, Berkeley California, 1997.

Bibliography

Aune, David, E., *Prophecy in Early Christianity and the Ancient Mediterranean World,* William B. Eerdmanns Publishing Company, Grand Rapids, Michigan, 1983.

Bach, Richard, *Jonathan Livingston Seagull,* Avon Books, An Imprint of HarperCollins*Publishers,* New York, 1970.

Betz, H. D., "The Sermon on the Mount: Its Literary Genre and Function", in JR59 (1979).

Black, Rufus, interviewed by Peter Thompson for *UCA Funds Management News,* Melbourne, April 2010.

Bonhoeffer, Dietrich, *The Cost of Discipleship,* Macmillan, New York, 1966.

Borg, Marcus, *The Heart of Christianity: Rediscovering a Life of Faith,* HarperSanFrancisco, 2003.

Brooks, Phillips, *Phillips Brooks Year Book: Selections from the Writings of the Rte Rev Phillips Brooks,* Boston, 2005.

Chesterton, G. K., *What's Wrong with the World,* London, 1910.

Chrysostom, John, *Homilies Against the Jews,* 1.3, 2.3, 4.3.

Conybeare, Fred. Cornwallis, *Myth, Magic and Morals: A Study of Christian Origins,* Watts & Co., London, 1910.

Crossan, John Dominic, *The Essential Jesus: Original Sayings and Earliest Images,* HarperSanFrancisco, New York, 1998.

Crossan, John Dominic, *God and Empire: Jesus Against Rome, then and now,* HarperSanFrancisco, New York, 2007.

Crossan, John Dominic, *Victory and Peace or Justice and Peace?,* Lecture published on DVD by 'Living the Questions', 2005.

Davies, W. D., *The Setting of the Sermon on the Mount,* Cambridge University Press, Cambridge, 1964.

Dawkins, Richard, *Atheists for Jesus,* Richard Dawkins Foundation, published on his web site, Tuesday April 11, 2006.

Dawkins, Richard, *The Greatest Show on Earth: The Evidence for Evolution,* Bantam Press, London, 2009.

Delbridge, A and J.R.L. Bernard (General Editors), *The Macquarie Concise Dictionary,* Third Edition, Macquarie University, Sydney, NSW, 1998.

Einstein, Albert, *The World as I See It,* Philosophical Library, New York, 1949.

Flannery, Tim, *Here on Earth: An Argument for Hope,* Text Publishing, Melbourne, 2010.

Galambush, Julie, *Christianity's Forgotten Jews,* HarperCollins, San Francisco, 2005.

Gandhi, Mohandas, in *Mahatma Gandhi: Essays and Reflections,* Sarvepalli Radhakrishnan, Jaico Publishing House, Mumbai, 1957.

Goldman, Robert N., *Einstein's God,* Jason Aronson, Northvale NJ, 1977.

Guardini, Romano, in *"Proclaiming the Sacred in a Modern World",* Robert King (Ed.), Liturgy Training Publications, September 1995.

Gülen, M. Fethullah, *Pearls of Wisdom,* The Light Inc., New Jersey, 2005.

Hick, John, *Evil and the God of Love,* Macmillan/Palgrave Press, London, 2007.

Josephus, Flavius, *Antiquities,* 17.10.10

Lucretius, *De Rerum Natura,* reprinted by Oxford University Press, 1947.

Kagawa, Toyohiko, *Love the Law of Life,* SCM Press, London, 1934.

Kelly, J. N. D., *Early Christian Doctrines,* Second Edition, Adam and Charles Black, London, 1960.

King, Martin Luther, *"Loving your Enemies",* sermon delivered on November 17, 1957.

Küng, Hans, "A Global Ethic", in *A Parliament of Souls: Conversations with 28 Spiritual Leaders from Around the World*, Michael Tobias, Jane Morrison and Bettina Gray (Eds.), KQED Books, San Francisco, 1995.

Kushner, Lawrence, in the Foreword to *Our Lives as Torah: Finding God in Our Own Stories*, Carol Ochs, Jossey-Bass, San Francisco, 2001.

Lowry, Somerset Corry, *A Man There Lived in Galilee*, No. 176 *Australian Hymn Book*, A Collins Liturgical Publication, Blackburn Victoria, 1987.

Merton, Thomas, *Gandhi on Non-Violence: Selections from the Writings of Mahatma Gandhi*, New Directions, New York, 1965.

Mill, John Stuart, *On Liberty*, in *India: its Administration and Progress*, Sir John Strachey.

Miner, Horace, "Body Ritual Among the Nacirema", *in The American Anthropologist*, Vol. 58 (1956).

Neville-Wright, David and Halafoff, Anna (Eds.), *Terrorism and Social Exclusion: Misplaced Trust – Common Security*, Edward Elgar Publishing, Cheltenham UK, 2010.

Niebuhr, Reinhold, *Moral Man and Immoral Society*, Charles Scribner's Sons, New York, 1932.

Obama, Barack, *The Audacity of Hope: Thoughts on Reclaiming the American Dream*, Crown Publishers, New York, 2006.

Roig-Franzia, Manuel, "United by loss, worshippers find new meaning in a shared, open-air faith", in *Washington Post*, January 18, 2010.

Schaff, Philip (Ed.), *Nicene and Post-Nicene Fathers*, Vol. 6, William Findlay (Tr.), Buffalo, NY, Christian Literature Publishing Company, 1888.

Stark, Rodney, *The Rise of Christianity: A Sociologist Reconsiders History*, Princeton University Press, 1996.

St Augustine of Hippo, *Sermon, Nature and Grace* (415), cited in Michael Marshall, *The Restless Heart: The Life and Influence of St Augustine*, Eerdmans, Grand Rapids, 1987.

Stendahl, Krister, in "An Interview with Krister Stendahl", Yehezkel Landau (interviewer and writer), *Harvard Divinity School*

Bulletin, Vol. 35, No. 1, Winter 2007.

Stitch, Wilhelmina, *Then Joy Stepped In,* in A. L. Alexander (Compiler), *Poems that Touch the Heart,* Doubleday, NY, 1986 (new enlarged edition).

Tolstoy, Leo, *The Kingdom of God is Within You: Christianity not as a Mystic Religion but as a New Theory of Life,* University of Nebraska Press, 1984, reprint from 1894 edition.

Trudinger, Paul, *Honest to Jesus,* Frye Publishing, Winnipeg, Canada, 1983.

Wildman, Wesley J, "What's Radical about Christian Ethics?", in *Focus,* Boston University School of Theology Alumni Magazine, Fall, 2007.

Wink, Walter, *Engaging the Powers: Discernment and Resistance in a World of Domination,* Augsburg Press, Minneapolis, 1992.